ON HISTORY

ALSO BY ERIC HOBSBAWM

Labouring Men
Industry and Empire
Bandits
Revolutionaries
Worlds of Labour
Nations and Nationalism Since 1780

The Age of Revolution 1789–1848
The Age of Capital 1848–1875
The Age of Empire 1875–1914
Age of Extremes 1914–1991

ON HISTORY

Eric Hobsbawm

THE NEW PRESS

Published in the United States by The New Press, New York
Distributed by W.W. Norton & Company, Inc., New York

The New Press was established in 1990 as a not-for-profit alternative to the large,
commercial publishing houses currently dominating the book publishing industry.
The New Press operates in the public interest rather than for private gain,
and is committed to publishing, in innovative ways, works of educational, cultural,
and community value that might not normally be commercially viable.
The New Press's editorial offices are located at the City University of New York.

Production management by Kim Waymer, The New Press
Printed in the United States of America

9 8 7 6 5 4 3 2 1

CONTENTS

Preface   vii

PREFACE

The least philosophically minded historians can hardly avoid general reflections about their subject. Even when they can, they may not be encouraged to do so, for the demand for lectures and symposia, which tends to increase as a historian gets older, is more easily met by generalities than by actual research. In any case the contemporary slant of interest is towards conceptual and methodological questions of history. Theoreticians of all kinds circle round the peaceful herds of historians as they graze on the rich pastures of their primary sources or chew the cud of each other's publications. Sometimes even the least combative feel impelled to face their attackers. Not that historians, the present author among them, are uncombative, at least when dealing with each other's writings. Some of the most spectacular academic controversies have been fought on their fields of battle. So it is not surprising that someone who has been in the business for fifty years should in the course of time have produced the reflections on his subject which are now brought together in this collection of papers.

Short and unsystematic though several of them are – in most of them the limits of what can be said in a fifty-minute lecture show through – they are nevertheless an attempt to grapple with a coherent set of problems. These are of three overlapping kinds. First, I am concerned with the uses, and abuses, of history in both society and politics, and with the understanding and, I hope, reshaping of the world. More specifically I discuss its value for other disciplines, especially in the social sciences. To this extent these papers are, if you like, advertisements for my trade. Second, they are about what has been happening among historians and other scholarly enquirers into the past. They include both surveys and critical assessments of various historical trends and fashions and interventions in debates, for instance, about postmodernism and cliometrics. Third, they are about my own kind of history, that is to say about the central problems which all serious historians ought to confront, about the historical interpretation I have found most useful when doing so, and also about the ways in which the history I have written bears the marks of a man of my age, background, beliefs and life-experience.

Readers will probably find that every paper is in one way or another relevant to all of them.

My views on all these matters should be clear from the text. Nevertheless, I want to add a word or two of clarification on two themes of this book.

First, about *telling the truth about history*, to use the title of a book by friends and colleagues of the author.[1] I strongly defend the view that what historians investigate is real. The point from which historians must start, however far from it they may end, is the fundamental and, for them, absolutely central distinction between establishable fact and fiction, between historical statements based on evidence and subject to evidence and those which are not.

It has become fashionable in recent decades, not least among people who think of themselves as on the left, to deny that objective reality is accessible, since what we call 'facts' exist only as a function of prior concepts and problems formulated in terms of these. The past we study is only a construct of our minds. One such construct is in principle as valid as another, whether it can be backed by logic and evidence or not. So long as it forms part of an emotionally strong system of beliefs, there is, as it were, no way in principle of deciding that the biblical account of the creation of the earth is inferior to the one proposed by the natural sciences: they are just different. Any tendency to doubt this is 'positivism', and no term indicates a more comprehensive dismissal than this, unless it is empiricism.

In short, I believe that without the distinction between what is and what is not so, there can be no history. Rome defeated and destroyed Carthage in the Punic Wars, not the other way round. How we assemble and interpret our chosen sample of verifiable data (which may include not only what happened but what people thought about it) is another matter.

Actually, few relativists have the full courage of their convictions, at least when it comes to deciding such questions as whether Hitler's Holocaust took place or not. However, in any case, relativism will not do in history any more than in law courts. Whether the accused in a murder trial is or is not guilty depends on the assessment of old-fashioned positivist evidence, if such evidence is available. Any innocent readers who find themselves in the dock will do well to appeal to it. It is the lawyers for the guilty ones who fall back on postmodern lines of defence.

Second, about the Marxist approach to history with which I am associated. Though it is imprecise, I do not disclaim the label. Without

Marx I would not have developed any special interest in history, which, as taught in the first half of the 1930s in a conservative German *Gymnasium* and by an admirable Liberal master in a London grammar school, was not an inspiring subject. I would almost certainly not have come to earn my living as a professional academic historian. Marx, and the fields of activity of young Marxist radicals, gave me my subjects of research and inspired the way I wrote about them. Even if I thought large parts of Marx's approach to history needed junking, I would still continue to pay my respects, profound though not uncritical, to what the Japanese call a *sensei*, an intellectual master to whom one owes a debt that cannot be repaid. As it happens, I continue (with qualifications to be found in these papers) to find Marx's 'materialist conception of history' the best guide by far to history, as the great fourteenth-century scholar Ibn Khaldun described it, namely as:

> the record of human society, or world civilization; of the changes that take place in the nature of that society ...; of revolutions and uprisings by one set of people against another, with the resulting kingdoms and states with their various ranks; of the different activities and occupations of men, whether for gaining their livelihood or in various sciences and crafts; and in general, of all the transformations that society undergoes by its very nature.[2]

It is certainly the best guide to those like myself whose field has been the rise of modern capitalism and the transformations of the world since the end of the European Middle Ages.

But what exactly is a 'Marxist historian' as distinct from a non-Marxist historian? Ideologists on both sides of the secular wars of religion through which we have lived for much of this century have attempted to establish neat dividing lines and incompatibilities. On the one hand the authorities of the late USSR could not bring themselves to translate any of my books into Russian, even though their author was actually known to be a member of a Communist Party, and an editor of the English edition of the Collected Works of Marx and Engels. By the criteria of their orthodoxy they were not 'Marxist'. On the other hand, more recently, no 'respectable' French publisher has so far been found willing to translate my *Age of Extremes*, presumably on the grounds that it is ideologically too shocking for Parisian readers, or, more likely, for those expected to review the book if it were translated. Yet, as my papers try to show, the history of the discipline which investigates the past has, from the end of the nineteenth century, at least until intellectual nebulosity began to settle over the historiographical landscape in the 1970s, been one of convergence and not separation. The parallelism between the *Annales* school in France and the Marxist historians in Britain has often been noted. Each side saw the other engaged on a similar historical project, though with a different intellectual genealogy, and though, presumably, the politics of their most prominent exponents were far from the same. Interpretations once identified exclusively with Marxism, even with what I have called 'vulgar-Marxism' (see below, pp. 145–7) have penetrated conventional history to an extraordinary degree. Half a century ago, it is safe to say, at least in Britain, only a Marxist historian would have suggested that the emergence of the theological concept of purgatory in the European Middle Ages was best explained by the shift in the economic base of the Church from reliance on the gifts of a small number of rich and powerful nobles to a broader financial base. Yet who could possibly classify either the eminent Oxford medievalist Sir Richard Southern, or Jacques Le Goff, whose book he reviewed along these lines in the 1980s, as an ideological, still less a political, follower or sympathizer of Marx?

I think this convergence is welcome evidence for one of the central theses of these essays, namely that history is engaged on a coherent intellectual project, and has made progress in understanding how the world came to be the way it is today. Naturally I would not want to suggest that one cannot or should not distinguish between Marxist and non-Marxist history, miscellaneous and ill-defined though the cargo of both these containers is. Historians in Marx's tradition – and this does not include all who call themselves by that name – have a significant contribution to make to this collective endeavour. But they are not alone. Nor should their, or anyone's, work be judged by the political labels they or others attach to their lapels.

The essays collected here have been written at different times over the past thirty years, mainly as lectures and contributions to conferences or symposia, sometimes as book reviews or contributions to those peculiar academic cemeteries, the *Festschriften* or collections of studies presented to an academic colleague on some occasion calling for celebration or appreciation. The public for which I have written ranges from general audiences, mainly at universities, to specialized groups of professional historians or economists. Chapters 3, 5, 7, 8, 17 and 19 are published for the first time, although a version of Chapter 17 in the original German text, given as a lecture in connection with the annual German *Historikertag*, was published in *Die Zeit*. Chapters 1 and 15 were first published in the *New York Review of Books*, Chapters 2 and 14 in the historical review *Past and Present*, Chapters 4, 11 and 20 have appeared in *New Left Review*, Chapter 6 in *Daedalus*, the review of the American Academy of Arts and Sciences, Chapters 10 and 21 in *Diogenes*, published under the auspices of UNESCO. Chapter 13 appeared in *Review*, under the auspices of Fernand Braudel Center of the State University of New York at Binghamton, Chapter 18 was published as a pamphlet by the University of London. Details of the *Festschriften* for which Chapters 9 and 16 were written are given at the head of these chapters, as, in general, are the dates of the original texts and, where necessary, the occasion of their original composition. I thank all these, where necessary also for permission to republish.

E. J. Hobsbawm
London 1997

CHAPTER 1

Outside and Inside History

This paper was given as a lecture opening the academic year 1993–4 at the Central European University in Budapest, that is to say it was addressed to a body of students essentially drawn from the formerly communist countries in Europe and the former USSR. It was subsequently published as 'The New Threat to History' in the New York Review of Books, *16 December 1992, pp. 62–5, and, in translation, in a number of other countries.*

It is an honour to be asked to open this academic year of the Central European University. It is also a curious sensation to do so, since, though I am a second-generation English-born British citizen, I am also a central European. Indeed, as a Jew I am one of the characteristic members of the central European diaspora of peoples. My grandfather came to London from Warsaw. My mother was Viennese, and so is my wife, though she now speaks better Italian than German. My wife's mother still spoke Hungarian as a little girl and her parents, at one stage of their lives in the old monarchy, had a store in Hercegovina. My wife and I once went to Mostar to trace it, in the days when there was still peace in that unhappy part of the Balkans. I have had some connections with Hungarian historians myself in the old days. So I come to you as an outsider who is also, in an oblique way, an insider. What can I say to you?

I want to say three things to you.

The first concerns central and eastern Europe. If you come from there, and I assume that almost all of you do, you are citizens of countries whose status is doubly uncertain. I am not claiming that uncertainty is a monopoly of central and east Europeans. It is probably more universal today than ever. Nevertheless, your horizon is particularly cloudy. In my own lifetime every country in your part of Europe has been overrun by war, conquered, occupied, liberated and reoccupied. Every state in it has a different shape from the one it had when I was born. Only six of the twenty-three states which now fill

1

the map between Trieste and the Urals were in existence at the time of my birth, or would have been if they had not been occupied by some army: Russia, Rumania, Bulgaria, Albania, Greece and Turkey, for neither post-1918 Austria nor post-1918 Hungary is really comparable to Habsburg Hungary and Cisleithania. Several came into existence after the First World War, even more since 1989. They include several countries which had never in history had the status of independent statehood in the modern sense, or which had it briefly – for a year or two, for a decade or two – and then lost it, though some have since regained it: the three little Baltic states, Belarus, Ukraine, Slovakia, Moldova, Slovenia, Croatia, Macedonia, not to go further eastwards. Some were born and died in my lifetime, like Yugoslavia and Czechoslovakia. It is perfectly common for the elderly inhabitant of some central European city to have had, successively, the identity documents of three states. A person of my age from Lemberg or Czernowitz has lived under four states, not counting wartime occupations; a man from Munkacs may well have lived under five, if we count the momentary autonomy of Podkarpatska Rus in 1938. In more civilized times, as in 1919, he or she might have been given the option which new citizenship to choose, but since the Second World War he or she has been more likely to be either forcibly expelled or forcibly integrated into the new state. Where does a central and eastern European belong? Who is he or she? The question has been a real one for great numbers of them, and it still is. In some countries it is a question of life and death, in almost all it affects and sometimes determines their legal status and life-chances.

However, there is another and more collective uncertainty. The bulk of central and eastern Europe belongs to that part of the world for which diplomats and United Nations experts since 1945 have tried to devise polite euphemisms: 'under-developed' or 'developing', that is to say, relatively or absolutely poor and backward. In some respects there is no sharp line between the two Europes, but rather a slope to the east and to the west of what we might call the main mountain-range or crest of European economic and cultural dynamism, which ran from north Italy across the Alps to northern France and the Low Countries, and was prolonged across the Channel into England. It can be traced in the medieval trade routes and the distribution map of gothic architecture, as well as in the figures for the regional GDP within the European Community. In fact, today this region is still the backbone of the European Community. However, insofar as there is a historical line separating 'advanced' from 'backward' Europe it ran, roughly, through the middle of the Habsburg Empire. I know that people are sensitive in these matters. Ljubljana thinks of itself as a great deal nearer the centre of civilization than, say, Skopje, and Budapest than Belgrade, and the present government in Prague does not even wish to be called 'central-European' for fear of being contaminated by contact with the East. It insists that it belongs exclusively to the West. However, my point is that no country or region in central and eastern Europe thought of itself as being at that centre. All looked somewhere else for a model of how really to be advanced and modern, even, I suspect, the educated middle class of Vienna, Budapest and Prague. They looked to Paris and London, just as the intellectuals of Belgrade and Ruse looked to Vienna – even though by most accepted standards the present Czech Republic and parts of the present Austria formed part of the advanced industrial part of Europe, and culturally Vienna, Budapest and Prague had no reason at all to feel inferior to anyone else.

The history of backward countries in the nineteenth and twentieth centuries is the history of trying to catch up with the more advanced world by imitating it. The nineteenth-century Japanese took Europe as their model, the west Europeans after the Second World War imitated the American economy. The story of central and eastern Europe in the twentieth century is, broadly, that of trying to catch up by following several models one after the other and failing. After 1918, when most of the successor countries were new, the model was Western democracy and economic liberalism. President Wilson – is the main station in Prague named after him again? – was the region's patron saint, except for the Bolsheviks who went their own way. (Actually, they too had foreign models: Rathenau and Henry Ford.) This did not work. The model broke down politically and economically in the 1920s and 1930s. The Great Depression eventually broke multinational democracy even in Czechoslovakia. A number of these countries then briefly tried or flirted with the fascist model, which looked like the economic and political success story of the 1930s. (We are inclined to forget that Nazi Germany was remarkably successful in overcoming the Great Depression.) Integration in a Great German economic system did not work either. Germany was defeated.

After 1945 most of these countries chose, or found themselves being made to choose, the Bolshevik model, which was essentially a model for modernizing backward agrarian economies by planned industrial revolution. It was therefore never relevant to what is now the Czech Republic and to what was until 1989 the German Democratic Republic, but it was relevant to most of the region, including the USSR. I do not have to tell you about the economic deficiencies and flaws of the system, which eventually led to its breakdown, and still less about the intolerable, the increasingly intolerable political systems it imposed on central and eastern Europe. Still less do I have to remind you of the incredible sufferings it imposed on the peoples of the former USSR, particularly in the iron age of Joseph Stalin. And yet I must say, although many of you will not welcome my saying so, that up to a point it worked better than anything since the break-up of the monarchies in 1918. For the common citizens of the more backward countries in the region – say Slovakia and much of the Balkan peninsula – it was probably the best period in their history. It broke down because economically the system became increasingly rigid and unworkable, and especially because it proved virtually incapable of generating or making economic use of innovation, quite apart from stifling intellectual originality. Moreover, it became impossible to hide the fact from the local populations that other countries had made far more material progress than the socialist ones. If you prefer putting it another way, it broke down because ordinary citizens were indifferent or hostile, and because the regimes themselves had lost faith in what they were pretending to do. Still, however you look at it, it failed in the most spectacular manner in 1989–91.

And now? There is another model which everyone rushes to follow, parliamentary democracy in politics and the extremes of free-market capitalism in economics. In the present form it is not really a model, but chiefly a reaction against what has gone before. It may settle down to become something more workable – if it is allowed to settle down. However, even if it were to do so, in the light of history since 1918 there is not much likelihood that this region, possibly with marginal exceptions, will succeed in joining the club of the 'really' advanced and up-to-date countries. The results of imitating President Reagan and Mrs Thatcher have proved disappointing even in countries which have not been laid waste in civil war, chaos and anarchy. I should add that the results of following the Reagan–Thatcher model in the countries of its origin have not been brilliantly successful either, if you will permit a British understatement.

So, on the whole, the people of central and eastern Europe will go on living in countries disappointed in their past, probably largely disappointed with their present, and uncertain about their future. This is a very dangerous situation. People will look for someone to blame for their failures and insecurities. The movements and ideologies most likely to benefit from this mood are not, at least in this generation, those which want a return to some version of the days before 1989. They are more likely to be movements inspired by xenophobic nationalism and intolerance. The easiest thing is always to blame the strangers.

This brings me to my second and main point, which is much more directly relevant to the work of a university, or at least to that part of the work which concerns me as a historian and university teacher. For history is the raw material for nationalist or ethnic or fundamentalist ideologies, as poppies are the raw material for heroin addiction. The past is an essential element, perhaps *the* essential element, in these ideologies. If there is no suitable past, it can always be invented. Indeed, in the nature of things there is usually no entirely suitable past, because the phenomenon these ideologies claim to justify is not ancient or eternal but historically novel. This applies both to religious fundamentalism in its current versions – the Ayatollah Khomeini's version of an Islamic state is no older than the early 1970s – and to contemporary nationalism. The past legitimizes. The past gives a more glorious background to a present that doesn't have much to celebrate. I recall seeing somewhere a study of the ancient civilization of the cities of the Indus valley with the title *Five Thousand Years of Pakistan*. Pakistan was not even thought of before 1932–3, when the name was invented by some student militants. It did not become a serious political demand until 1940. As a state it has existed only since 1947. There is no evidence of any more connection between the civilization of Mohenjo Daro and the current rulers of Islamabad than there is of a connection between the Trojan War and the government in Ankara, which is at present claiming the return, if only for the first public exhibition, of Schliemann's treasure of King Priam of Troy. But 5,000 years of Pakistan somehow sounds better than forty-six years of Pakistan.

In this situation historians find themselves in the unexpected role of political actors. I used to think that the profession of history, unlike that of, say, nuclear physics, could at least do no harm. Now I know it can. Our studies can turn into bomb factories like the workshops in which the IRA has learned to transform chemical fertilizer into an explosive. This state of affairs affects us in two ways. We have a responsibility to historical facts in general, and for criticizing the politico-ideological abuse of history in particular.

I need say little about the first of these responsibilities. I would not have to say anything, but for two developments. One is the current fashion for novelists to base their plots on recorded reality rather than inventing them, thus fudging the border between historical fact and fiction. The other is the rise of 'postmodernist' intellectual fashions in Western universities, particularly in departments of literature and anthropology, which imply that all 'facts' claiming objective existence are simply intellectual constructions – in short, that there is no clear difference between fact and fiction. But there is, and for historians, even for the most militantly anti-positivist ones among us, the ability to distinguish between the two is absolutely fundamental. We cannot invent our facts. Either Elvis Presley is dead or he isn't. The question can be answered unambiguously on the basis of evidence, insofar as reliable evidence is available, which is sometimes the case. Either the present Turkish government, which denies the attempted genocide of the Armenians in 1915, is right or it is not. Most of us would dismiss any denial of this massacre from serious historical discourse, although there is no equally unambiguous way to choose between different ways of interpreting the phenomenon or fitting it into the wider context of history. Recently Hindu zealots destroyed a mosque in Aodhya, ostensibly on the grounds that the mosque had been imposed by the Muslim Moghul conqueror Babur on the Hindus in a par-ticularly sacred location which marked the birthplace of the god Rama. My colleagues and friends in the Indian universities published a study showing (a) that nobody until the nineteenth century had suggested that Aodhya was the birthplace of Rama and (b) that the mosque was almost certainly not built in the time of Babur. I wish I could say that this has had much effect on the rise of the Hindu party which provoked the incident, but at least they did their duty as historians, for the benefit of those who can read and are exposed to the propaganda of intolerance now and in the future. Let us do ours.

Few of the ideologies of intolerance are based on simple lies or fictions for which no evidence exists. After all, there was a battle of Kosovo in 1389, the Serb warriors and their allies were defeated by the Turks, and this did leave deep scars on the popular memory of the Serbs, although it does not follow that this justifies the oppression of the Albanians, who now form 90 per cent of the region's population, or the Serb claim that the land is essentially theirs. Denmark does not claim the large part of eastern England which was settled and ruled by Danes before the eleventh century, which continued to be known as the Danelaw and whose village names are still philologically Danish.

The most usual ideological abuse of history is based on anachronism rather than lies. Greek nationalism refuses Macedonia even the right to its name on the grounds that all Macedonia is essentially Greek and part of a Greek nation-state, presumably ever since the father of Alexander the Great, King of Macedonia, become the ruler of the Greek lands on the Balkan peninsula. Like everything about Macedonia, this is a far from a purely academic matter, but it takes a lot of courage for a Greek intellectual to say that, historically speaking, it is nonsense. There was no Greek nation-state or any other single political entity for the Greeks in the fourth century BC, the Macedonian Empire was nothing like a Greek or any other modern nation-state, and in any case it is highly probable that the ancient Greeks regarded the Macedonian rulers, as they did their later Roman rulers, as barbarians and not as Greeks, though they were doubtless too polite or cautious to say so. Moreover, Macedonia is historically such an inextricable mixture of ethnicities – not for nothing has it given its name to French mixed-fruit salads (*macédoine*) – that any attempt to identify it with a single nationality cannot be correct. In fairness, the extremes of emigrant Macedonian nationalism should also be dismissed for the same reason, as should all the publications in Croatia which somehow try to turn Zvonimir the Great into the ancestor of President Tudjman. But it is difficult to stand up against the inventors of a national schoolbook history, although there are historians in Zagreb University, whom I am proud to count as friends, who have the courage to do so.

These and many other attempts to replace history by myth and invention are not merely bad intellectual jokes. After all, they can determine what goes into schoolbooks, as the Japanese authorities knew, when they insisted on a sanitized version of the Japanese war in China for use in Japanese classrooms. Myth and invention are essential to the politics of identity by which groups of people today, defining themselves by ethnicity, religion or the past or present borders of states, try to find some certainty in an uncertain and shaking world by saying, 'We are different from and better than the Others.' They are our concern in the universities because the people who formulate those myths and inventions are educated people:

schoolteachers lay and clerical, professors (not many, I hope), journalists, television and radio producers. Today most of them will have gone to some university. Make no mistake about it. History is not ancestral memory or collective tradition. It is what people learned from priests, schoolmasters, the writers of history books and the compilers of magazine articles and television programmes. It is very important for historians to remember their responsibility, which is, above all, to stand aside from the passions of identity politics – even if we feel them also. After all, we are human beings too.

How serious an affair this may be is shown in a recent article by the Israeli writer Amos Elon about the way in which the genocide of the Jews by Hitler has been turned into a legitimizing myth for the existence of the state of Israel. More than this: in the years of right-wing government it was turned into a sort of national ritual assertion of Israeli state identity and superiority and a central item of the official system of national beliefs, alongside God. Elon, who traces the evolution of this transformation of the concept of the 'Holocaust' argues, following the recent Minister of Education of the new Israeli Labour government, that history must now be separated from national myth, ritual and politics. As a non-Israeli, though a Jew, I express no views about this. However, as a historian I sadly note one observation by Elon. It is that the leading contributions to the scholarly historiography of the genocide, whether by Jews or non-Jews, were either not translated into Hebrew, like Hilberg's great work, or were translated only with considerable delay, and then sometimes with editorial disclaimers. The serious historiography of the genocide has not made it any less of an unspeakable tragedy. It was merely at variance with the legitimizing myth.

Yet this very story gives us ground for hope. For here we have mythological or nationalist history being criticized from within. I note that the history of the establishment of Israel ceased to be written in Israel essentially as national propaganda or Zionist polemic about forty years after the state came into being. I have noticed the same in Irish history. About half a century after most of Ireland won its independence, Irish historians no longer wrote the history of their island in terms of the mythology of the national liberation movement. Irish history, both in the Republic and in the North, is passing through a period of great brilliance because it has succeeded in so liberating itself. This is still a matter which has political implications and risks. The history that is written today breaks with the old tradition which stretches from the Fenians to the IRA, still fighting in the name of the old myths with guns and bombs. But the fact that a new generation has grown up which can stand back from the passions of the great traumatic and formative moments of their countries' history is a sign of hope for historians.

However, we cannot wait for the generations to pass. We must resist the *formation* of national, ethnic and other myths, as they are being formed. It will not make us popular. Thomas Masaryk, founder of the Czechoslovak Republic, was not popular when he entered politics as the man who proved, with regret but without hesitation, that the medieval manuscripts on which much of the Czech national myth was based were fakes. But it has to be done, and I hope those of you who are historians will do it.

That is all I wanted to say to you about the duty of historians. However, before I close, I want to remind you of one other thing. You, as students of this university, are privileged people. The odds are that, as alumni of a distinguished and prestigious institute you will, if you choose, have a good status in society, have better careers and earn more than other people, though not so much as successful businessmen. What I want to remind you of is something I was told when I began to teach in a university. 'The people for whom you are there', said my own teacher, 'are not the brilliant students like yourself. They are the average students with boring minds who get uninteresting degrees in the lower range of the second class, and whose examination scripts all read the same. The first-class people will look after themselves, though you will enjoy teaching them. The others are the ones who need you.'

That applies not only to the university but to the world. Governments, the economy, schools, everything in society, is not for the benefit of the privileged minorities. We can look after ourselves. It is for the benefit of the ordinary run of people, who are not particularly clever or interesting (unless, of course, we fall in love with one of them), not highly educated, not successful or destined for success – in fact, are nothing very special. It is for the people who, throughout history, have entered history outside their neighbourhoods as individuals only in the records of their births, marriages and deaths. Any society worth living in is one designed for them, not for the rich, the clever, the exceptional, although any society worth living in must provide room and scope for such minorities. But the world is not made for our personal benefit, nor are we in the world for our personal benefit. A world that claims that this is its purpose is not a good, and ought not to be a lasting, world.

CHAPTER 2

The Sense of the Past

The following chapters try to sketch the relations of past, present and future, all of which are the historian's concern. The present chapter is based on my introductory paper to the 1970 conference on 'The Sense of the Past and History' of the journal Past and Present. *It was published in number 55 of that journal (May 1972) under the title 'The Social Function of the Past: Some Questions'.*

All human being are conscious of the past (defined as the period before the events directly recorded in any individual's memory) by virtue of living with people older than themselves. All societies likely to concern the historian have a past, for even the most innovatory colonies are populated by people who come from some society with an already long history. To be a member of any human community is to situate oneself with regard to one's (its) past, if only by rejecting it. The past is therefore a permanent dimension of the human consciousness, an inevitable component of the institutions, values and other patterns of human society. The problem for historians is to analyse the nature of this 'sense of the past' in society and to trace its changes and transformations.

I

For the greater part of history we deal with societies and communities for which the past is essentially the pattern for the present. Ideally each generation copies and reproduces its predecessor so far as is possible, and considers itself as falling short of it, so far as it fails in this endeavour. Of course a total domination of the past would exclude all legitimate changes and innovations, and it is improbable that there is any human society which recognizes no such innovation. It can take place in two ways. First, what is officially defined as the

10

'past' clearly is and must be a particular selection from the infinity of what is remembered or capable of being remembered. How great the scope of this formalized social past is in any society naturally depends on circumstances. But it will always have interstices, that is matters which form no part of the system of conscious history into which men incorporate, in one way or another, what they consider important about their society. Innovation can occur in these interstices, since it does not automatically affect the system, and therefore does not automatically come up against the barrier: 'This is not how things have always been done.' It would be interesting to enquire what kinds of activities tend to be thus left relatively flexible, apart from those which appear to be negligible at one time, but may turn out not to be so at a later date. One may suggest that, other things being equal, technology in the widest sense belongs to the flexible sector, social organization and the ideology or the value system to the inflexible. However, in the absence of comparative historical studies the question must be left open. Certainly there are numerous extremely tradition-bound and ritualized societies which have in the past accepted the relatively sudden introduction of new crops, new means of locomotion (such as horses among North American Indians) and new weapons, without any sense of disturbing the pattern set by their past. On the other hand there are probably others, insufficiently investigated, which have resisted even such innovation.

The 'formalized social past' is clearly more rigid, since it sets the pattern for the present. It tends to be the court of appeal for present disputes and uncertainties: law equals custom, age wisdom in illiterate societies; the documents enshrining this past, and which thereby acquire a certain spiritual authority, do the same in literate or partly literate ones. A community of American Indians may base its claim to communal lands on possession from time immemorial, or on the memory of possession in the past (very likely systematically passed on from one generation to the next), or on charters or legal decisions from the colonial era, these being preserved with enormous care: both have value as records of a past which is considered the norm for the present.

This does not exclude a certain flexibility or even *de facto* innovation, insofar as the new wine can be poured into what are at least in form the old containers. Dealing in second-hand cars appears to be a quite acceptable extension of dealing in horses to gypsies, who still maintain nomadism at least in theory as the only proper mode of life. Students of the process of 'modernization' in twentieth-century India have investigated the ways in which powerful and rigid traditional systems can be stretched or modified, either consciously or in practice, without being officially disrupted, that is in which innovation can be reformulated as non-innovation.

In such societies conscious and radical innovation is also possible, but it may be suggested that it can be legitimized in only a few ways. It may be disguised as a return to or rediscovery of, some part of the past which has been mistakenly forgotten or abandoned, or by the invention of an anti-historical principle of superior moral force enjoining the destruction of the present/past, for example a religious revelation or prophecy. It is not clear whether in such conditions even anti-historical principles can lack all appeal to the past, that is whether the 'new' principles are normally – or always? – the reassertion of 'old' prophecies, or of an 'old' genre of prophecy. The historians' and anthropologists' difficulty is that all recorded or observed cases of such primitive legitimization of major social innovations occur, almost be definition, when traditional societies are thrown into a context of more or less drastic social change, that is when the rigid normative framework of the past is strained to breaking-point and may therefore be unable to function 'properly'. Though change and innovation which comes by imposition and importation from outside, apparently unconnected with internal social forces, need not in itself affect the system of ideas about novelty held within a community – since the problem whether it is legitimate is solved by *force majeure* – at such times even the extreme traditionalist society must come to some sort of terms with the surrounding and encroaching innovation. It may of course decide to reject it *in toto*, and withdraw from it, but this solution is rarely viable for lengthy periods.

The belief that the present should reproduce the past normally implies a fairly slow rate of historic change, for otherwise it would neither be nor seem to be realistic, except at the cost of immense social effort and the sort of isolation just referred to (as with the Amish and similar sectarians in the modern USA). So long as change – demographic, technological or otherwise – is sufficiently gradual to be absorbed, as it were, by increments, it can be absorbed into the formalized social past in the form of a mythologized and perhaps ritualized history, by a tacit modification of the system of beliefs, be 'stretching' the framework, or in other ways. Even very drastic single steps of change may be so absorbed, though perhaps at great psycho-social costs, as with the forced conversion of Indians to Catholicism after the Spanish conquest. If this were not so it would be impossible for the very substantial amount of cumulative historical change which every recorded society has undergone to have taken place, without destroying the force of this sort of normative traditionalism. Yet is still dominated much of rural society in the nineteenth and even twentieth centuries, though 'what we have always done' must plainly have been very different, even among Bulgarian peasants in 1850 from what it had been in 1150. The belief that 'traditional society' is static and unchanging is a myth of vulgar social science. Nevertheless, up to a certain point of change, it can remain 'traditional': the mould of the past continues to shape the present, or is supposed to.

Admittedly to fix one's eyes upon the traditional peasantry, however great its numerical importance, is somewhat to bias the argument. In most respects such peasantries are often merely one part of a more comprehensive socio-economic or even political system within which *somewhere* changes take place uninhibited by the peasant version of tradition, or within the framework of traditions allowing for greater flexibility, for example urban ones. So long as rapid change somewhere within the system does not change the internal institutions and relations in ways for which the past provides no guide, localized changes can take place rapidly. They may even be absorbed back into a stable system of beliefs. Peasants will shake their heads over city-dwellers, notoriously and proverbially 'always seeking something new', the respectable city-dwellers over the nobility at court, dizzily pursuing an ever changing and immoral fashion. The dominance of the past does not imply an image of social immobility. It is compatible with cyclical views of historic change, and certainly with regression and catastrophe (that is failure to reproduce the past). What it is incompatible with is the idea of continuous progress.

II

When social change accelerates or transforms the society beyond a certain point, the past must cease to be the pattern of the present, and can at best become the model for it. 'We ought to return to the ways of our forefathers' when we no longer tread them automatically, or can be expected to. This implies a fundamental transformation of the past itself. It now becomes, and must become, a mask for innovation, for it no longer expresses the repetition of what has gone before, but actions which are by definition different from those that have gone before. Even if the literal attempt to turn the clock back is made, it does not really restore the old days, but merely certain parts of the formal system of the conscious past, which are now functionally different. The most ambitious attempt to restore the peasant society of Morelos (Mexico) under Zapata to what it had been forty years earlier – to expunge the era of Porfirio Diaz and return to the *status quo ante* – demonstrates this. In the first place it could not restore the past literally, since this involved some reconstruction of what could not be accurately or objectively remembered (for example the precise boundaries of common lands in dispute between different communities), not to mention the construction of 'what ought to have been' and was therefore believed, or at least imagined, to have actually existed. In the second place, the hated innovation was not a mere alien body which had somehow penetrated the social organism like some bullet lodged in the flesh and which could be surgically removed, leaving the organism substantially as it was. It represented one aspect of a social change which could not be isolated from others, and consequently could be eliminated only at the cost of changing far more than the operation envisaged. In the third place, the sheer social effort of turning the clock back almost inevitably mobilized forces which had more far-reaching effects: the armed peasants of Morelos became a revolutionary power outside their state, though their horizons were local or at best regional. Restoration under the circumstances turned into social revolution. Within the borders of the state (at least so long as the power of the peasants lasted) it probably turned the hands of the clock back further than they had actually stood in the 1870s, cutting links with a wider market economy which had existed even then. Seen in the national perspective of the Mexican revolution, its effect was to produce a historically unprecedented new Mexico.[1]

Granted that the attempt to restore a lost past cannot literally succeed, except in trivial forms (such as the restoration of ruined buildings), attempts to do so will still be made and will normally be selective. (The case of some backward peasant region attempting to restore *all* of what still existed in living memory is analytically comparatively uninteresting.) What aspects of the past will be singled out for the effort of restoration? Historians are likely to note the frequency of certain calls for restoration – in favour of the old law, the old morality, the oldtime religion and so on, and might well be tempted to generalize from this. But before they do so they ought perhaps to systematize their own observations and seek guidance from social anthropologists and others whose theories might be relevant. Moreover, before taking too super-structural a view of the matter, they might recall that attempts to restore an actual dying or dead economic structure are by no means unknown. The hope of a return to an economy of petty peasant proprietorship, though it might be little more than a big-city pastoral in nineteenth-century Britain (it was not, at least initially, shared by the actual landless rural labourers), was nevertheless an important element in radical propaganda, and occasionally more actively pursued.

A distinction ought nevertheless to be made, even in the absence of a useful general model of such selective restoration, between symbolic and effective attempts of this kind. The call for a restoration of old morality or religion is intended to be effective. If successful, then ideally *no* girl will have, say, premarital sexual intercourse or *everyone* will attend church. On the other hand the desire to restore, literally, the bombed fabric of Warsaw after the Second World War, or conversely to pull down particular records of innovation such as the Stalin monument in Prague, is symbolic, even allowing for a certain aesthetic element in it. One might suspect that this is so because what people actually wish to restore is too vast and vague for specific acts of restoration, for example past 'greatness' or past 'freedom'. The relationship between effective and symbolic restoration may indeed be complex, and both elements may always be present. The literal restoration of the fabric of parliament on which Winston Churchill insisted could be justified on effective grounds, that is the preservation of an architectural scheme which favoured a particular pattern of parliamentary politics, debate and ambience essential to the functioning of the British political system. Nevertheless, like the earlier choice of the neo-gothic style for the buildings, it also suggests a strong symbolic element, perhaps even a form of magic which, by restoring a small but emotionally charged part of a lost past, somehow restores the whole.

Sooner or later, however, it is likely that a point will be reached when the past can no longer be literally reproduced or even restored. At this point the past becomes so remote from actual or even remembered reality that it may finally turn into little more than a language for defining certain not necessarily conservative aspirations of today in historical terms. The Free Anglo-Saxons before the Norman Yoke, or Merrie England before the Reformation, are familiar examples. So, to take a contemporary illustration, is the 'Charlemagne' metaphor, which has been used, ever since Napoleon I, to propagate various forms of partial European unity, whether by conquest from the French or German side or by federation, and which patently is not intended to re-create anything even remotely like the Europe of the eighth and ninth centuries. Here (whether its proponents actually believe in it or not), the demand to restore or re-create a past so remote as to have little relevance to the present may equal total innovation, and the past thus invoked may become an artefact or, in less flattering terms, a fabrication. The name 'Ghana' transfers the history of one part of Africa to another, geographically remote and historically quite different. The Zionist claim to return to the pre-diaspora past in the land of Israel was in practice the negation of the *actual* history of the Jewish people for more than 2,000 years.[2]

Fabricated history is familiar enough, yet we ought to distinguish between those uses of it which are rhetorical or analytic and those which imply some genuine concrete 'restoration'. The English radicals of the seventeenth to nineteenth centuries hardly intended to return to pre-conquest society; the 'Norman Yoke' for them was primarily an explanatory device, the 'Free Anglo-Saxons' at best an analogy or the search for a genealogy, such as will be considered below. On the other hand modern nationalist movements, which can almost be defined, in Renan's words, as movements which forget history or rather get it wrong, because their objectives are historically unprecedented, nevertheless insist on defining them to a greater or lesser extent in historical terms and actually attempt to realize parts of this fictitious history. This applies most obviously to the definition of the national territory, or rather to territorial claims, but various forms of deliberate archaism are familiar enough, from the Welsh neo-Druids to the adoption of Hebrew as a spoken secular language and the Ordensburgen of National Socialist Germany. All these, it must be repeated, are not in any sense 'restorations' or even 'revivals'. They are innovations using or purporting to use elements of a historic past, real or imaginary.

What kinds of innovation proceed in this manner, and under what conditions? Nationalist movements are the most obvious, since history is the most easily worked raw material for the process of manufacturing the historically novel 'nations' in which they are engaged. What other movements operate in this way? Can we say that certain types of aspiration are more likely than others to adopt this mode of definition, for example those concerning the social cohesion of human groups, those embodying the 'sense of the community'? The question must be left open.

III

The problem of systematically rejecting the past arises only when innovation is recognized both as inescapable and as socially desirable: when it represents 'progress'. This raises two distinct questions, how innovation as such is recognized and legitimized, and how the situation arising from it is to be specified (that is how a model of society is to be formulated when the past can no longer provide it). The former is more easily answered.

We know very little about the process which has turned the words 'new' and 'revolutionary' (as used in the language of advertising) into synonyms for 'better' and 'more desirable', and research is badly needed here. However, it would seem that novelty or even constant innovation is more readily accepted as far as it concerns the human control over non-human nature, for example science and technology, since so much of it is obviously advantageous even to the most tradition-bound. Has there ever been a serious example of Luddism directed against bicycles or transistor radios? On the other hand, while certain socio-political innovations may appear attractive to some groups of human beings, at least prospectively, the social and human implications of innovation (including technical innovation) tend to meet with greater resistance, for equally obvious reasons. Rapid and constant change in material technology may be hailed by the very people who are profoundly upset by the experience of rapid change in human (for example sexual and family) relations, and who might actually find it hard to conceive of constant change in such relations. Where even palpably 'useful' material innovation is rejected, it is generally, perhaps always, because of the fear of the social innovation, that is disruption, it entails.

Innovation which is so obviously useful and socially neutral that it is accepted almost automatically, at all events by people to whom technological change is familiar, raises virtually no problem of legitimation. One would guess (but has the subject actually been investigated?) that even so essentially traditionalist an activity as popular institutional religion has found little difficulty in accepting it. We know of violent resistance to any change in the ancient holy texts, but there appears to have been no equivalent resistance to, say, the cheapening of holy images and icons by means of modern technological processes, such as prints and oleographs. On the other hand certain innovations require legitimation, and in periods when the past ceases to provide any precedent for them, this raises very grave difficulties. A single dose of innovation, however great, is not so troublesome. It can be presented as the victory of some permanent positive principle over its opposite, or as a process of 'correction' or 'rectification', reason prevailing over unreason, knowledge over ignorance, 'nature' over the 'unnatural', good over evil. But the basic experience of the past two centuries has been constant and continued change, which cannot be so dealt with except sometimes, at the cost of considerable casuistry, as the constantly necessary application of permanent principles to circumstances ever changing in ways which remain rather mysterious, or by exaggerating the strength of the surviving forces of evil.[3]

Paradoxically, the past remains the most useful analytical tool for coping with constant change, but in a novel form. It turns into the discovery of history as a process of directional change, of development or evolution. Change thus becomes its own legitimation, but it is thereby anchored to a transformed 'sense of the past'. Bagehot's *Physics and Politics* (1872) is a good nineteenth-century example of this; current concepts of 'modernization' illustrate more simple-minded versions of the same approach. In brief, what legitimates the present and explains it is not now the past as a set of reference points (for example Magna Carta), or even as duration (for example the age of parliamentary institutions) but the past as a process of becoming the present. Faced with the overriding reality of change, even conservative thought becomes historicist. Perhaps, because hindsight is the most persuasive form of the historian's wisdom, it suits them better than most.

But what of these who also require foresight, to specify a future which is unlike anything in the past? To do so without some sort of example is unusually difficult, and we find those most dedicated to innovation often tempted to look for one, however implausible, including in the past itself, or in what amounts to the same thing, 'primitive society' considered as a form of man's past coexisting with his present. Nineteenth- and twentieth-century socialists doubtless used 'primitive communism' merely as an analytical prop, but the fact that they used it at all indicates the advantage of being able to have a concrete precedent even for the unprecedented, or at least an example of ways of solving new problems, however inapplicable the actual solutions of the analogous problems in the past. There is, of course, no theoretical necessity for specifying the future, but in practice the demand to predict or to set up a model for it is too strong to be shrugged off.

Some sort of historicism, that is the more or less sophisticated and complex extrapolation of past tendencies into the future, has been the most convenient and popular method of prediction. At all events the shape of the future is discerned by searching the process of past development for clues, so that paradoxically, the more we expect innovation, the more history becomes essential to discover what it will be like. This procedure may range from the very naive – the view of the future as a bigger and better present, or a bigger and worse present so characteristic of technological extrapolations or pessimistic social anti-utopias – to the intellectually very complex and high-powered; but essentially history remains the basis of both. However, at this point a contradiction arises, whose nature is suggested by Karl Marx's simultaneous conviction of the inevitable supersession of capitalism by socialism, and extreme reluctance to make more than a few very general statements about what socialist and communist society would actually be like. This not merely common sense: the capacity to discern general tendencies does not imply the capacity to forecast their precise outcome in complex and in many respects unknown circumstances of the future. It also indicates a conflict between an essentially historicist mode of analysing how the future will come about, which assumes a continuing process of historical change, and what has so far been the universal requirement of programmatic models of society, namely a certain stability. Utopia is by nature a stable or self-reproducing state and its implicit a-historicism can be avoided only by those who refuse to describe it. Even less utopian models of the 'good society' or the desirable political system, however designed to meet changing circumstances, tend also to be designed to do so by means of a relatively stable and predictable framework of institutions and values, which will not be disrupted by such changes. There is no theoretical difficulty in defining social systems in terms of continuous change, but in practice there seems little demand for this, perhaps because an excessive degree of instability and unpredictability in social relations is particularly disorienting. In Comtean terms 'order' goes with 'progress', but the analysis of the one tells us little about the desirable design of the other. History ceases to be of use at the very moment when we need it most.[4]

We may therefore still be forced back upon the past, in a way analogous to the traditional use of it as a repository of precedents, though now making our selection in the light of analytical models or programmes which have nothing to do with it. This is particularly likely in the design of the 'good society', since most of what we know about the successful functioning of societies is what has been empirically learned in the course of some thousands of years of living together in human groups in a variety of ways, supplemented perhaps by the recently fashionable study of the social behaviour of animals. The value of historical enquiry into 'what actually happened' for the solution of this or that specific problem of present and future is undoubted, and has given a new lease of life to some rather old-fashioned historical activities, provided they are teamed with rather new-fangled problems. Thus what happened to the poor displaced by the massive railway building or the nineteenth century in the hearts of great cities can and ought to throw light on the possible conse-quences of massive urban motorway building in the late twentieth century, and the various experiences of 'student power' in medieval universities[5] are not without bearing on projects to change the constitutional structure of modern universities. Yet the nature of this often arbitrary process of dipping into the past for assistance in forecasting the future requires more analysis than it has so far received. By itself it does not replace the construction of adequate social models, with or without historical enquiry. It merely reflects and perhaps in some instances palliates their present inadequacy.

IV

These casual remarks are far from exhausting the social uses of the past. However, though no attempt to discuss all other aspects can be made here, two special problems may be mentioned briefly: those of the past as genealogy and as chronology.

The sense of the past as a collective continuity of experience remains surprisingly important, even to those most dedicated to innovation and the belief that novelty equals improvement: as witness the universal inclusion of 'history' in the syllabus of every modern educational system, or the search for ancestors (Spartacus, More, Winstanley) by modern revolutionaries whose theory, if they are Marxists, assumes their irrelevance. What precisely did or do modern Marxists gain from the knowledge that there were slave rebellions in ancient Rome which, even supposing their aims to have been com-munist, were by their own analysis doomed to failure or to produce results which could have little bearing on the aspirations of modern communists? Clearly the sense of belonging to an age-old tradition of rebellion provides emotional satisfaction, but how and why? Is it analogous to the sense of continuity which infuses history syllabuses and makes it apparently desirable for schoolchildren to learn of the existence of Boadicea or Vercingetorix, King Alfred or Joan of Arc as part of that body of information which (for reasons which are assumed to be valid but are rarely investigated) they are 'supposed to know about' as Englishmen or Frenchmen? The pull of the past as continuity and tradition, as 'our ancestors', is strong. Even the pattern of tourism bears witness to it. Our instinctive sympathy with the sentiment should not, however, lead us to overlook the difficulty of discovering why this should be so.

This difficulty is naturally much smaller in the case of a more familiar form of genealogy, that which seeks to buttress an uncertain self-esteem. Bourgeois parvenus seek pedigrees, new nations or movements annex examples of past greatness and achievement to their history in proportion as they feel their actual past to have been lacking in these things – whether this feeling is justified or not.[6] The most interesting question concerning such genealogical exercises is whether or when they become dispensable. The experience of modern capitalist society suggests that they may be both permanent and transitional. On the one hand late-twentieth-century *nouveaux riches* still aspire to the characteristics of the life of an aristocracy which, in spite of its political and economic irrelevance, continues to represent the highest social status (the country château, the Rhineland managing director hunting elk and boar in the implausible surroundings of socialist republics, and so on). On the other, the neo-medieval, neo-Renaissance and Louis xv buildings and décor of nineteenth-century bourgeois society gave way at a certain stage to a deliberately 'modern' style, which not only refused to appeal to the past, but developed a doubtful aesthetic analogy between artistic and technical innovation. Unfortunately the only society in history which so far gives us adequate material for studying the comparative pull of ancestors and novelty is Western capitalist society in the nineteenth and twentieth centuries. It would be unwise to generalize on the strength of a sample of one.

Finally, the problem of chronology, which takes us to the opposite extreme of possible generalization, since it is hard to think of any known society which does not for certain purposes find it convenient to record the duration of time and the succession of events. There is, of course, as Moses Finley has pointed out, a fundamental difference between a chronological and a non-chronological past: between

Homer's Odysseus and Samuel Butler's, who is naturally and quite unHomerically conceived of as a middle-aged man returning to an ageing wife after twenty years' absence. Chronology is, of course, essential to the modern, historical sense of the past, since history is directional change. Anachronism is an immediate alarm-bell for the historian, and its emotional shock-value in a thoroughly chronological society is such as to lend itself to easy exploitation in the arts: *Macbeth* in modern dress today benefits from this in a way in which a Jacobean *Macbeth* obviously did not.

At first sight it is less essential to the traditional sense of the past (pattern or model for the present, storehouse and repository of experience, wisdom and moral precept). In such a past events are not necessarily believed to exist simultaneously, like the Romans and Moors who fight one another in Spanish Easter processions, or even out of time: their chronological relation to each other is merely irrelevant. Whether Horatius of the Bridge contributed his example to later Romans before or after Mucius Scaevola is of interest only to pedants. Similarly (to take a modern example) the value of the Maccabees, the defenders of Masada and Bar Kokhba, for modern Israelis has nothing to do with their chronological distance from them and from one another. The moment when real time is introduced into such a past (for example, when Homer and the Bible are analysed by the methods of modern historical scholarship) it turns into something else. This is a socially disturbing process and a symptom of social transformation.

Yet for certain purposes historical chronology, for example in the form of genealogies and chronicles, is evidently important in many (perhaps in all?) literate, or even illiterate, societies, though the ability of literate ones to maintain permanent written records makes it possible for them to devise uses for them which would seem to be impracticable in those relying purely oral transmission. (However, though the limits of oral historical memory have been investigated from the point of view of the requirements of the modern scholar, historians have given less attention to the question how far they are inadequate to the social requirements of their own societies.)

In the broadest sense all societies have myths of creation and development, which imply temporal succession: first things were thus, then they changed thus. Conversely, a providential conception of the universe also implies some kind of succession of events, for teleology (even if its objects have already been achieved) is a kind of history. Moreover, it lends itself excellently to chronology, where such exists:

as witness the various millennial speculations or the debates about the year 1000 AD, which pivot on the existence of a system of dating.[7] In a more precise sense, the process of commenting on ancient texts of permanent validity or of discovering the specific applications of eternal truth implies an element of chronology (for example, the search for precedent). It is hardly worth mentioning that even more precise calculations of chronology may be required for a variety of economic, legal, bureaucratic, political and ritual purposes, at least in literate societies which can keep a record of them, including, of course, the invention of favourable and ancient precedents for political purposes.

In some instances the difference between such chronology and that of modern history is clear enough. The lawyers' and bureaucrats' search for precedent is entirely present-oriented. Its object is to discover the legal rights of today, the solution of modern administrative problems, whereas for the historian, however interested in their relation to the present, it is the difference of circumstances which is significant. On the other hand this does not seem to exhaust the character of traditional chronology. History, the unity of past, present and future, may be something that is universally apprehended, however deficient the human capacity to recall and record it, and some sort of chronology, however unrecognizable or imprecise by our criteria, may be a necessary measure of it. But even if this should be so, where are the demarcation lines drawn between the coexisting non-chronological and chronological past between the coexisting historical and non-historical chronologies? The answers are by no means clear. Perhaps they might throw light not only on the sense of the past of earlier societies, but on our own, in which the hegemony of one form (historical change) does not exclude the persistence, in different milieux and circumstances, of other forms of the sense of the past.

It is easier to formulate questions than answers, and this paper has taken the easier way rather than the more difficult. And yet, perhaps to ask questions, especially about the experiences we tend to take for granted, is not a valueless occupation. We swim in the past as fish do in water, and cannot escape from it. But our modes of living and moving in this medium require analysis and discussion. My object has been to stimulate both.

CHAPTER 3

What Can History Tell Us about Contemporary Society?

This chapter was originally given as a lecture to the University of California, Davis, on the occasion of its seventy-fifth anniversary in 1984. It had not previously been published. I have, where necessary, changed tenses from present to past, and eliminated some duplication with other chapters.

What can history tell us about contemporary society? In asking this question I am not simply indulging in the usual self-defence of academics who occupy themselves with interesting but apparently quite useless subjects such as ancient Latin and Greek, literary criticism or philosophy, especially when they are trying to raise funds for them from people who can only see themselves paying out good money for things which have an obvious practical pay-off, such as improving nuclear weapons or making a few million dollars. I am formulating a question which everybody is asking, and has always asked for as long as we have human records.

For where we stand in regard to the past, what the relations are between past, present and future are not only matters of vital interest to all: they are quite indispensable. We cannot help situating ourselves in the continuum of our own life, of the family and group to which we belong. We cannot help comparing past and present: that is what family photo albums or home movies are there for. We cannot help learning from it, for that is what *experience* means. We may learn the wrong things – and plainly we often do – but if we don't learn, or have had no chance of learning, or refuse to learn from whatever past is relevant for our purpose, we are, in the extreme case, mentally abnormal. 'The child who burns its fingers keeps away from fire' says the old proverb – we rely on its learning from experience. Historians are the memory bank of experience. In theory the past – all the past, anything and everything that has happened to date – constitutes history. A lot of it is not the province of historians, but a good deal of it is. And, insofar as they compile and constitute the collective memory of the past, people in contemporary society have to rely on them.

The problem is not whether they do. It is what exactly they hope to get out of the past, and if so whether that is what historians should give them. Take an example, a way of using the past which is difficult to define, but patently felt to be important. An institution – say a university – celebrates its seventy-fifth anniversary. Why exactly? What – apart from a feeling of pride, or the occasion for having a good time, or some other incidental benefits, do we get out of such a celebration of an arbitrary chronological landmark in the history of an institution? We need and use history even if we don't know why.

But what can history tell us about contemporary society? For much the greater part of the human past – indeed even in western Europe, until the eighteenth century – it was assumed that it could tell us how that society, any society, should work. The past was the model for the present and the future. For normal purposes it represented the key to the genetic code by which each generation reproduced its successors and ordered their relationships. Hence the significance of the old, who represented wisdom in terms not only of lengthy experience, but of memory of how things were and were done, and therefore how they ought to be done. The term 'senate' for the senior branch of the US Congress and other parliaments records this assumption. In certain respects this is still so, as witness the concept of precedent in legal systems based on common (that is customary, that is traditional) law. But if today 'precedent' is mainly something which has to be reinterpreted or circumvented in order to fit circumstances which are obviously *not* like the past, it used to be, and sometimes still is, literally binding. I know of an Indian community in the Central Andes of Peru which has, since the late sixteenth century, consistently been in dispute about the possession of certain lands with the neighbouring haciendas or (since 1969) co-operatives. Generation after generation of illiterate older men took illiterate boys on to the disputed high pastures of the *puna* and showed them the boundaries of the communal land they had then lost. History is here literally the authority for the present.

This example takes us to another function of history. For, if the present was in some sense unsatisfactory, the past provided the model for reconstructing it in a satisfactory form. The old days were defined – often still are – as the good old days, and that is where society should return to. This view is still very much alive: all over the world people, and political movements, define utopia as nostalgia: a return to the good old morality, that old-time religion, the values of small-town America in 1900, the literal belief in Bible or Koran – which are ancient documents – and so on. But, of course, there are today few situations when a return to the past is, or even seems, literally possible. The return to the past is either the return to something so remote that it has to be reconstructed, a 'rebirth' or 'renaissance' of classical antiquity, after many centuries of oblivion – as the intellectuals of the fifteenth and sixteenth century saw it – or, more likely, a return to something that never existed at all, but has been invented for the purpose. Zionism, or for that matter any modern nationalism, could not conceivably be a return to a lost past, because the sort of territorial nation-states with the sort of organization it envisaged simply did not exist before the nineteenth century. It had to be revolutionary innovation masquerading as restoration. It had, in fact, to invent the history it claimed to bring to fruition. As Ernest Renan said a century ago: 'Getting history wrong is an essential part of being a nation.' It is the professional business of historians to dismantle such mythologies, unless they are content – and I am afraid national historians have often been – to be the servants of ideologists. This is an important, if negative, contribution of history to telling us about contemporary society. Historians are not usually thanked by politicians for making it.

Now for the most part this sort of lesson from history of accumulated and coagulated experience is no longer significant. The present is patently not, it cannot be, a carbon-copy of the past; nor can it be modelled on it in any operational sense. Since industrialization began, the novelty of what every generation brings is much more striking than its similarity to what has gone before. Yet there is still a very large part of the world and of human affairs in which the past retains its authority, and where therefore history or experience in the genuine old-fashioned sense still operates as it did in the days of our ancestors. And, before going on to more complex matters, I think I should remind you of this.

Let me give you a concrete and utterly contemporary example: the Lebanon. It isn't only the basic situation of that collection of armed religious minorities in and around some difficult mountain territory which hasn't changed for 150 years, but the details of their politics. A Jumblatt was the chieftain of the Druzes when they massacred the Maronites in 1860, and if you give names to a photograph of the leading politicians of Lebanon at any time since then, you will find they are the same names under different political labels and costumes. A few years ago a book about Lebanon by a mid-nineteenth-century Russian was translated into Hebrew, and an Israeli military man said, 'If we had been able to read that book, we would not have made all those mistakes in the Lebanon.' What he meant was: 'We ought to have known what the Lebanon was like.' A bit of elementary history would have helped to find out. But I am bound to add that history was not the only way to find out, though one of the easier ones. We professors are inclined to put too much down to ignorance. My guess is that there were plenty of people in and around Jerusalem and Washington who could and did give sound information about Lebanon. What they said did not fit into what Begin and Sharon and President Reagan and Secretary of State Shultz (or whoever took the decisions) wanted to hear. It takes two to learn the lessons of history or anything else: one to give the information, the other to listen.

The case of Lebanon is unusual, because there are after all few countries for which books written a century ago can still serve as guides to current politics – and even political leaders. On the other hand, plain historical experience without much theory can always tell us a good deal about contemporary society. This is partly because human beings stay much the same and human situations recur from time to time. Just as older people can often say 'I've seen this before,' so can historians, on the basis of the accumulated record of many generations. And this is rather relevant.

This is because modern social science, policy-making and planning have pursued a model of scientism and technical manipulation which systematically, and deliberately, neglects human, and above all historical, experience. The fashionable model of analysis and prediction is to feed all available current data into some notional or real supercomputer and let it come out with the answers. Plain human experience and understanding does not – or not yet, or only for highly specialized purposes – lend itself to this. And such a-historical or even anti-historical calculation is often unaware of being blind, and inferior to even the unsystematic vision of those who can use their eyes. Let me give you two examples, which are of some practical importance.

The first is economic. Ever since the 1920s – actually since about 1900 – some observers have been impressed by a secular pattern of the world economy of periods of about twenty to thirty years of economic expansion and prosperity alternating with periods of economic difficulties of about the same length. They are best known under the name of 'Kondratiev long waves'. Nobody has explained or even analysed them satisfactorily. Their existence has been denied by statisticians and others. And yet they are among the few historical periodicities which have allowed prediction. The crisis of the 1970s was so predicted – I risked such a prediction myself in 1968. And when the crisis came, historians, once again on the basis of the Kondratiev experience, dismissed the analyses of economists and politicians who predicted a rapid upturn every year from 1973. And we were quite right. Moreover, and again on the same basis, when I first gave this lecture in 1984, I was prepared to stick out my neck and predict that a return to the next long period of global economic boom was extremely unlikely before the end of the 1980s or the early 1990s. I had no theoretical justification for this: only the historical observation that this sort of pattern appears to have operated, give or take some distortions by major wars, since at least the 1780s. And, one more thing. Each of the 'Kondratievs' of the past not only formed a period in strictly economic terms, but also – not unnaturally – had political characteristics which distinguished it fairly clearly from its predecessor and its successor, in terms both of international politics and of the domestic politics of various countries and regions of the globe. That is also likely to continue.

My second illustration is more specific. During the Cold War there was a moment when the sensitive instruments of the US government recorded what looked like the launch of Russian nuclear missiles towards America. No doubt some general got ready for immediate action, while waiting for other sensitive instruments automatically to check up, at lightning speed, on these readings to see whether there had been some malfunction, or whether some harmless signals had been misread – in fact whether the Third World War had started or whether it hadn't. They concluded that it was okay, for the entire process was, inevitably, blind. The programming itself had to be based on the assumption that the worst could happen at any moment, for if it did there would be virtually no time for counter-measures. But, whatever the instruments said, it was as certain as anything can be that, in June 1980, when this incident occurred, nobody had deliberately pressed the nuclear button. The situation simply didn't look like it. I, and I hope we all, would have made this judgment, not for any theoretical reason – for a sudden surprise launch was not theoretically inconceivable – but simply because, unlike other instruments, the computer in our heads has, or can have, historical experience built into it.

So much for what one might call the old-fashioned, experiential use of history – the kind which Thucydides and Machiavelli would have recognized and practised. Now let me say a word about the much more difficult problem of what history can tell us about contemporary societies, insofar as they are quite *unlike* the past; insofar as they are without precedents. I don't mean just different. History, even when it generalizes most effectively – and in my view it is worth nothing much if it doesn't generalize – is always aware of unlikeness. The first lesson a professional historian learns is to watch out for anachronism, or differences in what at first sight seems to be the same, such as the British monarchy in 1797 and 1997. In any case history writing has traditionally grown out of the recording of specific and unrepeatable lives and events. No, what I mean is historical transformations which plainly make the past a fundamentally inadequate guide to the present. Though the history of Tokugawa Japan is relevant to Japan today, and the T'ang dynasty to China in 1997, it is no use pretending that either can be understood simply as modified prolongations of their past. And such rapid, profound, dramatic and continuing transformations are characteristic of the world since the late eighteenth century, and especially since the mid-twentieth.

Such innovation is now so general and evident that it is assumed to be the basic rule, particularly in societies like that of the USA, most of whose history falls into the era of constant revolutionary transformations, and by the young in such societies, for whom – at various moments of their development – everything in fact is a new discovery. In this sense we all grow up as Columbuses. One of the lesser functions of historians is to point out that innovation is not and cannot be absolutely universal. No historian will give a moment's credence to the claim that someone today has somehow discovered an absolutely new way of enjoying sex, a so-called 'G-spot' which was unknown to humanity before. Given the finite number of things that can be done between sexual partners of whatever kind, the length of time and the number of people who have been doing it all over the globe, and the persistent interest of human beings in exploring the subject, it can safely be assumed that absolute novelty is out of the question. Sexual practices and attitudes to them certainly change, as do the costumes and décor of what is often a form of private bedroom theatre of social and biographical symbolism. For obvious reasons S/M in motorcycle gear could not be part of it in the days of Queen Victoria. Probably the sexual fashion-cycle changes more rapidly today than in the past, like all other fashion-cycles. But history is a useful warning against confusing fashion with progress.

Still, what else can history say about the unprecedented? At bottom this is a question about the direction and the mechanism of human evolution. For, like it or not – and there are plenty of historians who don't like it – there is one central question in history which cannot be avoided, if only because we all want to know the answer to it. Namely: how did humanity get from caveman to space-traveller, from a time when we were scared by sabre-toothed tigers to a time when we are scared by nuclear explosions – that is scared not by the hazards of nature but by those we have created ourselves? What makes this an essentially historical question is that human beings, though recently rather taller and heavier than ever before, are biologically much the same as at the beginning of the historical record, which is not actually very long: perhaps 12,000 years since the first city, perhaps a bit longer since the invention of farming. We are almost certainly not more intelligent than the ancient Mesopotamians or Chinese. And yet the way human societies live and operate has been utterly transformed. Hence, incidentally, the irrelevance of socio-biology for this particular purpose. Hence also, I would add with a little more hesitation, the irrelevance of a certain type of social anthropology, which concentrates on what various types of human societies have in common: both Eskimos and the Japanese. For, if we fix our attention on what is permanent, we cannot explain what has obviously been transformed, unless we believe that there can be no historical change but only combination and variation.

Let me be quite clear. The purpose of tracing the historical evolution of humanity is not to foresee what will happen in future, even though historical knowledge and understanding are essential to anyone who wants to base their actions and plans on something better than clairvoyance, astrology or just plain voluntarism. The only result of a horse-race which historians can tell us with absolute confidence is one that has already been run. Still less is it to discover or devise legitimations for our hopes – or fears – for human destiny. History is not a secular eschatology, whether we conceive its objective as unending universal progress or a communist society or whatever. These are things we read into it, but cannot derive from it. What it can do is to discover the patterns and mechanisms of historical change in general, and more particularly of the transformations of human societies during the past few centuries of dramatically accelerated and widened change. This, rather than forecasts or hopes, is what is directly relevant to contemporary society and its prospects.

Now such a project requires an analytical framework for the analysis of history. Such a framework must be based on the one element of directional change in human affairs which is observable and objective, irrespective of our subjective or contemporary wishes and value-judgments, namely the persistent and increasing capacity of the human species to control the forces of nature by means of manual and mental labour, technology and the organization of production. Its reality is demonstrated by the growth of the human population of the globe throughout history, without significant setbacks, and the growth – particularly in the past few centuries – of production and productive capacity. Personally, I don't mind calling this progress, both in the literal sense of a directional process and because few of us will not regard it as a potential or actual improvement. But, never mind what we call it, any genuine attempt to make sense of human history must take this trend as its starting-point.

Here lies the crucial importance of Karl Marx for historians, for he built his conception and analysis of history on this basis – and so far no one else has. I don't mean Marx is right, or even that he is adequate, but that his approach is indispensable, as Ernest Gellner put it (and nobody was less of a Marxist than this notable scholar):

> Whether or not people positively believe in the Marxist scheme, no coherent, well-articulated rival pattern has emerged, West or East, and as people must need think against some kind of grid, even (or perhaps especially) those who do not accept the Marxist theory of history tend to lean upon its ideas when they wish to say what they do positively believe.[1]

In other words, no serious discussion of history is possible which doesn't refer back to Marx or, more exactly, which does not start where he starts. And that means, basically – as Gellner accepts – a materialist conception of history.

Now an analysis of the process of history raises a number of questions which are directly relevant to us. To take one obvious one. For most of recorded history most human beings were engaged in basic food production: say 80–90 per cent of the population. Today, as North America demonstrates, a farming population of the order of

3 per cent of the inhabitants of one country can produce enough food to feed not only the other 97 per cent but a large slice of the rest of the world population. Again, for most of the industrial era the production of manufactured goods and services, even when it was not labour-intensive, required a vast and growing labour force, but at present this is rapidly ceasing to be the case. For the first time in history it is no longer necessary that the bulk of humanity must, in the biblical phrase, 'eat thy bread in the sweat of thy face'. This happens to be a development of very recent history. The decline of the peasantry in the Western world, though long predicted, did not become dramatic until the 1950s and 1960s, and the decline of the socially necessary productive labour force outside farming – though, interestingly enough, envisaged by, of all people, Marx – is even more recent, and is still masked, or more than offset, by the rise of tertiary employment. And, of course, both are still regional rather than global phenomena. Now such a basic transformation in the secular occupational structure of humanity cannot but have far-reaching consequences, since the entire value-system of most men and women, at least since the end of Marshall Sahlins' era of 'stone-age affluence', has been geared to the need to labour as an inescapable fact, the bottom line of human existence.

History has no simple formula for discovering the exact consequences of this change, or solutions for the problems it is likely to create, or has already created. But it can pinpoint *one* urgent dimension of the problem, namely the need for social redistribution. For most of history the basic mechanism for economic growth has been the appropriation of the social surplus generated by man's capacity to produce by minorities of one kind or another for purposes of investment in further improvement, though it has not always been so used. Growth operated through inequality. Now hitherto this has been to some extent offset by the enormous growth in total wealth which, as Adam Smith pointed out, made even the labourer in developed economies materially better off than the Red Indian chieftain, and which, by and large, made each generation better off than its predecessors. But they have shared in these benefits, in however modest a way, through participation in the productive process – that is through having jobs, or as peasants and craftsmen being able to earn incomes by selling their output on the market. For peasant self-sufficiency has dramatically declined in the developed world.

Now suppose a majority of the population is no longer needed for production. What do they live on? And – equally important in a business economy – what happens to the mass market based on their purchases, on which that economy has increasingly come to depend, first in the USA, later in other countries? In one way or another they have to live by public transfer payments, such as pensions, and other forms of social security and welfare – that is by a political and administrative mechanism of social redistribution. In the past thirty years this welfare mechanism has expanded enormously and, on the strength of the greatest economic boom in history, on a remarkably generous scale in a number of countries. The enormous growth of the state sector, in other words public employment, much of which is also a form of hand-out – in both West and East has also had analogous effects. On the one hand welfare expenditure for income maintenance, health and social care and education now – or anyway in 1977 – forms between half and two-thirds of total public expenditure in the leading OECD countries, and on the other in these countries anything between 25 per cent and about 40 per cent of the total of household incomes comes from public employment and social security.

To this extent a mechanism of redistribution has already come into existence, and, where it has, it is safe to say that the chances that it will be dismantled are negligible. So much for the Reaganite dream of returning to the economics of President McKinley. But note two things. First, as we can see, this mechanism, through the tax burdens it imposes, creates genuine pressures on what is in the West still the major engine of economic growth, namely entrepreneurial profits, especially during a period of economic difficulties. Hence the current pressures to dismantle it. But, second, this mechanism was not designed for an economy in which the *majority* might be surplus to productive requirements. On the contrary, it was constructed for, and supported by, a period of unexampled full employment. And, third, it is designed, like any poor law, to provide a minimum income, though this is today more generous than was ever thought conceivable even in the 1930s.

So, even if we suppose that it works well and is extended, the mechanism is likely, in the conditions I have envisaged, to increase and intensify economic and every other kind of inequality, as between the superfluous majority and the rest. So what happens then? The traditional assumption, that economic growth, though destroying some employment, generates even more somewhere else, can no longer be relied on.

In some ways this internal inequality is analogous to the familiar, and growing, inequality between the minority of rich and developed or developing countries and the poor and backward world. In both cases the gap is growing, and looks like growing wider. In both cases economic growth through a market economy, however impressive, has plainly *not* been an automatically effective mechanism for diminishing internal or international inequalities, even though it has tended to increase the industrialized sector of the globe, and may be in the process of redistributing wealth and power within it – for example, from the USA to Japan.

Now leaving morality and ethics and social justice to one side, this situation creates, or intensifies, serious problems – economic and political. Since the inequalities built into these historical developments are inequalities of power as well as welfare, it is possible to dismiss them in the short run. This is in fact what most of the powerful states and classes are tempted to do today. Poor people and poor countries are weak, and disorganized, and technically incompetent: relatively more so today than in the past. Inside our countries we can leave them to stew in ghettos, or as an unhappy underclass. We can protect the lives and environments of the rich behind electrified fortifications protected by private – and public – security forces. We can, to use a phrase of a British minister about Northern Ireland, try to settle for 'an acceptable level of violence'. Internationally, we can bomb them and beat them. As the poet wrote of the period of early twentieth-century imperialism:

> We have got
> The Maxim gun and they have not.

The only non-Western power that the West was scared of was the only one that could hit them at home: the USSR, and that has ceased to exist.

In short, it is assumed that the economy will somehow sort itself out once the present crisis gives way to another phase of global boom, because it always has in the past; and that the poor and discontented, at home and abroad, can be permanently contained. Perhaps the first is a reasonable assumption: but only if we also recognize that it is practically certain that the world economy, and the state structures and policies, and the international pattern of the developed world, which will emerge from the present 'Kondratiev' phase, will be profoundly, and dramatically, different from those of the 1950s–1970s, as was the case after the last general secular crisis period between the two world wars. That is one thing which history can tell us, on both theoretical and empirical grounds. The second is not a reasonable assumption at all, except in the short term. It may be reasonable to assume that the poor will no longer be mobilized for protest, pressure, social change and revolution nationally or internationally, in the ways they were between the 1880s and the 1950s, but not that they will remain permanently ineffective as political, or even military, forces – especially when they cannot be bought off by prosperity. That is another thing that history can tell us. What it can't tell us is what will happen: only what problems we will have to solve.

Let me conclude. In practice, I will admit, most of what history can tell us about contemporary societies is based on a combination of historical experience and historical perspective. It is the business of historians to know a lot more about the past than other people, and they cannot be good historians unless they have learned, with or without theory, to recognize similarities and differences. For instance, while most politicians in the past forty years read the international danger of war in terms of the 1930s – a replay of Hitler, Munich and the rest – most historians concerned with international politics, while naturally accepting that it was *sui generis*, were gloomily impressed with its similarities to the period before 1914. As long ago as 1965 one of them wrote a study of the pre-1914 armaments race under the title 'Yesterday's Deterrent'. Unfortunately one thing historical experience has also taught historians is that nobody ever seems to learn from it. Still, we must go on trying.

But more generally, and this is one reason why the lessons of history are so seldom learned or heeded, the world is up against two forces which obscure vision. One I have already mentioned. It is the a-historical, engineering, problem-solving approach by means of mechanical models and devices. This has produced marvellous results in a number of fields, but it has no perspective, and it cannot take account of anything not fed into the model or the device from the start. And one thing historians know is that we haven't fed all the variables into the model, and the other things outside are never equal. (This is one thing the history of the USSR and its fall should have taught us all.) The other I have also mentioned. It is the systematic distortion of history for irrational purposes. Why, to return to a point I made earlier, do all regimes make their young study some history in school? Not to understand their society and how it changes, but to approve of it, to be proud of it, to be or become good citizens of the USA or Spain or Honduras or Iraq. And the same is true of causes and movements. History as inspiration and ideology has a built-in tendency to become self-justifying myth. Nothing is a more dangerous blindfold than this, as the history of modern nations and nationalisms demonstrates.

It is the business of historians to try and remove these blindfolds, or at least to lift them slightly or occasionally – and, insofar as they do, they can tell contemporary society some things it might benefit from, even if it is reluctant to learn them. Fortunately, universities are the one part of the educational system where historians have been allowed, even encouraged, to do this. It was not always so, for the profession of history has grown up largely as a collection of people serving their regimes and justifying them. It is still by no means universally so. But to the extent that universities have become the places where a critical history can most easily be practised – one which is capable of assisting us in contemporary society – a university celebrating its anniversary is a good place in which to express these opinions.

CHAPTER 4

Looking Forward:
History and the Future

This paper was delivered at the London School of Economics as the first David Glass Memorial Lecture, and published separately by the LSE and in the New Left Review *125 (February 1981), pp. 3–19. It has been slightly shortened.*

The lectures of which this is the first are intended to commemorate David Glass. He was one of the most distinguished scholars to teach at the LSE, with which he was so long associated and whose reputation owes much to his presence there. I might add that he represented its finest traditions at a time when not everyone there did so: the traditions of understanding society in order to make it better, of an instinctive radicalism, of an institution whose students, like himself, were not born with silver spoons in their mouths. It is typical that he concluded his very first book on demography – of which he was in his lifetime the most eminent practitioner in Britain – with the call to 'provide conditions in which the working class is able to bring up children without thereby suffering from economic and social hardship'. He was proud to be the first social scientist to be elected to the Royal Society since the great Dr William Farr in 1855, because he saw himself (like Farr) as a social scientist *in* and *for* society, and not just about society.

So it is natural that the lectures devoted to his memory should be about 'social trends', which I understand to mean in the broad sense the enquiry into the direction of social development and what we can do about it. That implies looking into the future, so far as this is possible. This is a risky, frequently a disappointing, but also a necessary activity. And all prediction about the real world rests to a great extent on some sort of inferences about the future from what has happened in the past, that is to say from history. The historian ought therefore to have something relevant to say about the subject.

Conversely, history cannot get away from the future, if only because there is no line which divides the two. What I have just said now belongs to the past. What I am about to say belongs to the future. Somewhere between the two there is a notional but constantly moving point which, if you like, you can call the 'present'. There may be technical reasons for considering past and future differently, as any bookmaker knows. There may also be technical reasons for distinguishing present from past. We cannot ask the past for *direct* answers to any questions which have not already been put to it, though we can use our ingenuity as historians to read indirect answers into what it has left behind. Conversely, as every pollster knows, we can ask the present any answerable question, though by the time it is answered and recorded it will also, strictly speaking, belong to the past, albeit the recent past. Nevertheless past, present and future form a continuum.

Moreover, even when historians and philosophers want to make a sharp distinction between past and future, as some do, nobody else will follow them. All human beings and societies are rooted in the past – that of their families, communities, nations or other reference groups, or even of personal memory – and all define their position in relation to it, positively or negatively. Today as much as ever: one is almost tempted to say 'more than ever'. What is more, the overwhelmingly large part of conscious human action which is based on learning, memory and experience constitutes a vast mechanism for constantly confronting past, present and future. People cannot help trying to forecast the future by some form of reading the past. They have to. The ordinary processes of conscious human life, not to mention public policy, require it. And of course they do so on the justified assumption that, by and large, the future is systematically connected with the past, which in turn is not an arbitrary con-catenation of circumstances and events. The structures of human societies, their processes and mechanisms of reproduction, change and transformation, are such as to restrict the number of things that can happen, determine some of the things that will happen, and make it possible to assign greater or lesser probabilities to much of the rest. This implies a certain (admittedly limited) range of pre-dictability – but, as we all know, this is by no means the same as successful forecasting. Still, it is worth bearing in mind that unpredictability looms so large mainly because arguments about prediction tend to concentrate, for obvious reasons, on those parts of the future where uncertainty appears to be greatest, and not on those where it is least. Meteorologists are not needed to tell us that spring will follow winter.

My own view is that it is desirable, possible and even necessary to forecast the future to some extent. This implies neither that the future is determined nor, even if it were, that it is knowable. It does not imply that there are no alternative choices or outcomes, and even less that forecasters are right. The questions I have in mind are rather: How much prediction? Of what kind? How can it be improved? And where do historians fit into this? Even if anyone can answer these questions, there will still be much of the future about which we can know nothing, for theoretical or practical reasons, but at least we may concentrate our efforts more effectively.

However, before I consider these questions, let me reflect for a moment on the reasons not only why the function of prognosis is so unpopular among many historians, but also why so little intellectual effort has gone into improving it, or considering its problems, even among those historians firmly committed to its desirability and practicability, such as Marxists. The answer, you may say, is obvious. The track-record of historical prediction is, to put it moderately, patchy. Every one of us who has made predictions has frequently fallen flat on his or her face. The safest thing is to avoid prophecy by claiming that our professional activities stop at yesterday, or to confine ourselves to the studied ambiguities which used to be the speciality of ancient oracles and are still the stock-in-trade of newspaper astrologers. But in fact, a poor predictive record has not stopped other people, disciplines or pseudo-disciplines from forecasting. There is a large industry devoted to it today, undeterred by its failures and uncertainties. The Rand Corporation has even in despair re-established an updated version of the Oracle of Delphi (I am not joking; the name of this peculiar game is the 'Delphi technique') by asking selected groups of experts to consult their chicken's entrails and then drawing conclusions from such consensus as may or may not emerge. Moreover, there are plenty of examples of good predictions among historians, social scientists and academically unclassifiable observers. If you do not wish to have Marx quoted at you, let me refer you to de Tocqueville and Burckhardt. Unless we assume, what is unlikely, that these are purely random hits, we must accept that they are based on methods which are worth enquiring into if we are to concentrate our fire on targets we can expect to hit and improve our ratio of bull's-eyes to misses. And, conversely, the reasons for notorious flops are worth enquiring into with the same object.

One such set of reasons is, unfortunately, the force of human desire. Both human and meteorological prediction are unreliable and uncertain enterprises, though they cannot be dispensed with. On the other hand those who use meteorology know that they cannot – or, if you prefer, cannot yet – change the weather. They aim to plan their actions in such a way as to make the best use of what they cannot change. Individual human beings probably use forecasts in much the same way in the comparatively rare cases where they take effective action upon them. My late father-in-law, having concluded correctly that Austria could not avoid Hitler, transferred his business from Vienna to Manchester in 1937 – but not many other Viennese Jews were as logical as he. However, collectively human beings are inclined to look to historical forecasts for knowledge which will enable them to alter the future; not only, as it were, when to stock up with suntan lotion but when to create sunshine. Since some human decisions, large or small, clearly do make a difference to the future, this expectation is not to be entirely dismissed. However, it affects the process of forecasting, generally adversely. Thus, unlike meteorology, historical forecasts are accompanied by a running commentary from those who think they are impossible or undesirable on various grounds, usually because we don't like what they tell us. Historians also suffer the disadvantage of lacking solid bodies of customers who, whatever their ideology, need weather forecasts regularly and urgently: sailors, farmers and the rest.

We are surrounded by people, notably in politics, who proclaim the need to learn the lessons of the past when they do not already proclaim that they have already discovered them, but since virtually all of them are chiefly interested in using history to justify what they would have wanted to do anyway, unfortunately this provides little incentive to improve the predictive capacities of historians.

However, we cannot only blame the customers. The prophets too must take their share of the blame. Marx himself was committed to a specific goal of human history, communism, and a specific role for the proletariat *before* he developed the historical analysis which, as he believed, demonstrated its ineluctability – indeed before he knew very much about the proletariat. Insofar as his predictions preceded his historical analysis, they cannot be said to rest on it, though this does not necessarily make them wrong. We must at the very least be careful to distinguish predictions based on analysis from those based on desire. Thus in the famous passage on the historical tendency of capitalist accumulation, Marx's forecast of the expropriation of the

individual capitalist through 'the immanent laws of capitalist production itself' (that is through the concentration of capital and the
necessity for an increasingly social form of the labour process, the
conscious use of technology and the planned exploitation of the
resources of the globe) rests on a different and more significant
historical–theoretical analysis than the forecast that the proletariat
itself will as a class be the 'expropriator of the expropriators'. The
two forecasts, though linked, are not identical, and indeed we may
accept the first without accepting the second.

All of us who have made predictions – and who has not? – know
these psychological, or if you prefer ideological, temptations. Nor
have we avoided them. If historical predicters were as neutral about
the social depressions and anticyclones they forecast as meteorologists,
historical prognosis would be more advanced than it is. Together
with sheer ignorance, this is, I believe, the major obstacle in the
forecaster's way. It is a much more serious one than the fact that
predictions can be falsified by the conscious actions of people who
are aware of them. There is little empirical evidence that such action
has so far been taken often or effectively. The safest empirical
generalization about history is still that nobody heeds even its obvious
lessons much – as any student of the agrarian policies of socialist
regimes or of Mrs Thatcher's economic policies will confirm. Oedipus
unfortunately remains a parable of humanity confronted with the
future, but, alas, with one major difference: Oedipus genuinely wanted
to avoid killing his father and marrying his mother (as the Oracle
correctly foretold), but could not. Most prophets and their customers
are apt to argue that unpleasant forecasts are in some ways avoidable
because they are unpleasant, that they do not mean what they say,
or that something will turn up to invalidate them.

As I have suggested, there is already a large forecasting industry.
Most of it is concerned with the effect of future developments on
fairly specific activities, mainly in the fields of economics and civil
and military technology. It therefore asks a fairly specific and restricted
set of questions which can be to some extent isolated, even though
of course they may be affected by a vast range of variables. There is
also an enormous amount of prediction which, whether or not it
bears on public or private practice, is not intended to foretell the
actual future but to confirm or falsify. Hence it is normally made in
conditional form. In principle it does not matter whether verification
occurs in the real future or in a specially constructed future such as
a laboratory situation from which all elements extrinsic to the matter

in hand have been eliminated. There are also propositions, mostly of the logico-mathematical type, which establish consequences. If a real situation happens to correspond to these, they may be said to predict such consequences.

Historical prediction differs from all other forms of forecasting in two ways. In the first place, historians are concerned with the real world in which other things are never equal or negligible. To this extent they know that there is no ideal global laboratory in which we could, as is theoretically conceivable, construct a situation where market prices would have a predictable relation to the monetary supply. Historians are by definition concerned with complex and changing ensembles and even their most specific and narrowly defined questions make sense only within this context. Unlike, say, the forecasters of large travel agencies, historians are interested in future trends in holiday-making not because they are our primary concern – though we may do specialist research in the field – but in relation to the rest of changing British society and culture in a changing world. In this respect history resembles disciplines like ecology, though it is wider and more complex. While we can and must single out particular strands from the seamless web of interactions, if we were not interested primarily in the web itself we should not be doing ecology or history. Historical forecasting is therefore, in principle, designed to provide the general structure and texture which, at least potentially, includes the means of answering all the specific forecasting questions which people with special interests may wish to make – of course insofar as they are answerable at all.

In the second place, as theorists historians are not concerned with forecasting as confirmation. Many of their predictions could not in any case be tested within the lifetime of this or the next generations, any more than the predictions of historical disciplines in the natural sciences can be – for example, those of climatologists about future ice ages. We may trust the climatologists more than the historians, but we still cannot verify them. To say that analyses of the tendencies of social change must 'be formulated as verifiable predictive propositions' shows kindness to our children and grandchildren but unkindness to poor old Vico, Marx, Max Weber and incidentally Darwin, because it constricts the scope of social analysis and misunderstands history, whose essence is to study complex transformations over time. It is, one might say, a matter of convenience that history concentrates on the data already available, and not on those which the future has not yet made available. Prediction may or may not be desirable to test it, but it emerges automatically from making statements about the continuum between past, present and future, because this implies references to the future; even if many historians may prefer to avoid actually extending their statements forward. To adapt Auguste Comte's phrase, *savoir* is not *pour prévoir* but *prévoir* is part of *savoir*, foreseeing is part of knowing.

And historians are constantly foreseeing, if only retrospectively. Their future happens to be the present or a more recent past compared to a more remote past. The most conventional and 'anti-scientific' historians are perpetually analysing the consequences of situations and events, or alternative counterfactual possibilities, the emergence of one era out of its predecessor. Some who do so most assiduously, like Lord Dacre (Hugh Trevor-Roper) in his Oxford valedictory, use it to argue against predictability, but they use techniques of prediction to do so. Now the methods elaborated to analyse historical causes, consequences and alternatives with the benefit of the futurologists' ultimate but inaccessible weapon, namely hindsight, are relevant to forecasters, since they are in principle similar. Their value rests not only on the enormous accumulation of actual historical experiences of all kinds which may serve to guide the present; not only on the record of past predictions which may be tested against actual outcomes in order to determine why there were right or wrong; and not only on the very considerable practical experience and judgment which historians have acquired over the generations in pursuing their activities. It rests chiefly on two things. First, historians' forecasts, retrospective though they be, are precisely about the complex and all-embracing reality of human life, about the other things which are never equal, and which are in fact not 'other things', but the system of relationships from which statements about human life in society can never be entirely abstracted. And second, any historical discipline worthy of the name attempts to discover precisely those patterns of interaction in society, those mechanisms and tendencies of change and transformation, and those directions of the transformation in society, which alone provide an adequate framework for forecasting that is more than what has been called 'statistical projections based on compilations of empirical data within categories of perhaps little theoretical significance'. More even than the sort of imaginative presentiment or *Ahnung*, to use Burckhardt's term, which is the historian's equivalent of flying by the seat of one's pants. I do not undervalue it: but it is not enough. And here, if you will excuse a brief commercial, lies the unique value of Marx and those who, whether Marxists or not, adopt a similar approach to historical development.

These predictions by means of history use two methods, generally in combination: the prediction of tendencies by means of generalization, or modelling; and the prediction of actual events or outcomes by means of a sort of path analysis. Predicting the continued decline of the British economy is an example of the first, predicting the future of Mrs Thatcher's government is an example of the second. Predicting something like the Russian or Iranian Revolutions (which we happen to know in one case, but not yet in the other) combines the two methods. Both are required, if only because actual events do make a difference to at least some tendencies, as the division of Germany in 1945 has to the analysis of social trends in what are now two very different countries [as became evident after they were reunited in 1990]. Now the present margin of uncertainty about future events is so large – even when they can subsequently be shown to have been far from uncertain, like a 'fixed' boxing-match – that we can only narrow it to a set of alternative scenarios. We can also neglect some unpredictables as trivial, but this usually implies a judgment of significance in the light of our questions. Still, many such unpredictables are accepted as insignificant today: we may not know whether an American president will be assassinated, but analysis and experience suggest that it is unlikely to make much difference. Others are commonly accepted as trivial and may be left to the sort of politician for whom a week is a long time in politics and the sort of historian who thirsts to know exactly what Sir Stafford Northcote wrote to R. A. Cross on 8 October 1875. Others plainly can't. Nevertheless, we can do more than merely present the customer with an array of equally probable scenarios, preferably broken down into a series of binary choices, as in the Jewish jokes in which every situation contains two possibilities. This is where the historian's exercises in retrospective prediction can provide guidance.

It may be useful at this point to look at a particular exercise in retrospective forecasting in this light: the Russian Revolution, an episode where hindsight may actually be checked against contemporary foresight. Since this inevitably involves some consideration of might-have-beens, such retrospective prediction could be regarded as a form of counterfactual history (that is history as it might have happened but did not). So it is, but it ought nevertheless to be distinguished from the commonest and most publicized form of counterfactual speculation in this field, that of the 'cliometricians'. It is not my object to deny the interest of such cost-benefit analyses of the past – for that is what they amount to – or to discuss their validity. I merely observe that in the form made fashionable in quantitative economic history, they usually have nothing to do with assessing historical probabilities. A slave economy may have been economically viable, efficient and a good business proposition – I am not entering that debate – but the question whether it was likely to last is not affected by these propositions, only the arguments about its capacity to last. In fact it disappeared everywhere in the nineteenth century, and its decline and fall were confidently and correctly forecast. Forecasting, retrospective or not, is about assessing probabilities, or it is about nothing.

A Russian revolution was widely expected, irrespective of the particular and unpredictable circumstances of its actual outbreak in 1905 and 1917. Why? Clearly because a structural analysis of Russian society and its institutions led to the belief that Tsarism was unlikely to overcome its internal weaknesses and contradictions. If correct, such an analysis would in principle override minor might-have-beens – as indeed it did. Even if we grant that in theory good policy and able rulers might have done the trick, they could only do so, as it were, by pushing Sisyphus' stone all the way uphill in order to make it roll down in the right direction. In fact, Tsarism had effective policies and good statesmen from time to time and an astonishing record of economic growth, which has misled some liberals into the belief that all might have come right but for accidents such as the war and Lenin. It was not enough. The odds were against Tsarism, even if Lenin as a politician was wise to leave open the possibility that, for example, Stolypin's agrarian policy might have proven successful.

Why did a number of people, against most Western aspirations and expectations (including those of Russian Marxists, Lenin among them) come to doubt that a Russian revolution would result in a bourgeois-democratic government of the Western type? Because it soon became clear that the liberals or any other middle-class groups were too weak to achieve this solution. Indeed the weakness of the Russian middle class was revealed between 1905 and 1917 at a time when the Russian bourgeoisie were growing much stronger and more self-confident than they had been before 1900. Too confident in 1917, it has been argued by at least one good historian, who believes that the radicalization of the urban workers in 1917 was precipitated by an attempt to reimpose control in the factories which it was no longer able to do. Today such forward prediction would be easier, if only because we have learned since 1914 how historically specific the conditions for stable liberal-democratic regimes are, how conditional the commitment of bourgeoisie and middle strata to such regimes, and how precarious they may be. In the light of these lessons of history – not by an means unpredictable if we remember Burckhardt and other conservative forecasters – we might have considered the possibility of a non-democratic but capitalist alternative to Bolshevism: perhaps a military–bureaucratic regime. But given the collapse of the armed forces in 1917 we can see that this was not at all probable.

On the other hand, the actual outcome in October 1917 certainly seemed among the least likely options in 1905 and hardly more likely in February 1917: a Russia committed to install socialism under Bolshevik leadership. Even Marxists unanimously held that the conditions for proletarian revolution in Russia *alone* were simply not present. Kautsky and the Mensheviks argued, logically enough, that the attempt was bound to fail. In any case the Bolsheviks were a minority. So improbable was this outcome that it is still fashionable to ascribe the October Revolution entirely to Lenin's decision to make a sort of putsch in the brief period when it had a chance of success. There were of course structural reasons why such an outcome was not as totally implausible as it seemed. We know that Marxist governments have come to power by revolution precisely in the sort of countries Marxists didn't expect them to. (We also know, incidentally, that such revolutions can have quite different outcomes.) Lenin himself had already in 1908 drawn attention to this kind of 'inflammable material in world politics' and anticipated what was later to be called the 'weakest link' theory of revolutionary prospects. However, there was no way of predicting, as distinct from hoping for, a Bolshevik victory, and still less lasting success. Nevertheless, predictive analysis was far from impossible. It was indeed the basis of Lenin's policy. It is utterly absurd to see Lenin as a voluntarist. Action was a function of what was possible, and nobody mapped the changing territory on the march more carefully than he did nor with a more ruthless sense of what was impossible. Indeed the Soviet regime survived – and in doing so turned itself into something far from his original expectations – just because, time and again, he recognized what had to be done, like it or not. Even had he wanted to be a voluntarist like Mao, he was in no position to be one in 1917, since he could not make anything whatever happen by taking decisions: he did not automatically control even his party and that party did not control much. It is only after revolutionaries have become governments that they can make people do things – within limits which even strong governments do not always recognize.

We need not follow Lenin's analysis, since he was interested in only one outcome, but we can make a parallel analysis. To put it briefly, the basic question in 1917 was not who would take over in Russia, but whether anyone would establish an effective regime. The reasons why the provisional government couldn't succeed, failing immediate peace – which raised problems in any case – are clear. The Bolsheviks won: (a) because unlike almost everybody else on the left they were ready to take over; (b) because they were consistently more ready to recognize and take account of what was happening at the grassroots; (c) because – largely for this reason – they gained control of the situation in Petrograd and Moscow; and, only lastly, (d) because at the crucial moment they were ready to seize power. The only alternative to Bolshevism in October was *de facto* anarchy. Various possible scenarios might be constructed for that situation, the most plausible of which would be a more extreme version of what in fact happened – namely the eventual secession of the marginal regions of the empire, civil war and the establishment of various regional and uncoordinated counter-revolutionary warlord regimes, one of which might eventually have gained control of the capital and attempted the long task of establishing itself as a central government. In short, the choice was between a Bolshevik government and no government.

It is at this point that the fog which conceals the landscape of the future cannot be more than thinned. As Lenin himself saw clearly, the survival of the regime was much more uncertain than its initial establishment. It no longer depended on a form of political 'surfing' – finding the big wave and riding it – but on a conjuncture of domestic and international variables which could not be foreseen. Moreover, insofar as future developments now depended on *policy* – that is on conscious, possibly erroneous and certainly variable decisions – the course of the future itself was skewed by their intervention. Thus the Bolshevik decision to set up a new International, but refuse entry to all but those conforming to Bolshevik criteria, might have appeared sensible when other European revolutions seemed imminent or possible in 1919–20; but the split between social democrats and communists and their mutual hostility has remained, creating unforeseen problems for both ever since, in varying and quite different circumstances. Here the difference between foresight and hindsight becomes crucial. At all events prediction is interrupted by passages of darkness which can only be lit up retrospectively, when we know what 'had to happen' simply because nothing else actually happened. To the extent that the survival of the Bolshevik Revolution depended upon international circumstances, one might have put one's money on it from late 1918, although for some months after October 1917 its future was not effectively predictable. On the other hand, given its survival and permanence, prediction came into its own again. Unfortunately I can think of no realistic forecast which ought to have envisaged the long-term future of the USSR as very different from what it has actually become. It is possible to envisage alternative scenarios which would have been very much less cruel and intellectually disastrous, but none which would not have disappointed many of the high hopes of 1917.

The purpose of my brief exercise (to which Chapter 19 returns) is not to show that the course of history was inevitable, but to consider the scope and limits of prediction. Such an exercise allows us to identify long-odds outcomes such as that Tsarism could have saved itself, and odds-on outcomes such as a Russian revolution, a non-liberal post-revolutionary regime and, in broad outline, much of subsequent Soviet development. It allows us to disentangle Lenin's personal contribution from much of the obfuscation which surrounds it. It allows us to identify yes–no situations such as the choice between Bolshevism and no government, and situations with a wide range of options. It explains the reasons for Lenin's confidence about seizing power in October and his uncertainty about maintaining it. It allows us to specify the conditions of survival and their calculability or incalculability. It also allows us to distinguish between the relative analytical predictability of processes which nobody controls – such as most of Russian history in 1917 – and those where the exercise of effective command and planning confuse the issue. I do not share the naive belief of an American sociologist that, because 'social change [is] increasingly both organized and institutionalized ... the future is partly predictable because it will resemble in part what it is now intended to be'. In fact, the tendencies of Soviet development were and are predictable only to the degree that Soviet policy (given its aims) recognized what had to be done. Alas, what makes human planning, however powerful, so frustrating for prophets as well as politicians, is the contrast between its limited capacity and the limited consequences of 'getting it right', and the potentially enormous consequences of getting it wrong. As Napoleon knew well, one battle lost can sometimes change the situation more than ten battles won. And finally, such an exercise enables us to assess the numerous forecasters in this much predicted field. It is a curious reflection on the vast literature that, so far as I know, it has never been surveyed systematically in order to assess historic predictability, even though it was and is full of past and present forecasts.

Predicting social trends is in one respect easier than predicting events, since it rests precisely on the discovery which is the basis of all social sciences: that it is possible to generalize about populations and over periods of time without bothering about the shifting tangle of decisions, events, accidents and possibilities – on the ability to say something about the wood without knowing each tree. So far as trends are concerned, this requires a certain minimal span of time. To this extent it can be called long-run as distinct from short-term prediction, though the particular 'long run' may be comparatively short even by the time-span of human long-term predictions which is limited to a century or so at most. At least I can think of no prediction which is not millennial – in both senses of the word – beyond this. But one familiar drawback of such long-term predictions is that it is almost impossible to assign a proper time-scale to them. We may know what is likely to happen, but not when. That the USA and the USSR would become the giants among the world's powers was correctly predicted by the 1840s, on the grounds of their size and resources, but only a fool would have committed himself to an exact date of, say, 1900.

Some such predictions happen more slowly than most observers expected. For instance the failure of the peasantry to disappear in developed countries could be used as an argument against the mid-nineteenth-century prediction that it would. On the other hand, some happen faster than expected. That the division of a vast sector of the world into colonies administered by a handful of states would not last, could be and was predicted. Yet it is doubtful whether many people in the days of Joe Chamberlain could have expected almost the entire rise and disappearance of this variant of imperialism to take place within the lifetime of a single man – I am thinking of Winston Churchill, who lived from 1874 to 1965. Some are both faster and slower than is predictable. The speed with which the peasantry began to disappear after its lengthy and successful survival is astonishing. In Colombia, where in 1960 the rural population was estimated at some 67 per cent of the total, it had halved or more than halved by the late 1970s. Such predictions are significant even if we don't know when they will come true. If we believe that the chances of the Jews establishing themselves permanently by conquest in a Middle Eastern enclave are not much greater in the long run than the chances of the Crusaders were, then this has obvious policy implications for those who care about their survival, whether we can set dates or not. However, the point I wish to make is simply that the question 'what will happen' is methodologically quite different from the question 'when it will happen'.

The only chronological predictions I know which command some confidence are those based on some regular periodicity behind which we suspect an explicable mechanism, even when we don't understand it. Economists are the greatest searchers for such periodicities, although demography also implies some (if only through the succession and maturation of generations and age-cohorts). Other social sciences have also claimed to have discovered periodicities, but few of them are of much help except in very specialized forecasting. For example, if the anthropologist Kroeber is correct, the dimensions of women's dresses 'alternate with fair regularity between maxima and minima which in most cases average about fifty years apart'. (I express no opinion about this claim, whatever its salience to the rag trade.) However, as already noted (pp. 27–8 above), at least one species of periodicity has shown a wider, if largely enigmatic relevance, even though I know of no explanation of these so-called 'Kondratiev long waves' which is widely accepted, and even though their existence has been doubted by sceptics. But they do enable us to make predictions not only about the economy, but also, in a more general form, about the social, political and cultural scenes which accompany the alternating cycles. The periodization of nineteenth- and twentieth-century history which historians of Europe find most useful does, in fact, coincide largely with Kondratiev waves. Unfortunately for forecasters, such predictive aids are rare.

Leaving chronology aside, the historian is in fact recognized as essential even to the most common and powerful form of prediction in the social sciences, which is based on theoretical propositions or models (basically of the mathematical type) applied to any kind of reality. This is both invaluable and inadequate. Invaluable because, if we establish a logically compelling relationship between variables, argument must cease. If mankind uses up limited resources at a faster rate than they can be replaced or substituted by alternatives, then sooner or later they will run out, and the only question, as with oil reserves, is when. No prediction beyond the purely empirical is possible without constructions based on such propositions. But they are inadequate because by themselves they are too general to throw much light on concrete situations, and any attempt to use them directly for forecasting is therefore doomed. That is why David Glass pointed out that demography, which is, I suppose with economics and linguistics, the most developed of the social sciences by the fashionable criterion of similarity to physics, has had a terrible predictive record. Thus the basic Malthusian proposition that population cannot permanently rise beyond the limits imposed by the availability of the means of subsistence is both undeniable and valuable. However, by itself it can tell us nothing about the past, present and future relationship between population growth and the means of subsistence. It cannot predict or retrospectively explain a crisis describable in malthusian terms such as the Irish famine. If we want to explain why Ireland had such a crisis in the 1840s and Lancashire didn't, we cannot do so with the Malthusian model, but must do so in terms of factors analysable without reference to it. Conversely, if we forecast a famine in Somalia, it is not on the tautological ground that people starve if there is not enough food for them. In short, demographic theory can make conditional predictions which are not forecasts, and forecasts which are not based on its models. On what are they based?

In so far as Malthus himself forecast tendencies – wrongly – he relied on certain historical data, on population growth and on assigning would-be empirical magnitudes, which have proved arbitrary, to future increases in food productivity, which have proved unrealistic. The demographic or economic forecaster must not only translate his variables into real quantities, which is problematical enough: he must also constantly go outside his own theoretical analysis and his own specialist domain into the broad territory of total history, past or present. Why did Western fertility cease to fall after the 1930s, thus forcing the revision of all projections of future population? It is the historian's business to answer such questions, and in doing so to throw light on possible future changes. Why do some now believe that the rate of demographic growth in third-world countries may slow down with industrialization and urbanization? Not only because there is some evidence that it has done so (that is historical data), but because of a supposed analogy with the demographic history of developed countries (that is a historical generalization). Fortunately demographers are aware of all this; more so than economists, if one compares the flourishing discipline of historical demography with the retrospective econometrics which passes for history among them. David Glass, I need not remind you, held a post for much of his life as a sociologist and not demographer, and, apart from his wide interests in other fields, was a strikingly erudite and acute historian. He was a great demographer because he knew that 'the competence of demographers is relevant to only part of the field. The main burden of work will have to fall upon historians and sociologists.'

I am bound to say, however, that historians, like social scientists, are fairly helpless when confronted with the future, not only because we all are, but because they have no clear idea of what exactly the ensemble or system they are investigating is, and – in spite of Marx's superb pioneering – exactly how its various elements interact. What exactly is 'society' (singular or plural) which is our concern? Ecologists may claim to delimit their eco-systems, but few students of human society, except some anthropologists dealing with small, isolated and 'primitive' communities, claim they can do the same; especially not in the modern world. We grope our way. The most historians can claim is that, unlike most social sciences, we cannot sidestep the problems of our ignorance. Unlike them, we are not tempted into striving for fake precision in imitation of the more prestigious natural sciences; and that, after all, we and the anthropologists have an unparalleled knowledge of the varieties of human social experience. And perhaps also that we alone in the field of human studies *must* think in terms of historical change, interaction and transformation. History alone provides orientation and anyone who faces the future without it is not only blind but dangerous, especially in the era of high technology.

Let me give you an extreme example. In June 1980, you may recall, the American observational system reported that Russian missiles were on their way and for several minutes the US nuclear arsenal automatically moved towards action, until it all turned out to be a computer error. If the porter were to come into this theatre *now* to inform us that nuclear war had broken out, it would not take three minutes for even pessimistic human beings to conclude that he must be wrong, and for essentially historical reasons. It is most unlikely that a world war would break out without some preliminary crisis, however short, or some other premonitory signs, and our experience of the past months, weeks or even days has simply not shown any of this evidence. If we were in the middle of something like the Cuban Missile Crisis of 1962, of course, we might be less confident. In short, we have a rational model in our minds on how world wars break out or are likely to, based on a combination of analysis and information about the past. On this basis we assess probabilities while not necessarily excluding possibilities unless they are so remote as not to be worth taking into account. I don't suppose that Canada today spends much time planning against a war with the United States, or, in spite of appearances, Britain against a French invasion. Failing such assessments, however, we are tempted to assume that *anything* can happen at any time – an assumption which also underlies horror movies and the expectations of UFO fans. Or, if we wish to confine ourselves to cases where practical precautions can be taken, we follow the equally irrational procedure of formulating a 'worst case' and preparing for that, especially when we shall be blamed as functionaries if things go wrong. It is equally irrational because the worst case is not more likely than the best case, and there is a substantial difference between taking precautions against the worst cases and taking steps to meet that case: for example, in 1940 when the British government wanted to put all German and Austrian refugees behind barbed wire.

The psychological equivalent of 'worst case' thinking is paranoia or hysteria. Indeed it is at times of tension and fear such as those that we live in [this was written at the height of the second Cold War], that hysteria and a-historicity combine. The worst is expected, not only among those professionally committed to envisaging it – like military men, secret services and the thriller-writers they so often imitate – but also among quite sensible people who develop geo-political fits at the thought of Afghanistan or some Cuban (as distinct from French) troops in some parts of Africa. And, more seriously, our failure to understand the world becomes mechanized, and we set up automated systems geared to the worst case, which are set in motion by signs which mistakenly read 'attack'. Short of the intervention of practical historians, only equally automatic technical cross-checks showing that the signs have been mechanically misread can stop the process of destruction. These false alarms are, in a sense, the hair-raising *reductio ad absurdum* of facing the future a-historically. I don't actually expect that, if or when war breaks out, it will be triggered off by a blind technical malfunction. But the fact that it could, and just possibly might, does illustrate the indispensable role of historical rationality in assessing the future and the human action required to meet it.

How should I conclude? Historians are not prophets in the sense that they can or should try to write the headlines of next year's or next century's BBC World Service news bulletins. Neither are we or ought we to be in the eschatological department of the prophecy business. I know that some thinkers, including historians, have seen the process of history as the unfolding of human destiny to some happy or unhappy end in the future. This kind of belief is morally preferable to the view, so common in American social sciences of the confident 1950s, that human destiny has already found its resting-place in some current society right now, with Omaha as its new Jerusalem. It is certainly not so easily falsifiable; but it is unhelpful. True, man is, in the words of the philosopher Ernst Bloch, a hoping animal. We dream forward. There is plenty of reason to. Historians, like other human beings, are entitled to have their idea of a desirable future for mankind, to fight for it and to be cheered up if they discover that history seems to be going their way, as it sometimes does. In any case it is not a good sign of the way the world is going when men lose confidence in the future, and *Götterdämmerung* scenarios replace utopias. However, the historian's job of finding out where we have come from and whither we are going ought not to be affected *as a job* by whether we like the prospective results.

Let me put it in paradoxical form. It is equally unhelpful to dismiss Marx because we dislike his demonstration that capitalism and bourgeois society are temporary historical phenomena, and to embrace him simply because we are for socialism, which he thought would succeed them. I believe Marx discerned some basic tendencies with profound insight; but we do not know actually what they will bring. Like so much of the future predicted in the past, when it comes it may be unrecognizable, not because the predictions were wrong but because we were wrong to put a particular face and costume to the interesting stranger whose arrival we were told to expect. I don't say we should go as far as Schumpeter, who was both a conservative and a great respecter of Marx's extraordinary analytical vision, and claim that 'to say that Marx ... admits of interpretation in a conservative sense is only saying that he can be taken seriously'. But we should remember that hope and prediction, though inseparable, are not the same.

This still leaves plenty that historians can contribute to our exploration of the future: to discovering what human beings can and cannot do about it; to establish the settings and consequently the limits, potentialities and consequences of human action; to distinguish between the foreseeable and the unforeseeable and between different kinds of foresight. For one thing, they can help to bring into disrepute those absurd and dangerous exercises in constructing mechanical automata for prediction, popular among some seekers after scientific status: people who – I am again quoting a real sociologist – think the way to predict revolutions is to quantify the question 'how extensive and rapid must early modernization be in order for it to produce social revolution' by means of 'the collection of comparative data, both cross-sectional and temporal'. It is not Marxists who do this. They can and ought to bring into disrepute the even more dangerous exercises in futurology which think out the unthinkable as an alternative to thinking out the thinkable. They can keep the statistical extrapolators in check. They can actually say something about what is likely to happen and even more about what isn't. They won't be listened to much – that is of the essence of history. But just possibly they might be listened to a bit more if they actually spent more time in assessing and improving their capacity to say something about the future, and in advertising it a bit better. In spite of everything, they have something to advertise.

CHAPTER 5

Has History Made Progress?

How has history-writing – at least in my fields of interest – developed? What are its relations with the social sciences? These are the questions discussed in the following group of chapters.

'Has History Made Progress?' (previously unpublished) was given as a somewhat belated Inaugural Lecture at Birkbeck College in 1979.

Has history made progress? The question is natural enough for someone approaching retirement who looks back on some forty years of studying history as undergraduate, research student and, since 1947, teacher at Birkbeck College. It is almost another way of asking: what have I been doing with my professional life? Almost, but not quite. For the question assumes that the term 'progress' has some application to a subject such as history. Has it?

There are academic disciplines to which it obviously applies, and others to which one would say – or at least I would say – that it does not. In a way the distinction today is visible in our libraries. The natural sciences, in which progress is not seriously to be doubted by any rational observer, can hardly any longer use books, except for the purpose of relatively elementary teaching and the occasional short-lived synthesis of their field, because their rate of obsolescence is proportionate to their rate of progress, which in my – in our – lifetime has been prodigious. There are no classics to be read, except by those with a sense of *pietas* towards their great predecessors or an interest in the history of the sciences. What survives of Newton or Clerk Maxwell or Mendel has been absorbed into the wider and demonstrably less inadequate understanding of the physical universe; and, conversely, the average mediocre graduate student of physics today has a better understanding of this universe than Newton had. Historians and other analysts of the process and development of the natural sciences know that their progress is far from linear, but its existence cannot be doubted.

On the other hand if we consider literary criticism, which is the only form of the study of the creative arts habitually practised in universities, progress is neither demonstrable nor plausible, except in the relatively trivial forms of erudition and technical sophistication. Twentieth-century literature is not better than seventeenth-century literature, nor is the criticism of Dr Johnson worse than that of Dr Leavis, or for that matter Roland Barthes, only different. No doubt the great bulk of academic or other critical writings drop out of sight, except that of PhD students, but if they survive it is not because they are more recent and have therefore replaced their predecessors, but because they are by authors who – for reasons difficult to define – are considered to demonstrate particular perspicacity and understanding. Of course there is a part of literary studies which is simply a specialized form of history, whether of literature or of literary criticism, and my observation applies to this as little as to other similar subjects taught not as criticism but as history, that is the history of art. English departments read books, and perhaps for this reason also generate books.

There are other disciplines to which the concept of 'progress' seems equally difficult to apply at least globally: for instance, philosophy or law. Plato was not rendered obsolete by Descartes, Descartes by Kant, Kant by Hegel; nor can we detect a process of accumulating wisdom which assimilates and absorbs in later work what turns out to be permanently true in the earlier. Indeed very often we observe merely the continuation or revival of old, often indeed of ancient, debates in contemporary terms, rather like those productions in the mode of the 1920s or the 1970s of Shakespearean dramas with which theatrical producers make their reputations. This is no more a criticism of such disciplines than it would be to observe that, while modern competitive athletics shows progress, in that people today run faster and jump greater distances than fifty years ago and will presumably continue to improve their records, no similar tendency can be observed in the ever changing but essentially unchanged duels of the chess-players.

Now history has plainly something in common with this second kind of discipline, if only because historians not only write but above all read books, including quite old ones. On the other hand, historians do become obsolete, though probably at a rather slower rate than scientists. We don't read Gibbon as we still read Kant or Rousseau, for their relevance to our own problems. We read him, though certainly with enormous admiration for his scholarship, not to learn about the Roman Empire but for his literary merits; that is to say most practising historians don't read him at all, except in their leisure hours. If we read the works of older historians at all, it is either because they have provided us with some permanent corpus of historical raw material, such as an unsuperseded edition of medieval chronicles, or because they happen to have been interested in a topic which has not attracted subsequent work, but which, for one reason or another, we happen to have become interested in again: in other words, because on this topic they are *not* old historians. This is the economic basis of the historical reprint industry. But, of course, the very fact that a book may thus surface again more than a century after its original publication raises, at least by implication, precisely the question I am asking myself this afternoon: can we speak of 'progress' in history, and if so what is its character?

It is obviously not progress in the sense that historians have become more learned, or more intelligent. They have certainly not become more erudite; though they have access to more knowledge. I am not sure whether they have become more intelligent, though there is a case to be made here. History has not, over the past century or two, been a discipline which required great intellectual powers. I have at one stage of my career had close contact with a discipline which does call for considerable brain-power, or at least nimbleness, namely economics at Cambridge, UK and USA, and I have never forgotten this salutary but depressing experience of trying to keep up with a much cleverer body of people. I don't say that historians fifty years ago did not include people of equal intelligence, although it was and still is to some extent possible for a person to make a fine contribution and – not quite the same – a great reputation in history armed with little more than a capacity for very hard work and some detective-like ingenuity. It may even be argued that the very hostility to theory and generalization which characterized so much orthodox academic history in the long period when it was dominated by the tradition of the great Ranke encouraged the intellectually unadventurous, who were also often the intellectually undemanding. On the other hand there have been countries and periods in which history attracted the very opposite type of minds, for instance in France since the 1930s, where one particular approach to history – that generally identified with the so-called *Annales* school – actually became for some decades the central discipline in the country's social sciences. In any case, there has been no shortage of historians who were also pretty bright. What could perhaps be claimed is that today, for certain types of history – for instance, those which require the use of concepts and models from some other disciplines in the social sciences, or of philosophy – a degree of braininess is required comparable to that needed in those disciplines. Some history at least is no longer an intellectual soft option. But that is a comparatively trivial point.

In what significant way can one say that history has progressed? There is no obvious answer to this question, insofar as there is no agreement among historians about what they are trying to do, or for that matter about what their subject-matter is. To take one example, everything that happened in the past is history; everything that happens now is history. While I have been pursuing my profession it has lengthened by some forty years, incidentally turning both me and my contemporaries – and all of you – into the subject-matter of history as well as its students or observers. All historical study therefore implies making a selection, a tiny selection, of some things out of the infinity of human activities in the past, and of what affected those activities. But there is no generally accepted criterion for making such a selection, and to the extent that there is one at any given time, it is likely to change. When historians thought history was largely determined by great men, their selection was obviously different from what it is when they don't. This is what provides so strong and effective a set of fortifications behind which the historical die-hards (and those who reject history) can make their stand, and a guarantee that it will never be quite their last stand.

Anyone who investigates the past according to recognized criteria of scholarship is a historian, and that is about all that the members of my profession will agree about. How can I deny the right to that title of even the most mindless antiquarian chronicler of trivia? They may seem trivia now, but not tomorrow. After all, a great deal of historical demography, a subject which has been transformed in the last twenty years, rests on material originally collected by genealogists, either for reasons of snobbery or, as in the case of the Mormons in Salt Lake City, for theological purposes, which non-Mormons do not share. Historians are therefore constantly haunted by introspection or pursued by philosophical and methodological challengers of one kind or another.

One way to avoid such debates is to see what actually has been happening in historical research over the past few generations and to ask whether this indicates a systematic tendency of development in the subject. This does not prove 'progress', but it may well show that there is more to this discipline than a sort of academic canoe bobbing up and down on the waves of personal taste, of current politics and ideology, or even merely of fashion.

Let us turn back to the middle 1890s, which form so important a turning-point in the history of the modern natural sciences. History as a respectable academic subject had been firmly established. The archives were ordered, the standard journals which still exist had been founded fairly recently – the *English Historical Review*, the *Revue Historique*, the *Historische Zeitschrift*, the *American Historical Review* are all, broadly speaking, children of the last third of the nineteenth century – and the nature of the discipline seemed clear. The great historians were formidable figures in public life – in Britain they included both bishops and peers. Its principles and methods were expounded by the French, and Lord Acton even thought the time had come for a definitive Cambridge Modern History which would both ratify the progress of the subject and, presumably, make the question of its further progress otiose. Less than fifty years later even the University of Cambridge, the home of lost causes in, at all events, modern history, felt it was so obsolete that it had to be completely replaced. Yet even at this moment of triumph there were sceptics.

The challenge essentially concerned the nature of the subject-matter of history – which at that stage was overwhelmingly narrative and descriptive, political and institutional, or what was later to be lampooned in the English satire *1066 and All That*; the challenge also concerned the possibility of historical generalization. Essentially it came from the social sciences and from outsiders who believed that history should be a special form of social science. The bulk of established historians rejected this challenge totally. The matter was argued out with surprising bitterness in the mid-1890s in Germany in connection with the challenge of one historical heretic who now seems to us not very heterodox, Karl Lamprecht. History, said the orthodox, was essentially descriptive. People, events, situations were so different that no generalizations about society were possible. There could therefore be no 'historical laws'.

Now in fact two interrelated matters were at issue here. The first was the actual selection from the past which made up the essential subject-matter of orthodox history. It dealt primarily with politics, and in the modern period with the politics, and especially the foreign policies, of nation-states. It concentrated on great men. While it recognized that other aspects of the past might be investigated, it tended to leave these to sub-disciplines such as the history of culture or economic history whose relations to history proper were left obscure, except insofar as they formed the subject-matter of policy decisions. In short, its selection was both narrow and, as was even then evident, politically rather biased. But, secondly, it rejected any attempt to bring the various aspects of the past into a systematic structural or causal relation to one another, especially any attempt to derive politics from economic and social factors, and above all any models of the evolutionary development of human societies (though its own practice implied such a model), any model of stages of historical development. Such things, as Georg von Below said, might be popular among natural scientists, philosophers, economists, jurists or even some theologians – but they had no place in history.

This view was in fact a mid- and late-nineteenth century reaction against the earlier developments of history, notably in the eighteenth century. However, that is not my concern here. And in any case the eighteenth-century historians and historically mined economists and sociologists, whether in Scotland or Göttingen, were technically as yet unable to solve their problem of a genuinely comprehensive history which should establish the general regularities of social organization and social change, bring them into relation with the institutions and events of politics, and also take account of the uniqueness of events and the peculiarities of conscious human decision. My point is that the extreme position which represented the Rankean orthodoxy dominant in Western universities was challenged not merely on ideological grounds, but because of its narrowness and inadequacy; and that it was fighting a rearguard action, though an entrenched one.

I stress the first point, because orthodoxy itself preferred to regard the challenge as an ideological, and more specifically a socialist or even a Marxist one. Not for nothing did the polemicists of the *Historische Zeitschrift* in the mid-1890s insist that what they were against was the 'collectivist' as against the 'individualist' conception of history, and against a 'materialist conception of history'; and everybody knew what that meant. But it wasn't ideological. Even if we leave aside all those sciences and disciplines which, unlike the historians, refused to see history – at least from their perspective – as just one damned thing after another undertaken preferably by kings and great men, the revolt against orthodoxy was not confined to any single ideology. It included followers of both Marx and Comte as well as people like Lamprecht, who were politically and ideologically far from rebellion. It included the followers of Max Weber and Durkheim. In France, for instance, the rebellion against historical orthodoxy –

the so-called 'history of events' – owes very little indeed to Marxism, for historical reasons which don't concern us here. And orthodoxy was already in retreat well before 1914, even though effectively protected by its institutional strongholds. The eleventh edition of the *Encyclopaedia Britannica* (1910) already observed that, from the mid-nineteenth century, there had been a growing attempt systematically to substitute a materialist for an idealist framework of historical analysis, and that this had led to the rise of 'economic or sociological history'.

If I say that this tendency, which has continued to progress inexorably, was *general*, it is not because I wish to minimize the specific influence of Marx and Marxism on it and in it. I am the last person who would want to do so, and in any case even at the end of the nineteenth century few serious observers would have wished to do so. What I am trying to do is rather to show that historiography has been moving in one particular direction over a period of several generations, irrespective of the ideologies of its practitioners, and – what is more significant – against the enormously powerful and institutionally entrenched resistance of the historical profession. Before 1914, the pressure came largely from those outside history: from economists (who in some countries had a strong historical bias); from sociologists; in one case – France – from geographers; even from lawyers. If we think, for instance, of the crucial and much discussed question of the relations between society and religion, or more specifically between Protestantism and the rise of capitalism, the original classic texts, leaving aside the observations of Marx which formed the starting-point of this discussion, are those of Max Weber, a sociologist, and Troeltsch, a theologian. Later orthodoxy was undermined from within. In France the famous *Annales* – originally and characteristically called *Annales d'Histoire Economique et Sociale*, attacked the fortress of Paris from the provincial base of Strasbourg; in Britain the journal *Past and Present*, which established an international position with surprising rapidity in the 1950s, was started by a handful of Marxist outsiders, though it very soon broadened its base. In West Germany, the first and perhaps the last bastion of tradition, it was challenged in the 1960s by radical opponents of German nationalism and by people who deliberately sought their inspiration in the one or two historians of the Weimar period who could be regarded as democrats and republicans; and the main emphasis of this group is once again on explaining politics in terms of social and economic developments.

The trend, then, is not in doubt. You have merely to compare a standard British inter-war textbook of European history like Grant and Temperley's *Europe in the Nineteenth and Twentieth Centuries* with a standard contemporary work like John Roberts' *Europe 1880–1945* to see the extraordinary transformation in this type of literature since I was a student: and I am deliberately picking a modern author who would pride himself on being a sound middle-of-the-road man, or even a shade on the conservative side. The old book begins with a brief, sixteen-page chapter on Modern Europe which sketches the state system and the balance of power and the main continental states, adding a few remarks on the French *philosophes* – Voltaire, Rousseau and so on – and Liberty, Equality and Fraternity. The new book, first published forty years after the old, begins with what is essentially a long chapter on the economic structure of Europe, followed by a shorter chapter on 'society: institutions and assumptions', political patterns and religion: both these chapters – before we even reach international relations – cover some sixty pages each.

Essentially what we have seen over the twentieth century is precisely what the orthodox historians of the 1890s rejected completely: a rapprochement between history and the social sciences. Of course history cannot be more than partly subsumed under the heading of social or perhaps any science. Not that this should prevent some historians from concentrating on problems which could be and are also tackled by, say, historically minded demographers or economists. Anyway, it doesn't. Of course the rapprochement is not only from one side. If the historians have increasingly looked to various social sciences for methods and explanatory models, social sciences have increasingly tried to historicize themselves and in doing so looked to historians. And the professors of the late nineteenth century were quite right to reject the evolutionary schemata and explanatory models of contemporary social sciences as simple-minded and unrealistic, and most of the ones on offer today can still be legitimately rejected for that reason.

Yet the fact remains that history has moved away from description and narrative to analysis and explanation; from concentrating on the unique and individual to establishing regularities and to generalization. In a sense the traditional approach has been turned upside down.

Does all this constitute progress? Yes, it does, in a modest sort of way. I don't believe that history can get anywhere as a serious subject while it cuts itself off on various pretexts from the other disciplines which investigate the transformations of life on earth, or the evolution of our ancestors up to that arbitrary point when they began to leave behind certain sorts of records, or for that matter the structure and function of eco-systems and groups of social animals, of whom *Homo sapiens* is a special case. We are all agreed that this does not, cannot and ought not to exhaust the scope of history, but insofar as the tendency of historical work over the past generations has brought these other disciplines into closer relations with history, it has rendered possible a better understanding of what has made man what he is today than anything Ranke and Lord Acton did. For, after all, that is what history in the broadest sense is about: how and why *Homo sapiens* got from the palaeolithic to the nuclear era.

If we do not tackle the basic problem of the transformations of humanity, or at least if we do not see that part of its activities that is our specialist concern in the context of this transformation, which is still in progress, then we as historians are engaged in trivialities or intellectual or other parlour-games. Of course it is easy to find reasons why history should cut itself off from the other disciplines investigating man, or directly bearing on such investigation, but none of them is a good reason. They all amount to leaving the central job of the historian to non-historians (who know quite well that someone has to tackle it), and then using their failure to do this job properly as a further argument for keeping historians out of such bad company.

I have already said that this can't exhaust the activities of historians. It should also be obvious that history cannot be subsumed under the heading of some other discipline projected back into the past, such as a historical sociology or social biology. It is and must be *sui generis*, and in this respect the historical reactionaries are correct. This is partly for trivial reasons. Many historians and more of their readers happen to take a vivid interest in the fortunes of individual members of human populations which, say, an animal ecologist would rarely think it worth writing learned papers about, or they are interested in precisely those micro-events and micro-situations which are smoothed out of sight by the search for regularities. If they wanted to, biologists could treat the affairs of animals the way historians do those of humans. The novel *Watership Down* corresponds exactly to what an old-fashioned historian – indeed an ancient one, like Xenophon in his *Anabasis* – would write about rabbits. (I assume the author is zoologically sound.) But there are less trivial reasons also. For, whether or not we think the pre-occupation with the difference between Gladstone and Disraeli trivial, we can't write about animals in this way except fictionally, without making them in some way think, talk and act like what they are not, human beings. And human beings, as the socio-biologists need reminding, *are* different as well as similar to animals.

They make their own world and their own history. This evidently does not mean that they are free to do so as they consciously choose (whatever 'conscious choice' means), or that history can be understood by investigating men's intentions. It clearly can't. But it does mean that the transformations of human society are mediated by a number of phenomena which are specifically human (let's call them 'culture' in the widest sense of the word) and they operate through a number of institutions and practices which are at least in part conscious constructs – for instance, governments and policies. We can both construct and move about this furniture of human life among which we live – to what extent is one of the bigger historical questions – and, since we have language, we always have and express ideas about ourselves and our activities.

These things simply cannot be overlooked. West Germany and East Germany have plainly gone very different ways because each part has since 1945 adopted a very different set of institutions and policies based on different sets of ideas. I am not saying that it could not have happened otherwise. The problem of historical inevitability of determinism is quite a different problem – I don't propose to enter into it here – and the question of the role of consciousness and culture, or, in Marxist terms, of the relations between base and superstructure, has often been confused and obscured by mixing the two up. What I am saying is that history can't leave out consciousness, culture and purposive action within man-made institutions. May I add that I believe Marxism to be much the best approach to history because it is more clearly aware than other approaches of what human beings can do as the subjects and makers of history as well as what, as objects of history, they can't. And it is the best, incidentally, because, as the virtual inventor of the sociology of knowledge, Marx also evolved a theory about how the ideas of historians themselves are likely to be affected by their social being.

But let me return to the main question. Yes, there has been progress in history over the past three generations at least, mainly by the convergence of history and the social sciences, but it has been modest and this process may for the time being be in trouble. In the first place, its major advances were certainly achieved by a necessary simplification, which, now that the advance has been achieved, reveals certain drawbacks. That is why there is at present a distinct movement to re-emphasize that political history which was for so long demoted by the historical revolutionaries. Of course some of this new political history is little more than a reversion – often, as among the Cambridge historians, a deliberately neo-conservative reversion – to the most obsolete form of nineteenth-century archive-grubbing: who wrote what and to whom in the Cabinet during the Home Rule crisis or in 1931. Still, at its best, to quote Jacques Le Goff, 'political history [has] gradually ... return[ed] in force by borrowing the methods, spirit and theoretical approach of the very social science which has pushed it into the background', particularly for periods before the nineteenth century.

In the second place, with the enormous development of the social sciences, not least as a group of academic vested interests, the convergence of history with them is now producing divergence and fragmentation. We have a 'new' economic history which is chiefly current academic theory projected back into the past, and much the same for social anthropology, psychoanalysis, structural linguistics or any other discipline or pseudo-discipline which can help deserving young men and women to make a reputation by setting a new fashion or saying what nobody else has said before. Novelty as a label helps to sell history among professionals, as it helps to sell detergents among a wider public. My objection is not, of course, to historians borrowing techniques and ideas from other social sciences and integrating the latest developments in these sciences into their own work, so far as they are useful and relevant. It is to distributing the historical cargo into a series of non-communicating containers. There is no such thing as economic, or social, or anthropological, or psychoanalytical history: there is just history.

This tendency to fragmentation has been strengthened by a third phenomenon: the spectacular expansion of the field of historical studies, which is probably the most striking achievement of the past twenty or thirty years. As I said earlier, all history-writing is selection. We have now become far more aware than any previous generation of how narrow that selection usually is. To mention only a few topics which have recently become specialized fields or sub-disciplines, sometimes even with journals and societies, which are the scholar's equivalent of membership of the UN for Indian Ocean islands: the family, women, childhood, death, sexuality, ritual and symbolism (festivals and carnivals are much in fashion), food and cooking, climate, crime, the physical characteristics and health of human beings, not to mention the continents and regions, both geographical and social, previously unexplored or even undiscovered. They are not all new, but they now form part of the accepted field of historical study. You can read articles in leading journals about the perception of space in Madagascar and changes in the distribution of eye-colour among Frenchmen, and far more about the hitherto neglected history of the common people.

This imperialism or ecumenism of historical studies is a good thing. History is 'total', to use a fashionable phrase, though even the current range is only a selection of those things which happen to interest late-twentieth-century historians. And it is an even more welcome development, insofar as it tends to turn history into what I believe it ought to be, the general framework of at least the social sciences. Nevertheless, at the present stage of the game it does tend to turn major historical journals into something like antiques supermarkets. The various parts of the contents all come from the past, but beyond that they don't have much to do with each other.

Where do we go from here? I can't predict future developments, partly because (as in any other science) they may arise out of changes in the questions we ask and the models we accept as possible or desirable, which are difficult to predict ('paradigms' is the current phrase); partly because history is a very immature discipline in which, outside specialist fields – and even within them – there is no real consensus about what are the important and crucial basic problems; and partly because the historian himself is inside his subject in the way the practitioner of the non-human sciences isn't. I don't go along with the ultra-sceptics who claim that historians can do no more than write contemporary history in period costume, but it is unquestionable that we can only see it in some contemporary perspective. On the other hand I can say what I think some future developments might profitably be. Here are three.

First, the time is ripe to turn again to the transformations of human kind, which is the major question of history. And, incidentally, to ask why the entire itinerary from hunter-gatherers to modern industrial society was completed in only one region of the world and not in others. Once historians recognize that this is a common and central problem, which concerns students of medieval coronation rituals as much as those of the origins of the Cold War, they can contribute to it within the limits of their special interests. They might even extend the range of their subject on rational or at least operational grounds rather than haphazardly. Fortunately there is evidence that at least one large and crucial sector of the problem is once again debated as such a common concern by other than Marxist historians, namely the historical origin and development of capitalism. This may prove to be one of the more positive spin-offs of the present period of global economic crisis. Further progress is now possible; it may even be resuming.

Second, there is the central question of how things fit together. I don't mean by this where the major mechanisms of historical change and transformation are to be found, for this is already implicit in my first big problem. I mean rather the mode of interaction between different aspects of human life, between say economics, politics, family and sexual relations, culture in the wide or the narrow sense, or sensibility. It is patent that in nineteenth-century Europe, which has been my main field, all these things are determined by the triumph of the capitalist economy, or at any rate cannot possibly be analysed without seeing this as the central fact. But it is also clear that the triumph of this economy, even in its core regions, operated on and through the products of past history. It destroyed and created some things, but more often it adapted, co-opted and modified what was already there. Indeed, if you look at it from another perspective – say from that of the Japanese in the 1860s – a pre-existing society might see itself as adapting and co-opting capitalism as a way to keep itself viable. For this reason simple determinism or functionalism will not do.

I don't want to bore the non-historians among you with nineteenth-century examples, but let me transpose one aspect of the problem into the present. We have been living, since 1950, through perhaps the most massive social and cultural transformations yet recorded, and few will doubt that they derive from economic and techno-scientific developments. Few will doubt that they are in some way interconnected – if you prefer the jargon, they form a syndrome. But what exactly is the relation to the basic transformation of the rapid decline of the peasantry outside parts of Africa and Asia, of the crisis in the Roman Catholic Church, of the rise of rock'n'roll, the crisis in the global communist movement, the crisis in the traditional Western marriage and family patterns, the bankruptcy of the avant-garde arts, the scientists' interest in the historical development of the universe, the decline of the puritan work ethic and parliamentary government, and the unusually full coverage of the arts in, of all newspapers, the London *Financial Times*? And what are the interconnections between all these? Such questions are enormously interesting, enormously important, and quite enormously difficult. Still, historians must try their hand at them, again. They will get further than Montesquieu – they ought to get further than Marx.

There is a third set of problems, closer to the traditional interests of historians. What difference does the specificity of historical experience, events and situations make – or not make? This can include relatively trivial questions about such things as the role of some individual or decision, such as 'What would have happened if Napoleon had won the Battle of Waterloo?' They can include more interesting questions such as why the intellectual history of Germany and Austria in the nineteenth century, of England and Scotland in the eighteenth, was so different, though linguistically and culturally each pair of countries belonged together. They can, above all, include problems of great practical importance, as every economist knows who thinks he has discovered a recipe for economic growth which has worked excellently in some country or at some period, but not in another – for instance, in Sweden and Austria but not in Britain.

This raises questions not so much of research – though it may also do so – as of methodology: notably questions about comparative and counterfactual studies. History, after all, exists as a separate discipline distinct from other historically minded social sciences because in it other things are never equal. It might be defined as the study which *must* investigate the relationship of the things that are not equal with those that are. Even at the level of the apparently unique or unrepeatable – of, say, the effects of Mao's death or Lenin's arrival at the Finland Station – that is what distinguished history from anecdote and from the sort of documented narrative about which all we can say is that it is just as strange as, or stranger than, or (I am sorry to say quite often) more boring than, fiction. There are signs that both comparative and counterfactual exercises are now seriously interesting historians, though I am bound to say we have not got very far with them.

So let me conclude. History has made progress this century, in a lumbering and zig-zag manner, but genuine progress. In saying this I am implying that it belongs to the disciplines to which the word 'progress' can properly apply, that it is possible to arrive at a better understanding of a process which is objective and real, namely the complex, contradictory, but not adventitious, historical development of human societies in the world. I know that there are people who deny this. History is inevitably so deeply impregnated with ideology and politics that its very subject-matter and objects are from time to time called into question, especially when its findings are thought to lead to undesirable political consequences. That has been shown for German academic history in the period before, and indeed after, 1914. And history can be argued away into pure subjectivity or otherwise reduced, in a manner which is not open to critics of the natural or even most of the accepted social sciences.

That this is so, that we historians operate in the grey zone where the investigation of what *is* – even the choice of what *is* – is constantly affected by who we are and what we want to happen or not to happen: this is a fact of our professional existence. And yet we have a subject. I take my stand with that great and neglected philosopher of history who wrote his remarkable Prolegomena to Universal History just 600 years ago – between 1375 and 1381 – Ibn Khaldun (see Preface above, p. ix).

Significant contributions to carrying out Ibn Khaldun's programme had been made since history became something like a recognized discipline in the mid-eighteenth century. Some have been made in my lifetime. When I look back on over thirty years of research, teaching and writing I hope it can be said that I am making a small contribution too. But even if I am not, even if it is denied that there is any progress to be made, nobody can possibly deny that I am enjoying myself enormously.

CHAPTER 6

From Social History to the History of Society

*This paper, which raised some discussion at the time, was originally written
for a conference on Historical Studies Today organized in 1970 in Rome by*
Daedalus, *the journal of the American Academy of Arts and Sciences, and
was published in that journal and in the subsequent book,* Historical Studies
Today, *edited by Felix Gilbert and Stephen R. Graubard (New York, 1972),
of which it formed the first chapter. Much has happened in social history
since this survey of its development up to 1970, which is now itself a piece
of history. The author cannot but note with embarrassed astonishment that
it contained no reference at all to women's history. Admittedly this field had
scarcely begun to develop before the end of the 1960s, but neither I nor any
of the other contributors to the volume, among the most distinguished in the
profession − all males − appears to have been aware of the gap.*

I

The term social history has always been difficult to define, and until
recently there has been no great pressure to define it, for it has lacked
the institutional and professional vested interests which normally
insist on precise demarcations. Broadly speaking, until the present
vogue of the subject − or at least of the name − it was in the past
used in three sometimes overlapping senses. First, it referred to the
history of the poor or lower classes, and more specifically to the
history of the movements of the poor ('social movements'). The term
could be even more specialized, referring essentially to the history of
labour and socialist ideas and organizations. For obvious reasons this
link between social history and the history of social protest or socialist
movements has remained strong. A number of social historians have
been attracted to the subject because they were radicals or socialists
and as such interested in subjects of great sentimental relevance to
them.[1]

Second, the term was used to refer to works on a variety of human activities difficult to classify except in such terms as 'manners, customs, everyday life'. This was, perhaps for linguistic reasons, a largely Anglo-Saxon usage, since the English language lacks suitable terms for what the Germans who wrote about similar subjects – often also in a rather superficial ad journalistic manner – called *Kultur-* or *Sittengeschichte.* This kind of social history was not particularly oriented toward the lower classes – indeed rather the opposite – though the more politically radical practitioners tended to pay attention to them. It formed the unspoken basis of what may be called the residual view of social history, which was put forward by the late G. M. Trevelyan in his *English Social History* (1944) as 'history with the politics left out'. It requires no comment.

The third meaning of the term was certainly the most common and for our purposes the most relevant: 'social' was used in combination with 'economic history'. Indeed, outside the Anglo-Saxon world, the title of the typical specialist journal in this field before the Second World War always (I think) bracketed the two words, as in the *Vierteljahrschrift für Sozial u. Wirtschaftsgeschichte,* the *Revue d'Histoire E. & S.,* or the *Annales d'Histoire E. & S.* It must be admitted that the economic half of this combination was overwhelmingly preponderant. There were hardly any social histories of equivalent calibre to set beside the numerous volumes devoted to the economic history of various countries, periods and subjects. There were in fact not very many economic and social histories. Before 1939 one can think of only a few such works, admittedly sometimes by impressive authors (Pirenne, Mikhail Rostovtzeff, J. W. Thompson, perhaps Dopsch), and the monographic or periodical literature was even sparser. Nevertheless, the habitual bracketing of economic and social, whether in the definitions of the general field of historical specialization or under the more specialized banner of economic history, is significant.

It revealed the desire for an approach to history systematically different from the classical Rankean one. What interested historians of this kind was the evolution of the economy, and this in turn interested them because of the light it threw on the structure and changes in society, and more especially on the relationship between classes and social groups, as George Unwin admitted.[2] This social dimension is evident even in the work of the most narrowly or cautiously economic historians so long as they claimed to be historians. Even J. H. Clapham argued that economic history was of all varieties of history the most fundamental because it was the foundation of society.[3] The predominance of the economic over the social in this combination had, we may suggest, two reasons. It was partly owing to a view of economic theory which refused to isolate the economic from social, institutional and other elements, as with the Marxists and the German historical school, and partly to the sheer headstart of economics over the other social sciences. If history had to be integrated into the social sciences, economics was the one it had primarily to come to terms with. One might go further and argue (with Marx) that, whatever the essential inseparability of the economic and the social in human society, the analytical base of any historical enquiry into the evolution of human societies must be the process of social production.

None of the three versions of social history produced a specialized academic field of social history until the 1950s, though at one time the famous *Annales* of Lucien Febvre and Marc Bloch dropped the economic half of its subtitle and proclaimed itself purely social. However, this was a temporary diversion of the war years, and the title by which this great journal has now been known for a quarter of a century – *Annales: Économies, Sociétés, Civilisations* – as well as the nature of its contents, reflect the original and essentially global and comprehensive aims of its founders. Neither the subject itself, nor the discussion of its problems, developed seriously before 1950. The journals specializing in it, still few in number, were not founded until the end of the 1950s: we may perhaps regard the *Comparative Studies in Society and History* (1958) as the first. As an academic specialization, social history is therefore quite new.

What explains the rapid development and growing emancipation of social history in the past twenty years? The question could be answered in terms of technical and institutional changes within the academic disciplines of social science: the deliberate specialization of economic history to fit in with the requirements of the rapidly developing economic theory and analysis, of which the 'new economic history' is an example; the remarkable and worldwide growth of sociology as an academic subject and fashion, which in turn called for subsidiary historical service-branches analogous to those required by economics departments. We cannot neglect such factors. Many historians (such as the Marxists) who had previously labelled themselves economic because the problems they were interested in were plainly not encouraged or even considered by orthodox general history found themselves extruded from a rapidly narrowing economic history and accepted or welcomed the title of 'social historians', especially if their mathematics were poor. It is improbable whether in the atmosphere of the 1950s and early 1960s someone like R. H. Tawney would have been welcomed among the economic historians had he been a young researcher and not president of the Economic History Society. However, such academic redefinitions and professional shifts hardly explain much, though they cannot be overlooked.

Far more significant was the general historization of the social sciences which took place during this period, and may retrospectively appear to have been the most important development within them at this time. For my present purpose it is not necessary to explain this change, but it is impossible to avoid drawing attention to the immense significance of the revolutions and struggles for political and economic emancipation of colonial and semi-colonial countries, which drew the attention of governments, international and research organizations, and consequently also of social scientists, to what are essentially problems of historic transformations. These were subjects which had hitherto been outside, or at best on the margins of, academic orthodoxy in the social sciences, and had increasingly been neglected by historians.[4]

At all events essentially historical questions and concepts (sometimes, as in the case of 'modernization' or 'economic growth', excessively crude concepts) have captured even the discipline hitherto most immune to history, when not actually, like Radcliffe-Brown's social anthropology, actively hostile to it. This progressive infiltration of history is perhaps most evident in economics, where an initial field of growth economics, whose assumptions, though much more sophisticated, were those of the cookery book ('Take the following quantities of ingredients *a* through *n*, mix and cook, and the result will be the take-off into self-sustained growth'), has been succeeded by the growing realization that factors outside economics also determine economic development. In brief, it is now impossible to pursue many activities of the social scientist in any but a trivial manner without coming to terms with social structure and its transformations: without the history of societies. It is a curious paradox that the economists were beginning to grope for some understanding of social (or at any rate not strictly economic) factors at the very moment when the economic historians, absorbing the economists' models of fifteen years earlier, were trying to make themselves look hard rather than soft by forgetting about everything except equations and statistics.

What can we conclude from this brief glance at the historical development of social history? It can hardly be an adequate guide to the nature and tasks of the subject under consideration, though it can explain why certain more or less heterogeneous subjects of research came to be loosely grouped under this general title, and how developments in other social sciences prepared the ground for the establishment of an academic theory specially demarcated as such. At most it can provide us with some hints, at least one of which is worth mentioning immediately.

A survey of social history in the past seems to show that its best practitioners have always felt uncomfortable with the term itself. They have either, like the great Frenchmen to whom we owe so much, preferred to describe themselves simply as historians and their aim as 'total' or 'global' history, or as men who sought to integrate the contributions of all relevant social sciences in history, rather than to exemplify any one of them. Marc Bloch, Fernand Braudel, Georges Lefebvre are not names which can be pigeonholed as social historians except insofar as they accepted Fustel de Coulanges' statement that 'History is not the accumulation of events of all kinds which occurred in the past. It is the science of human societies.'

Social history can never be another specialization like economic or other hyphenated histories because its subject-matter cannot be isolated. We can define certain human activities as economic, at least for analytical purposes, and then study them historically. Though this may be (except for certain definable purposes) artificial or unrealistic, it is not impracticable. In much the same way, though at a lower level of theory, the old kind of intellectual history which isolated written ideas from their human context and traced their filiation from one writer to another is possible, if one wants to do that sort of thing. But the social or societal aspects of man's being cannot be separated from the other aspects of his being, except at the cost of tautology or extreme trivialization. They cannot, for more than a moment, be separated from the ways in which men get their living and their material environment. They cannot, even for a moment, be separated from their ideas, since their relations with one another are expressed and formulated in language which implies concepts as soon as they open their mouths. And so on. The intellectual historian may (at his risk) pay no attention to economics, the economic historian to Shakespeare, but the social historian who neglects either will not get far. Conversely, while it is extremely improbable that a monograph on Provençal poetry will be economic history or one on inflation in the sixteenth century intellectual history, both could be treated in a way to make them social history.

II

Let us turn from the past to the present and consider the problems of writing the history of society. The first question concerns how much societal historians can get from other social sciences, or indeed how far their subject is or ought to be merely the science of society insofar as it deals with the past. This question is natural, though the experience of the past two decades suggests two different answers to it. It is clear that social history has since 1950 been powerfully shaped and stimulated, not only by the professional structure of other social sciences (for example, their specific course requirements for university students), and by their methods and techniques, but also by their questions. It is hardly too much to say that the recent efflorescence of studies in the British industrial revolution, a subject once grossly neglected by its own experts because they doubted the validity of the concept of industrial revolution, is due primarily to the urge of economists (doubtless in turn echoing that of governments and planners) to discover how industrial revolutions happen, what makes them happen, and what socio-political consequences they have. With certain notable exceptions, the flow of stimulation in the past twenty years has been one way. On the other hand, if we look at recent developments in another way, we shall be struck by the obvious convergence of workers from different disciplines toward socio-historical problems. The study of millennial phenomena is a case in point, since among writers on these subjects we find people coming from anthropology, sociology, political science, history, not to mention students of literature and religions – though not, so far as I am aware, economists. We also note the transfer of men with other professional formations, at least temporarily, to work which historians would consider historical, as with Charles Tilly and Neil Smelser from sociology, Eric Wolf from anthropology, Everett Hagen and Sir John Hicks from economics.

Yet the second tendency is perhaps best regarded not as convergence but as conversion. For it must never be forgotten that if non-historical social scientists have begun to ask properly historical questions and to ask historians for answers, it is because they themselves have none. And if they have sometimes turned themselves into historians, it is because the practising members of our discipline, with the notable exception of the Marxists and others – not necessarily *Marxisants* – who accept a similar problematic, have not provided the answers.[5] Moreover, though there are now a few social scientists from other disciplines who have made themselves sufficiently expert in our field to command respect, there are more who have merely applied a few crude mechanical concepts and models. For every *Vendée* by a Tilly, there are, alas, several dozen equivalents of Rostow's *Stages*. I leave aside the numerous others who have ventured into the difficult territory of historical source material without an adequate knowledge of the hazards they are likely to encounter there, or of the means of avoiding and overcoming them. In brief, the situation at present is one in which historians, with all their willingness to learn from other disciplines, are required to teach rather than to learn. The history of society cannot be written by applying the meagre available models from other sciences; it requires the construction of adequate new ones – or, at least (Marxists would argue), the development of existing sketches into models.

This is not, of course, true of techniques and methods, where the historians are already net debtors to a substantial extent, and will, or at least ought to, go even more heavily and systematically into debt. I do not wish to discuss this aspect of the problem of the history of society, but a point or two can be made in passing. Given the nature of our sources, we can hardly advance much beyond a combination of the suggestive hypothesis and the apt anecdotal illustration without the techniques for the discovery, the statistical grouping and handling of large quantities of data, where necessary with the aid of division of research labour and technological devices, which other social sciences have long developed. At the opposite extreme, we stand in equal need of the techniques for the observation and analysis in depth of specific individuals, small groups and situations, which have also been pioneered outside history, and which may be adaptable to our purposes – for example, the participant observation of the social anthropologists, the interview-in-depth, perhaps even psychoanalytical methods. At the very least these various techniques can stimulate the search for adaptations and equivalents in our field, which may help to answer otherwise impenetrable questions.[6]

I am much more doubtful about the prospect of turning social history into a backward projection of sociology, as of turning economic history into retrospective economic theory, because these disciplines do not at present provide us with useful models or analytical frameworks for the study of long-run *historical* socio-economic transformations. Indeed the bulk of their thinking has not been concerned with, or even interested in, such changes, if we except such trends as Marxism. Moreover, it may be argued that in important respects their analytical models have been developed systematically, and most profitably, by abstracting from historical change. This is notably true, I would suggest, of sociology and social anthropology.

The founding fathers of sociology have indeed been more historically minded than the main school of neo-classic economics (though not necessarily more than the original school of classical political economists), but theirs is an altogether less developed science. Stanley Hoffmann has rightly pointed to the difference between the 'models' of the economists and the 'checklists' of the sociologists and anthropologists.[7] Perhaps they are more than mere checklists. These sciences have also provided us with certain visions, patterns of possible structures composed of elements which can be permuted and combined in various ways, vague analogues to Kekulé's ring glimpsed at the top of the bus, but with the drawback of unverifiability. At their best such structural–functional patterns may be both elegant and heuristically useful, at least for some. At a more modest level, they may provide us with useful metaphors, concepts or terms (such as 'role'), or convenient aids in ordering our material.

Moreover, quite apart from their deficiency as models, it may be argued that the theoretical constructions of sociology (or social anthropology) have been most successful by excluding history, that is directional or oriented change.[8] Broadly speaking, the structural–functional patterns illuminate what societies have in common in spite of their differences, whereas our problem is with what they have not. It is not what light Lévi-Strauss's Amazonian tribes can throw on modern (indeed on any) society, but on how humanity got from the cavemen to modern industrialism or post-industrialism, and what changes in society were associated with this progress, or necessary for it to take place, or consequential upon it. Or, to use another illustration, it is not to observe the permanent necessity of all human societies to supply themselves with food by growing or otherwise acquiring it, but what happens when this function, having been overwhelmingly fulfilled (since the neolithic revolution) by classes of peasants forming the majority of their societies, comes to be fulfilled by small groups of other kinds of agricultural producers and may come to be fulfilled in non-agricultural ways. How does this happen and why? I do not believe that sociology and social anthropology, however helpful they are incidentally, at present provide us with much guidance.

On the other hand, while I remain sceptical of most current economic theory as a framework of the historical analysis of societies (and therefore of the claims of the new economic history), I am inclined to think that the possible value of economics for the historian of society is great. It cannot but deal with what is an essentially dynamic element in history, namely the process – and, speaking globally and on a long time-scale, progress – of social production. Insofar as it does this it has, as Marx saw, historical development built into it. To take a simple illustration: the concept of the 'economic surplus', which the late Paul Baran revived and utilized to such good effect,[9] is patently fundamental to any historian of the development of societies, and strikes me as not only more objective and quantifiable, but also more primary, speaking in terms of analysis, than, say, the dichotomy Gemeinschaft–Gesellschaft. Of course Marx knew that economic models, if they are to be valuable for historical analysis, cannot be divorced from social and institutional realities, which include certain basic types of human communal or kinship organization, not to mention the structures and assumptions specific to particular socio-economic formations as cultures. And yet, though Marx is not for nothing regarded as one of the major founding fathers of modern sociological thought (directly and through his followers and critics), the fact remains that his major intellectual project Das Kapital took the form of a work of economic analysis. We are required to agree with neither his conclusions nor his methodology. But we would be unwise to neglect the practice of the thinker who, more than any other, has defined or suggested the set of historical questions to which social scientists find themselves drawn today.

III

How are we to write the history of society? It is not possible for me to produce a definition or model of what we mean by society here, or even a checklist of what we want to know about its history. Even if I could, I do not know how profitable this would be. However, it may be useful to put up a small and miscellaneous assortment of signposts to direct or warn off future traffic.

(1) The history of society is *history*; that is to say it has real

chronological time as one of its dimensions. We are concerned not only with structures and their mechanisms of persistence and change, and with the general possibilities and patterns of their transformations, but also with what actually happened. If we are not, then (as Fernand Braudel has reminded us in his article on 'Histoire et Longue Durée').[10] we are not historians. *Conjectural* history has a place in our discipline, even though its chief value is to help us assess the possibilities of present and future, rather than past, where its place is taken by *comparative* history; but actual history is what we must explain. The possible development or non-development of capitalism in imperial China is relevant to us only insofar as it helps to explain the actual fact that this type of economy developed fully, at least to begin with, in one and only one region of the world. This in turn may be usefully contrasted (again in the light of general models) with the tendency for other systems of social relations – for example the broadly feudal – to develop much more frequently and in a greater number of areas. The history of society is thus a collaboration between general models of social structure and change and the specific set of phenomena which actually occurred. This is true whatever the geographical or chronological scale of our enquiries.

(2) The history of society is, among other things, that of specific units of people living together and definable in sociological terms. It is the history of societies as well as of human society (as distinct from, say, that of apes and ants), or of certain types of society and their possible relationships (as in such terms as 'bourgeois' or 'pastoral society), or of the general development of humanity considered as a whole. The definition of a society in this sense raises difficult questions, even if we assume that we are defining an objective reality, as seems likely, unless we reject as illegitimate such statements as 'Japanese society in 1930 differed from English society'. For even if we eliminate the confusions between different uses of the word 'society', we face problems (a) because the size, complexity and scope of these units varies, for example at different historical periods or stages of development; and (b) because what we call society is merely one set of human interrelations among several of varying scale and comprehensiveness into which people are classifiable or classify themselves, often simultaneously and with overlaps. In extreme cases such as New Guinea or Amazon tribes, these various sets may define the same group of people, though this is in fact rather improbable. But normally this group is congruent neither with such relevant sociological units as the community, nor with certain wider systems

of relationship of which the society forms a part, and which may be functionally essential to it (like the set of economic relations) or non-essential (like those of culture).

Christendom or Islam exist and are recognized as self-classifications, but though they may define a *class* of societies sharing certain common characteristics, they are not societies in the sense in which we use the word when talking about the Greeks or modern Sweden. On the other hand, while in many ways Detroit and Cuzco are today part of a single system of functional interrelationships (for example, part of one economic system), few would regard them as part of the same society, sociologically speaking. Neither would we regard as one the societies of the Romans or the Han and those of the barbarians who formed, quite evidently, part of a wider system of interrelationships with them. How do we define these units? It is far from easy to say, though most of us solve – or evade – the problem by choosing some outside criterion: territorial, ethnic, political or the like. But this is not always satisfactory. The problem is more than methodological. One of the major themes of the history of modern societies is the increase in their scale, in their internal homogeneity, or at least in the centralization and directness of social relationships, the change from an essentially pluralist to an essentially unitary structure. In tracing this, problems of definition become very trouble-some, as every student of the development of national societies or at least of nationalisms knows.

(3) The history of societies requires us to apply, if not a formalized and elaborate model of such structures, then at least an approximate order of research priorities and a working assumption about what constitutes the central nexus or complex of connections of our subject, though of course these things imply a model. Every social historian does in fact make such assumptions and hold such priorities. Thus I doubt whether any historian of eighteenth-century Brazil would give the Catholicism of that society analytical priority over its slavery, or any historian of nineteenth-century Britain would regard kinship as central a social nexus as he or she would in Anglo-Saxon England.

A tacit consensus among historians seems to have established a fairly common working model of this kind, with variants. One starts with the material and historical environment, goes on to the forces and techniques of production (demography coming somewhere in between), the structure of the consequent economy – divisions of labour, exchange, accumulation, distribution of the surplus and so forth – and the social relations arising from these. These might be followed by the institutions and the image of society and its functioning which underlie them. The shape of the social structure is thus established, the specific characteristics and details of which, insofar as they derive from other sources, can then be determined, most likely by comparative study. The practice is thus to work outwards and upwards from the process of social production in its specific setting. Historians will be tempted, in my view rightly, to pick on one particular relation or relational complex as central and specific to the society (or type of society) in question, and to group the rest of the treatment around it – for example, Bloch's 'relations of interdependence' in his *Feudal Society*, or those arising out of industrial production, possibly in industrial society, certainly in its capitalist form. Once the structure has been established, it must be seen in its historical movement. In the French phrase 'structure' must be seen in 'conjuncture', though this term must not be taken to exclude other, and possibly more relevant, forms and patterns of historical change. Once again the tendency is to treat economic movements (in the broadest sense) as the backbone of such an analysis. The tensions to which the society is exposed in the process of historic change and transformation then allow the historian to expose, first, the general mechanism by which the structures of society simultaneously tend to lose and re-establish their equilibria, and, second, the phenomena which are traditionally the subject of interest to the social historians – for example, collective consciousness, social movements and the social dimension of intellectual and cultural changes.

My object in summarizing what I believe – perhaps wrongly – to be a widely accepted working plan of social historians is not to recommend it, even though I am personally in its favour. It is rather the opposite: to suggest that we try and make the implicit assumptions on which we work explicit and to ask ourselves whether this plan is in fact the best for the formulation of the nature and structure of societies and the mechanisms of their historic transformations (or stabilizations), whether other plans of work based on other questions can be made compatible with it, or are to be preferred to it, or can simply be superimposed to produce the historical equivalent of those Picasso portraits which are simultaneously displayed full-face and in profile.

In brief, if as historians of society we are to help in producing – for the benefit of all the social sciences – valid models of socio-historic dynamics, we shall have to establish a greater unity of our practice and our theory, which at the present stage of the game probably means in the first instance to watch what we are doing, to generalize it, and to correct it in the light of the problems arising out of further practice.

IV

Consequently, I should like to conclude by surveying the actual practice of social history in the past decade or two, in order to see what future approaches and problems it suggests. This procedure has the advantage that it fits in both with the professional inclinations of a historian and with what little we know about the actual progress of sciences. What topics and problems have attracted most attention in recent years? What are the growing-points? What are the interesting people doing? The answers to such questions do not exhaust analysis, but without them we cannot get very far. The consensus of workers may be mistaken, or distorted by fashion or – as is obviously the case in such a field as the study of public disorder – by the impact of politics and administrative requirements, but we neglect it at our peril. The progress of science has derived less from the attempt to define perspectives and programmes *a priori* – if it did we should now be curing cancer – than from an obscure and often simultaneous convergence upon the questions worth asking and, above all, those ripe for an answer. Let us see what has been happening, at least insofar as it is reflected in the impressionistic view of one observer.

Let me suggest that the bulk of interesting work in social history in the past ten or fifteen years has clustered around the following topics or complexes of questions:

(1) demography and kinship
(2) urban studies insofar as these fall within our field
(3) classes and social groups
(4) the history of 'mentalities' or collective consciousness or of 'culture' in the anthropologists' sense
(5) the transformation of societies (for example, modernization or industrialization)
(6) social movements and phenomena of social protest.

The first two groups can be singled out because they have already institutionalized themselves as fields, regardless of the importance of their subject-matter, and now possess their own organization, methodology and system of publications. Historical demography is a rapidly growing and fruitful field, which rests not so much on a set of problems as on a technical innovation in research (family reconstitution) that makes it possible to derive interesting results from material hitherto regarded as recalcitrant or exhausted (parish registers). It has thus opened a new range of sources, whose characteristics in turn have led to the formulation of questions. The major interest for social historians of historical demography lies in the light it sheds on certain aspects of family structure and behaviour, on the life-curves of people at different periods, and on intergenerational changes. These are important though limited by the nature of the sources – more limited than the most enthusiastic champions of the subject allow, and certainly by themselves insufficient to provide the framework of analysis of 'The World We Have Lost'. Nevertheless, the fundamental importance of this field is not in question, and it has served to encourage the use of strict quantitative techniques. One welcome effect, or side-effect, has been to arouse a greater interest in historical problems of kinship structure than social historians might have shown without this stimulus, though a modest demonstration effect from social anthropology ought not to be neglected. The nature and prospects of this field have been sufficiently debated to make further discussion unnecessary here.

Urban history also possesses a certain technologically determined unity. The individual city is normally a geographically limited and coherent unit, often with its specific documentation and even more often of a size which lends itself to research on the Ph. D. scale. It also reflects the urgency of urban problems which have increasingly become the major, or at least the most dramatic, problems of social planning and management in modern industrial societies. Both these influences tend to make urban history a large container with ill-defined, heterogeneous and sometimes indiscriminate contents. It includes anything about cities. But it is clear that it raises problems peculiarly germane to social history, at least in the sense that the city can never be an analytical framework for economic macro-history (because economically it must be part of a larger system), and politically it is only rarely found as a self-contained city-state. It is essentially a body of human beings living together in a particular way, and the characteristic process of urbanization in modern societies makes it, at least up to the present, the form in which most of them live together.

The technical, social and political problems of the city arise essentially out of the interactions of masses of human beings living in close proximity to one another; and even the ideas about the city (insofar as it is not a mere stage-set for the display of some ruler's power and glory) are those in which men – from the Book of Revelation on – have tried to express their aspirations about human communities. Moreover, in recent centuries it has raised and dramatized the problems of rapid social change more than any other institution. That the social historians who have flocked into urban studies are aware of this need hardly be said.[11] One may say that they have been groping toward a view of urban history as a paradigm of social change. I doubt whether it can be this, at least for the period up to the present. I also doubt whether many really impressive global studies of the larger cities of the industrial era have so far been produced, considering the vast quantity of work in this field. However, urban history must remain a central concern of historians of society, if only because it brings out – or can bring out – those specific aspects of societal change and structure with which sociologists and social psychologists are peculiarly concerned.

The other clusters of concentration have not so far been institutionalized, though one or two may be approaching this stage of development. The history of classes and social groups has plainly developed out of the common assumption that no understanding of society is possible without an understanding of the major components of all societies no longer based primarily on kinship. In no field has the advance been more dramatic and – given the neglect of historians in the past – more necessary. The briefest list of the most significant works in social history must include Lawrence Stone on the Elizabethan aristocracy, E. Le Roy Ladurie on the Languedoc peasants, Edward Thompson on the making of the English working class, Adeline Daumard on the Parisian bourgeoisie; but these are merely peaks in what is already a sizeable mountain range. Compared to these the study of more restricted social groups – professions, for instance – has been less significant.

The novelty of the enterprise has been its ambition. Classes, or specific relations of production such as slavery, are today being systematically considered on the scale of a society, or in inter-societal comparison, or as general types of social relationship. They are also now considered in depth, that is, in all aspects of their social existence, relations and behaviour. This is new, and the achievements are already striking, though the work has barely begun – if we except fields of specially intense activity, such as the comparative study of slavery. Nevertheless, a number of difficulties can be discerned, and a few words about them may not be out of place.

(1) The mass and variety of material for these studies is such that the pre-industrial artisan technique of older historians is plainly inadequate. They require co-operative teamwork and the utilization of modern technical equipment. I would guess that the massive works of individual scholarship will mark the early phases of this kind of research, but will give way on the one hand to systematic co-operative projects and on the other hand to periodic (and probably still single-handed) attempts at synthesis. This is evident in the field of work with which I am most familiar, the history of the working class. Even the most ambitious single work – E. P. Thompson's – is no more than a great torso, though it deals with a rather short period. (Jürgen Kuczynski's titanic *Geschichte der Lage der Arbeiter unter dem Kapitalismus*, as its title implies, concentrates only on certain aspects of the working class.)

(2) The field raises daunting technical difficulties, even where conceptual clarity exists, especially as regards the measurement of change over time – for example, the flow into and out of any specified social group, or the changes in peasant landholdings. We may be lucky enough to have sources from which such changes can be derived (for example, the recorded genealogies of the aristocracy and gentry as a group) or from which the material for our analysis may be constructed (for example, by the methods of historical demography, or the data on which the valuable studies of the Chinese bureaucracy have been based). But what are we to do, say, about Indian castes, which we also know to have contained such movements, presumably inter-generational, but about which it is so far impossible to make even rough quantitative statements?

(3) More serious are the conceptual problems, which have not always been clearly confronted by historians – a fact which does not preclude good work (horses can be recognized and ridden by those who can't define them), but which suggests that we have been slow to face the more general problems of social structure and relations and their transformations. These in turn raise technical problems, such as those of the possibly changing specification of the membership of a class over time, which complicates quantitative study. It also raises the more general problem of the multidimensionality of social groups. To take a few examples, there is the well-known Marxian duality of the term 'class'. In one sense it is a general phenomenon of all post-tribal history, in another a product of modern bourgeois

society; in one sense almost an analytical construct to make sense of otherwise inexplicable phenomena, in another a group of people actually seen as belonging together in their own or some other group's consciousness, or both. These problems of consciousness in turn raise the question of the language of class – the changing, often overlapping and sometimes unrealistic terminologies of such contemporary classification[12] about which we know as yet very little in quantitative terms. (Here historians might look carefully at the methods and preoccupations of social anthropologists, while pursuing – as L. Girard and a Sorbonne team are doing – the systematic quantitative study of socio-political vocabulary.)[13]

Again, there are degrees of class. To use Theodore Shanin's phrase,[14] the peasantry of Marx's 18th Brumaire is a 'class of low classness', whereas Marx's proletariat is a class of very high, perhaps of maximal 'classness'. There are the problems of the homogeneity or heterogeneity of classes; or, what may be much the same, of their definition in relation to other groups and their internal divisions and stratifications. In the most general sense, there is the problem of the relation between classifications, necessarily static at any given time, and the multiple and changing reality behind them.

(4) The most serious difficulty may well be the one which leads us directly toward the history of society as a whole. It arises from the fact that class defines not a group of people in isolation, but a system of relationships, both vertical and horizontal. Thus it is a relationship of difference (or similarity) and of distance, but also a qualitatively different relationship of social function, of exploitation, of dominance/subjection. Research on class must therefore involve the rest of society of which it is a part. Slave-owners cannot be understood without slaves, and without the non-slave sectors of society. It might be argued that for the self-definition of the nineteenth-century European middle classes the capacity to exercise power over people (whether through property, keeping servants or even – via the patriarchal family structure – wives and children), while not having direct power exercised over themselves, was essential. Class studies are therefore, unless confined to a deliberately restricted and partial aspect, analyses of society. The most impressive, like Le Roy Ladurie's, therefore go far beyond the limits of their title.

It may thus be suggested that in recent years the most direct approach to the history of society has come through the study of class in this wider sense. Whether we believe that this reflects a correct perception of the nature of post-tribal societies, or whether we merely put it down to the current influence of *Marxisant* history, the future prospects of this type of research appear bright.

In many ways the recent interest in the history of 'mentalities' marks an even more direct approach to central methodological problems of social history. It has been largely stimulated by the traditional interest in 'the common people' of many who are drawn to social history. It has dealt largely with the individually inarticulate, undocumented and obscure, and is often indistinct from an interest in their social movements or in more general phenomena of social behaviour, which today, fortunately, also includes an interest in those who fail to take part in such movements – for example, in the conservative as well as in the militant or passively socialist worker.

This very fact has encouraged a specifically dynamic treatment of culture by historians, superior to such studies as those of the 'culture of poverty' by anthropologists, though not uninfluenced by their methods and pioneering experience. They have been not so much studies of an aggregate of beliefs and ideas, persistent or not – though there has been much valuable thought about these matters, for example, by Alphonse Dupront[15] – as of ideas in action and, more specifically, in situations of social tensions and crisis, as in Georges Lefebvre's *Grande Peur*, which has inspired so much subsequent work. The nature of sources for such study has rarely allowed the historian to confine himself to simple factual study and exposition. He has been obliged from the outset to construct models, that is, to fit his partial and scattered data into coherent systems, without which they would be little more than anecdotal. The criterion of such models is or ought to be that its components should fit together and provide a guide both to the nature of collective action in specifiable social situations and to its limits.[16] Edward Thompson's concept of the 'moral economy' of pre-industrial England may be one such; my own analysis of social banditry has tried to base itself on another.

Insofar as these systems of belief and action are, or imply, images of society as a whole (which may be, as occasion arises, images seeking either its permanence or its transformation), and insofar as these correspond to certain aspects of its actual reality, they bring us closer to the core of our task. Insofar as the most successful such analyses have dealt with traditional or customary societies, even though sometimes with such societies under the impact of social transformation, their scope has been more limited. For a period characterized by constant, rapid and fundamental change, and by a complexity which puts society far beyond the individual's experience or even conceptual grasp, the models derivable from the history of culture have probably a diminishing contact with the social realities. They may not even any longer be very useful in constructing the pattern of aspiration of modern society ('what society ought to be like'). For the basic change brought about by the industrial revolution in the field of social thought has been to substitute a system of beliefs resting on unceasing *progress* toward aims which can be specified only as a *process*, for one resting on the assumption of permanent order, which can be described or illustrated in terms of some concrete social model, normally drawn from the past, real or imaginary. The cultures of the past measured their own society against such specific models; the cultures of the present can measure them only against possibilities. Still, the history of 'mentalities' has been useful in introducing something analogous to the discipline of the social anthropologists into history, and its usefulness is very far from exhausted.

I think the profitability of the numerous studies of social conflict, ranging from riots to revolutions, requires more careful assessment. Why they should attract research today is obvious. That they always dramatize crucial aspects of social structure because they are here strained to the breaking-point is not in doubt. Moreover, certain important problems cannot be studied at all except in and through such moments of eruption, which do not merely bring into the open so much that is normally latent, but also concentrate and magnify phenomena for the benefit of the student, while – not the least of their advantages – normally multiplying our documentation about them. To take a simple example: how much less would we know about the ideas of those who normally do not express themselves commonly or at all in writing but for the extraordinary explosion of articulateness which is so characteristic of revolutionary periods, and to which the mountains of pamphlets, letters, articles and speeches, not to mention the mass of police reports, court depositions and general enquiries bear witness? How fruitful the study of the great, and above all the well-documented, revolutions can be is shown by the historiography of the French Revolution, which has been studied longer and more intensively perhaps than any period of equal brevity, without visibly diminishing returns. It has been, and remains, an almost perfect laboratory for the historian.[17]

The danger of this type of study lies in the temptation to isolate the phenomenon of overt crisis from the wider context of a society undergoing transformation. This danger may be particularly great when we launch into comparative studies, especially when moved by the desire to solve problems (such as how to make or stop revolutions), which is not a very fruitful approach in sociology or social history. What, say, riots have in common with one another (for example, 'violence') may be trivial. It may even be illusory, insofar as we may be imposing an anachronistic criterion, legal, political or otherwise, on the phenomena – something which historical students of criminality are learning to avoid. The same may or may not be true of revolutions. I am the last person to wish to discourage an interest in such matters, since I have spent a good deal of professional time on them. However, in studying them we ought to define the precise purpose of our interest clearly. If it lies in the major transformations of society, we may find, paradoxically, that the value of our study of the revolution itself is in inverse proportion to our concentration on the brief moment of conflict. There are things about the Russian Revolution, or about human history, which can be discovered only by concentrating on the period from March to November 1917 or the subsequent Civil War; but there are other matters which cannot emerge from such a concentrated study of brief periods of crisis, however dramatic and significant.

On the other hand, revolutions and similar subjects of study (including social movements) can normally be integrated into a wider field which does not merely lend itself to, but requires, a comprehensive grasp of social structure and dynamics: the short-term social transformations experienced and labelled as such, which stretch over a period of a few decades or generations. We are dealing not simply with chronological chunks carved out of a continuum of growth or development, but with relatively brief historic periods during which society is reoriented and transformed, as the very phrase 'industrial revolution' implies. (Such periods may of course include great political revolutions, but cannot be chronologically delimited by them.) The popularity of such historically crude terms as 'modernization' or 'industrialization' indicates a certain awareness of such phenomena.

The difficulties of such an enterprise are enormous, which is perhaps why there are as yet no adequate studies of the eighteenth–nineteenth-century industrial revolutions as social processes for any country, though one or two excellent regional and local works are now available, such as Rudolf Braun on the Zurich countryside and John Foster on early-nineteenth-century Oldham.[18] It may be that a practicable approach to such phenomena can be at present derived not only from economic history (which has inspired studies of industrial revolution), but from political science. Workers in the field of the prehistory and history of colonial liberation have naturally been forced to confront such problems, though perhaps in an excessively political perspective, and African studies have proved particularly fruitful, though recent attempts to extend this approach to India may be noted.[19] In consequence the political science and political sociology dealing with the modernization of colonial societies can furnish us with some useful help.

The analytical advantage of the colonial situation (by which I mean that of *formal* colonies acquired by conquest and directly administered) is that here an entire society or group of societies is sharply defined by contrast with an outside force, and its various internal shifts and changes, as well as its reactions to the uncontrollable and rapid impact of this force, can be observed and analysed as a whole. Certain forces which in other societies are internal, or operate in a gradual and complex interaction with internal elements of that society, can here be considered for practical purposes and in the short run as entirely external, which is analytically very helpful. (We shall not of course overlook the distortions of the colonial societies – for example, by the truncation of their economy and social hierarchy – which also result from colonization, but the interest of the colonial situation does not depend on the assumption that colonial society is a replica of non-colonial.)

There is perhaps a more specific advantage. A central preoccupation of workers in this field has been nationalism and nation-building, and here the colonial situation can provide a much closer approximation to the general model. Though historians have hardly yet come to grips with it, the complex of phenomena which can be called national(ist) is clearly crucial to the understanding of social structure and dynamics in the industrial era, and some of the more interesting work in political sociology has come to recognize it. The project conducted by Stein Rokkan, Eric Allardt and others on 'Centre Formation, Nation-Building and Cultural Diversity' provides some very interesting approaches.[20]

The 'nation', a historical invention of the past 200 years, whose immense practical significance today hardly needs discussion, raises several crucial questions of the history of society, for example the change in the scale of societies, the transformation of pluralist, indirectly linked social systems into unitary ones with direct linkages (or the fusion of several pre-existing smaller societies into a larger social system), the factors determining the boundaries of a social system (such as territorial–political), and others of equal significance. To what extent are these boundaries objectively imposed by the requirements of economic development, which necessitate as the locus of, for example, the nineteenth-century-type industrial economy a territorial state of minimum or maximum size in given circumstances?[21] To what extent do these requirements automatically imply not only the weakening and destruction of earlier social structures, but also particular degrees of simplification, standardization, and centralization – that is, direct and increasingly exclusive links between 'centre' and 'periphery' (or rather 'top' and 'bottom')? To what extent is the 'nation' an attempt to fill the void left by the dismantling of earlier community and social structures by inventing something which could function as, or produce symbolic substitutes for, the functioning of a consciously apprehended community or society? (The concept of the 'nation-state' might then combine these objective and subjective developments.)

The colonial and ex-colonial situations are not necessarily more suitable bases for investigating this complex of questions than is European history, but in the absence of serious work about it by the historians of nineteenth- and twentieth-century Europe, who have been hitherto – including the Marxists – rather baffled by it, it seems likely that recent Afro-Asian history may form the most convenient starting-point.

V

How far has the research of recent years advanced us towards a history of society? Let me put my cards on the table. I cannot point to any single work which exemplifies the history of society to which we ought, I believe, to aspire. Marc Bloch has given us in *La Société féodale* a masterly, indeed an exemplary, work on the nature of social structure, including the consideration both of a certain type of society and of its actual and possible variants, illuminated by the comparative method, into the dangers and the much greater rewards of which I do not propose to enter here. Marx has sketched out for us, or allows us to sketch for ourselves, a model of the typology and the long-term historical transformation and evolution of societies which remains immensely powerful and almost as far ahead of its time as were the Prolegomena of Ibn Khaldun, whose own model, based on the interaction of different types of societies, has of course also been fruitful, especially in prehistory, ancient, and Oriental history. (I am thinking of the late Gordon Childe and Owen Lattimore.) Recently there has been important advances toward the study of certain types of society – notably those based on slavery in the Americas (the slave-societies of antiquity appear to be in recession) and those based on a large body of peasant cultivators. On the other hand the attempts to translate a comprehensive social history into popular synthesis strike me so far as either relatively unsuccessful or, with all their great merits, not the least of which is stimulation, as schematic and tentative. The history of society is still being constructed. I have in this essay tried to suggest some of its problems, to assess some of its practice, and incidentally to hint at certain problems which might benefit from more concentrated exploration. But it would be wrong to conclude without noting, and welcoming, the remarkably flourishing state of the field. It is a good moment to be a social historian. Even those of us who never set out to call ourselves by this name will not want to disclaim it today.

CHAPTER 7

Historians and Economists: I

This and the following chapter represent the slightly revised text of the Marshall Lectures to the Faculty of Economics, Cambridge University, which I was invited to give in 1980. They have not previously been published. Though much has happened since then in both economics and economic history – not least the award of the Nobel Prize in economics to economic historians critically considered here – the questions I tried to raise in these lectures are still unsettled, and the texts still seem worth publishing. However, in response to criticism I have modified my position slightly on some points. Later additions to this effect are in square brackets.

Though every Napoleonic soldier proverbially carried a marshal's baton in his knapsack, few Napoleonic soldiers seriously expected to have the occasion for taking it out. I was for many years in a similar position to the Napoleonic rank and file, and am therefore not merely honoured but also surprised by the invitation to give the Marshall Lectures, which I first heard given here, in the early 1950s, by Gunnar Myrdal. I was then a historian marginally linked to this university, operating on the fringes of the Economics Faculty as supervisor and examiner in economic history, while Cambridge refused me several jobs in two faculties over the years. The university then certainly had the most distinguished economics faculty in Britain and possibly in the world. I am therefore keenly aware that the invitation to give these lectures is a considerable distinction, for which I thank the Faculty.

But, if I speak to you with some satisfaction, I also do so with a strong admixture of defensive modesty. I am not an economist and, by the criteria of one school among my colleagues, not even a proper economic historian, though of course these criteria would also have excluded Sombart, Max Weber and Tawney. I am neither a mathematician nor a philosopher, two occupations in which economists sometimes seek refuge when too hard pressed by the real world, and whose propositions might seem relevant to them. In short, I speak as a layman. The only thing that encourages me to open my mouth, other than the pleasure of being on records as a Marshall Lecturer, is the feeling that, in the present state of your subject, economists may be prepared to listen to lay observations, on the ground that they cannot be less relevant to the present situation of the world than some of what they write themselves. Especially, one hopes, they may listen to a layman who appeals for a greater integration, or rather reintegration, of history into economics.

For economics, or rather that part of it which from time to time claims a monopoly of defining the subject, has always been the victim of history. For lengthy periods, when the world economy appears to be rolling on quite happily with or without advice, history encourages a good deal of self-satisfaction. Proper economics has the floor, improper economics is tacitly excluded, or consigned to the twilight world of past and present heterodoxy, the equivalent of faith-healing or acupuncture in medicine. Even Keynes, you may remember, made no marked distinction between Marx, J. A. Hobson and the otherwise unremembered Silvio Gesell. However, from time to time history catches economists at their brilliant gymnastics and walks off with their overcoats. The early 1930s were such a period, and we are living through another such. At least some economists are dissatisfied with the state of their subject. Historians may be able to contribute to clarification, if not to revision.

The topic I have chosen, 'Historians and Economists', is also one that has a specific relevance to Cambridge and its Economics Faculty, in which economic history and economics have since the days of Marshall been permanently and uneasily yoked together. The relationship has been complex and problematic for both sides. On the one hand Marshall's own theoretical apparatus was, as has often been observed, essentially static. It had difficulty in accommodating historical change and evolution. The appendix to the *Principles*, originally an introductory chapter, which summarizes economic history, has been rightly described by Schumpeter as reading 'like a series of trivialities'.[1] Indeed Marshall's own very considerable knowledge of economic history contributes little more than some decorative and illustrative flourishes to a theoretical structure designed without much room for such additions. Yet he was aware that economics was embedded in historical change and could not be abstracted from it without substantial loss in realism. He knew that economics needed history, but not how to fit history into his analysis. In this respect he was inferior not only to Marx but to Adam Smith. And while the Cambridge syllabus, like that of other economics faculties, has always so far (1980) included some economic history, its place in the syllabus, and the place of those who taught it, has in the past often been like that of the human appendix. It was unquestionably part of the organism, but its precise function, if any, was far from clear.

On the other hand the economic historians lived, and still to some extent live, an uneasy double life between the two disciplines which give them their name. In the Anglo-Saxon world, at least, there are normally two economic histories, whether we call them 'old' and 'new' or, as seems more realistic, economic history for historians and for economists. Basically the second kind is theory – mainly neo-classical theory – projected backwards. I shall have more to say about the 'new' economic history, or 'cliometrics'. For the moment I merely wish to point out that, while it has attracted persons of great ability and – in the case of at least one of them [since rewarded with a Nobel Prize], Professor Robert Fogel – admirable ingenuity in the exploration and exploitation of historical sources, it has so far been less than revolutionary. Professor Fogel himself has admitted that even in American economic history, on which most cliometricians initially concentrated, they may have altered, but have not replaced, the basic narratives of the growth of agriculture, the rise of manu-facturing, the evolution of banking, the spread of trade and much else that has been traced and documented by traditional methods.[2]

The old economic historians, even when competent in economics and statistics, have generally, and with good reason, distrusted the mere retrospective verification or falsification of propositions in current economic theory, and the deliberate narrowing of the 'new' economic history's field of vision. Even the holder of the Cambridge chair in economic history, J. H. Clapham, who had been picked by Marshall himself for his sense of economic analysis, and who had himself been a professor of economics, did not think that economic theory had a major role in his subject. Economic history does not imply suspicion of theory as such. If it implies some scepticism of neo-classical theory, it is because of its a-historicity and the highly restrictive nature of its models.

Economists and historians therefore live in uneasy coexistence. I suggest that this is unsatisfactory for both.

Economists need to reintegrate history, and this cannot be done simply by transforming it into retrospective econometrics. Economists need this reintegration more than historians, because economics is an applied social science, as medicine is an applied natural science. Biologists who do not see curing illness as their main job are not doctors, even when associated with medical schools. Economists who are not primarily concerned, directly or indirectly, with the operations of real economies which they wish to transform, improve or protect against deterioration, are better classed as sub-species of philosophers or mathematicians, unless they choose to occupy the space left vacant in our secular society by the decline of theology. I express no opinion here on the value of justifying the ways of Providence (or the Market) to man. Anyway, policy recommendations, positive or negative, are built into the subject. If this were not the case, no such subject as economics would have come into existence or would have survived. Admittedly, with the numerical growth, professionalization and academicization of this as of so many other disciplines, there has also developed a large body of work whose object is neither to interpret the world nor to change it, but to advance careers and score points off other practitioners of the subject. However, we may leave this aspect of the evolution of economics to one side.

History, whose subject is the past, is not in a position to be an applied discipline in this sense, if only because no way has yet been discovered to change what has already happened. At most we can make counterfactual speculations about hypothetical alternatives. Of course past, present and future are part of one continuum, and what historians have to say could therefore permit both forecasts and recommendations for the future. Indeed I hope that this is so. The skills of the historian are certainly not irrelevant for such a purpose. Nevertheless, my discipline is so defined that historians can only enter the field of present policy in an extracurricular manner, or insofar as history is an integral part of a wider conception of social science, as in Marxism. In any case, much of what we do must remain outside, namely all that distinguishes the unchangeable past from the theoretically changeable future, or, if you prefer, betting on known results from ante-post betting.

But do economists need the reintegration of history into economics? In the first place some economists patently call for history, 'in the hope that the past will supply answers which the present alone appears reluctant to yield'.[3] At a time when it is the staple of Martini conversation that the troubles of the British economy go back to the nineteenth century, history seems a natural component of any diagnosis of what is wrong with it, and may not be irrelevant to therapy. Nothing is more ridiculous than the assumption [increasingly common] that economic history is purely academic, whereas notorious pseudo-subjects like 'management' are in some way real and earnest. For long – to judge by the American profession, by far the largest in the world – the interest in history among economists declined, even as profoundly historical subjects moved into the centre of attention. Topics in economic history or the history of economic thought, declined from 13 per cent of all American doctoral dissertations in the first quarter of the century to 3 per cent in the first half of the 1970s. Conversely, economic growth, which stimulated no dissertations under that name at all until 1940, comprised 13 per cent of all theses, the largest single body of doctoral work, in the later period.

This is all the more odd since history and economics grew up together. If classical political economy is specifically associated with Britain it is, I suggest, not simply because Britain was a pioneer capitalist economy. After all, the other pioneer, the seventeenth-eighteenth-century Netherlands, was a less distinguished producer of economic theorists. It was because the Scottish thinkers who contributed so much to the discipline specifically refused to isolate economics from the rest of the historical transformation of society in which they saw themselves engaged. Men like Adam Smith saw themselves as living through a transition from what the Scots, probably earlier than anyone else, called a 'feudal system' of society to another kind of society. They wished to hasten and rationalize this transition, if only to avoid the probably deleterious political and social results of leaving the 'Natural Progress of Opulence' to its own devices, when it might turn into an 'unnatural and retrograde order'.[4] One might say that, if Marxists recognized barbarism as a possible alternative outcome of capitalist development, Smith recognizes it as a possible alternative outcome of feudal development. Hence it is as much an error to abstract classical political economy from the historical sociology to which Smith devoted the third book of his *Wealth of Nations* as it is to separate it from his moral philosophy. Similarly history and analysis remained integrated in Marx, the last of the great classical political economists. In a somewhat different and analytically less satisfactory manner they remained integrated with economics among the Germans. Let us recall that in the late nineteenth century Germany probably possessed more teaching posts in economics and a more voluminous literature in the field than the British and French combined.

In fact, the separation between history and economics did not make itself felt fully until the marginalist transformation of economics. It became a major issue in debate in the course of the now largely forgotten *Methodenstreit* of the 1880s, brought into the open by Carl Menger's provocative attack on the so-called 'historical school', which, in a particularly extreme form, then dominated German economics. However, it would be unwise to forget that the Austrian school, to which Menger belonged, was also engaged in passionate polemics against Marx.

In this battle of methodologies one side was eventually so completely successful that the issues, the arguments and even the existence of the defeated side have been largely forgotten. Marx survived in the schools insofar as the arguments against him could be conducted in the analytic mode of neo-classicism: he could be treated as an economic theorist, though a dangerously mistaken one. Schmoller and the other historicists could simply be dismissed as not serious economists at all in the analytical sense, or pigeonholed as merely 'economic historians', as happened to William Cunningham in Cambridge. Indeed, I think that this is the origin of economic history as an academic specialization in Britain. British economics, and especially Marshall, never excluded history and empirical observation – the other things which are so rarely equal – as systematically from analysis as the more extreme Austrians did. Nevertheless it narrowed its base and perspectives in a way that made them hard to incorporate, except in a trivial manner, if only by virtually leaving to one side for several generations dynamic problems such as economic development and fluctuations, indeed even static macro-economics. As Hicks has pointed out, under the circumstances even Marshall's thirst for realism 'was essentially myopic ... Marshallian economics is at its best when dealing with the firm or with the "industry"; it is much less capable of dealing with the whole economy, even the whole of the national economy.'[5]

It would be pointless to reopen the *Methodenstreit* of the 1880s, all the more so since it turned on a methodological dispute which, in this form, is no longer of great interest: that between the value of deductive and inductive methods. However, three observations may be worth making. First, at the time the victory did not seem anything like as clear-cut as we recognize it to be in retrospect. Neither German nor American economics followed the lead of Vienna, Cambridge and Lausanne at all readily. Second, the case for the winning side was essentially *not* based on the practical value of economic theory, as now defined. The third observation, based on hindsight, is that there is indeed no obvious correlation between the success of an economy and the intellectual distinction and prestige of its economic theorists, as measured by the retrospective criteria of neo-classical peer-group assessment. To put it bluntly, the fortunes of national economies appear to have little to do with the supply of good economists – at all events in the days when their opinions were not as readily available internationally as they are today. Germany, which has produced hardly any theorists who figure much, even in the footnotes of non-German textbooks, since Thünen, has clearly not suffered as a dynamic economy from this shortage. Pre-1938 Austria, where such theorists were plentiful, distinguished and consulted by governments, was not an advertisement for economic success until after 1945 when, as it happens, it had lost all its distinguished older theorists without acquiring comparable replacements. The practical significance of suppliers of good economic theory is not at all self-evident. We cannot be content with Menger's original analogy, which Schumpeter maintained to the end of his life, between pure theory as the biochemistry and physiology of economics, on which the surgery and therapy of applied economics are based. Unlike doctors, even economists who agree about the principles of economics may have diametrically opposite views about therapy. Furthermore, if successful treatment can be practised, as was evidently the case in Germany for most of the past century, by practitioners who do not necessarily accept the need for the theorists' biochemistry and physiology, then the relations between economic theory and practice clearly require further reflection.

In fact, as I have already hinted, the neo-classical case against the historicists accepted that their own theory had little relation to reality, though paradoxically their objection to the Marxists was that *their* pure theory (of value) was not a guide to real market pricing. Pure theorists could not deny that empirical enquiry (that is for the past, historical enquiry) could tell us more about the economy than whether it conformed to some theoretical proposition. (Indeed, we would today say that the validation of theoretical models by evidence from the real economy is rather more difficult than positive economics thought.) As far as policy and economic practice went, the role of pure theory was admitted to be quite secondary. Böhm-Bawerk deliberately excluded it from the battle of methods. 'It is only [in theory] that the question of method is in dispute,' he argued. 'In the province of practical social politics, for technical reasons, the historic–statistical method is so unquestionably superior that I do not hesitate to declare that a purely abstract–deductive legislative policy in economic and social matters would be as much of an abomination to me as to others.'[6] There are governments which could bear to be reminded of this. And Schumpeter, who was the most sophisticated and realistic mind among the Austrians, spelled it out even more clearly. 'Insofar as our theory is firmly founded, it fails when confronted with the most important phenomena of economic life.'[7]

Here, I think, Schumpeter's taste for provocation led him to make too sweeping a case against his own side. Pure theory did develop a practical dimension, only it turned out to be quite different from the one it was supposed to have before 1914.

It is beyond my scope to discuss the reasons why economic theory developed in this direction after 1870, though it is worth reminding ourselves that the differences between the two sides in the battle of methods were largely those between economic liberals or neo-liberals and believers in government intervention. Behind the dissatisfaction of the American institutionalists with neo-classical economics lay a belief in more social control of business, especially big business, and more state intervention than neo-classicists usually envisaged. The German historicists, who inspired so much American institutionalism, were essentially believers in a visible and not a hidden hand – the state's. This ideological or political element is obvious in the debate. It led economic heretics to treat pre-Keynesian neo-classicism as little more than a public-relations exercise for *laissez-faire* capitalism, an inadequate view, even if, for readers of Mises and Hayek, not a totally implausible one.

The point is rather that ideology could be so prominent in the debate, pure theory and history could glare at each other across a growing gap, one side could neglect practice and the other theory, just because both could regard the capitalist market-economy as essentially self-regulating. Both (except for the Marxists) could take its general and secular stability for granted. Pure theorists could regard practical applications as secondary, since theory contributed little except congratulation, unless governments proposed policies – mainly fiscal and monetary – which seriously interfered with the operations of the market. At this stage their relation to the conduct of their business by private enterprise and government was rather like that of film-reviewers and film-theorists to movie-makers before the 1950s. Conversely businessmen and – except in the fields of finance and fiscal policy – governments did not need more theory than was implicit in empirical common sense.

What business and government needed was information and technical expertise, which the pure theorists were not much interested in and did not provide. German administrators and executives thought they needed it more than British ones. So long as German social science fed them with a massive flow of admirably researched empirical studies, it did not matter to them that there was no German Marshall, Wicksell or Walras. Even the Marxists did not, for the moment, have to bother about the problems of a socialist economy, or any economy for which they were responsible, as witness the absence of any serious consideration of the problems of socialization. The First World War began to change this situation.

Paradoxically, the limits of a historicist or institutionalist approach which rejected pure theory became evident at precisely the moment when even capitalist economies, increasingly dependent on or dominated by their public sectors, had to be deliberately managed or planned. This required intellectual tools which historicists and institutionalists did not provide, however inclined to economic interventionism. We see a theory-based economics of management and planning emerging during the era of world wars. The hope of a return to 1913 'normalcy' somewhat postponed the adaptation of neo-classical economics, but after the 1929 slump it proceeded rapidly. The application of neo-classical theory to policy grew, as pure theorists abandoned their hitherto rather notable lack of interest in the numerical expression and testing of their concepts, for example in the possibilities of econometrics, which was institutionalized under this name in the 1930s. At the same time important instruments of operationalization became available, some derived from pre-marginalist classical political economy or macro-economics, via Marxism, like the input–output analysis which first appears in Leontiev's preparatory study for the Soviet plan of 1925, others from the mathematics of scientists applied to military-operations research, as with linear programming. Though the impact of neo-classical economic theory on socialist planning was also delayed, for historical and ideological reasons, in practice its applicability to non-capitalist economies has also been recognized since the Second World War.

Pure theory, operationalized and extended in this way, has thus proved to be more relevant to practice than Schumpeter thought in 1908. It really cannot any longer be said that it has no practical uses. However, in medical terms – if I may labour the old metaphor still further – it produces not physiologists or pathologists or diagnosticians, but body-scanning machines. Unless I am greatly mistaken, economic theory facilitate the choice between decisions, and perhaps develops techniques for making, implementing and monitoring decisions, but does not itself generate positive policy-making decisions. Of course it may be argued that this is not new. Whenever economic theory in the past has appeared to point unequivocally to a particular policy, do we not suspect – except in special cases – that the answers have been built into the demonstration of their ineluctability beforehand?

While the neo-classical theorists produced better policy tools than they originally suspected, their historicist and institutionalist adversaries have turned out worse than they expected at precisely the function on which they prided themselves, namely guiding an economically interventionist state. Here their old-fashioned positivism and lack of theory were to prove fatal. This is why Schmoller and Wagner and John R. Commons are now part of that history which they practised so assiduously. Yet there are two respects in which their contribution cannot be dismissed.

In the first place, as already suggested, they encouraged a really serious concrete study of that economic and social reality which Marshall was so concerned about. Before 1914 the Germans were constantly and rightly amazed at the sheer lack of interest of British economists in the actual data about their economy, and the consequent feebleness and patchiness of the quantitative information about it. Indeed, where British and German scholars treated the same subject factually, as Schulze-Gaevernitz and Sydney Chapman treated the British cotton industry, the superiority of the German work is hard to deny. Occasionally the shortage of native research actually led to the translation of German monographs on British subjects. Moreover, such empirical enquiries as were made in Britain before 1914 came, more often than not, from the economically heterodox, such as the Oxford economists who have been largely forgotten because they gravitated into social and public service (such as Hubert Llewellyn-Smith at the Board of Trade, and Beveridge) or from the strongly institutionalist Fabians whose sympathies in the battle of methods had been with the historicists, and whose London School of Economics was founded as an anti-Marshallian centre. The only serious British factual survey of economic concentration before 1914 was the work of a Fabian civil servant who was also chiefly responsible for setting up the first Census of Production in 1907.[8] Conversely, there was no equivalent to the massive series of applied monographs produced by the German Verein für Sozialpolitik on economic as well as social subjects. There was not, for many years to come, an equivalent to that institutionalist initiative, the American National Bureau of Economic Research. Since the Second World War we have perforce caught up to some extent, but between the wars it was certainly true that much of the argument between British economists was based on what has been called 'suggestive statistics' rather than on some of the detailed information already then available. In short, these debates tended to neglect information about the economy other than what was visible to the proverbial man on the Clapham omnibus, such as unemployment.

In the second place, the heterodox were considerably more alive both to the other things which are never equal and to the actual historical changes in the capitalist economy. There have been two major transformations of this economy in the past hundred years. The first, towards the end of the nineteenth century, is the one with which contemporaries tried to come to grips under such labels as 'imperialism', 'finance capitalism', 'collectivism' and others, the various aspects of change being recognized as somehow belonging together. The first of these shifts was noticed relatively soon, though not adequately analysed – but, I think exclusively, by people who were heterodox or marginal: by German historicists like Schulze-Gaevernitz or Schmoller, by J. A. Hobson, and, of course, by Marxists like Kautsky, Hilferding, Luxemburg and Lenin. Neo-classical theory had, at this stage, nothing to say about it. Indeed Schumpeter, lucid as always, argued in 1908 that 'pure theory' could have nothing to say about imperialism except platitudes and inexact philosophical reflections. When he himself eventually tried his hand at an explanation, it was on the improbable assumption that the new imperialism of the time had no intrinsic connection with capitalism, but was a sociologically explicable hangover from pre-capitalist society. Marshall was aware that some people held that economic concentration was the product of capitalist development, and were worried about trusts and monopolies. However, to the end of his life he regarded them as special cases. His belief in the efficacy of free trade and the free entry into industries of new competitors seemed unshaken. True, as a realist he never made the assumption of perfect competition, but he showed few signs of recognizing that the capitalist economy no longer operated as it had in the 1870s. Yet when *Industry and Trade* was published in 1919, it was no longer reasonable to assume that these matters, however important in Germany and the USA, were of no significance in Britain. It was not until the Great Slump that neo-classical theory adjusted itself to 'imperfect competition' as the economic norm.

The second major shift is that developed during, or rooted in, the quarter-century that followed the Second World War. While it was now obvious that a return to the world of the 1920s was neither possible nor desirable, it cannot be said that the new phase of the world economy was adequately analysed by orthodox economists in its own historical terms. Even, it must be said, the strongest surviving heterodox school, the Marxists, was much more reluctant to take a realistic look at post-war capitalism than Marxists had been in the 1890s and 1900s. The marked revival in Marxist theorizing in the abstract, contrasted rather unhappily with the fumbling manner in which Marxists came to grips, or until the 1970s avoided coming to grips, with the realities of the world around them. Nevertheless, insofar as a historically new reality was recognized, it was from a position on the margins. J. K. Galbraith formulated his vision of 'The New Industrial State', already implicit in his earlier books on 'American Capitalism' and 'The Affluent Society', primarily in terms of the metropolitan economy of large corporations, largely independent of the 'market'. One notes in passing that he was received much more favourably by lay readers, who understood what he was talking about, than by his colleagues. From Santiago the economists of the UN Economic Commission for Latin America criticized the belief that comparative costs destined the third world to produce primary products, and called for its industrialization. However, it was not until after the end of the 'Golden Age' in the early 1970s that the two phenomena were put together – this time largely by heterodox neo-Marxists – in the vision of a transnational phase of capitalism in which the large firm, and not the nation-state, is the institution through which the dynamic of capitalist accumulation is expressed. [In the 1980s and 1990s this was to become the common currency of a revived neo-liberalism. Whether this formulation underestimates the role of the national economy need not concern us here.]

While the heterodox were perhaps not as quick off the mark in recognizing a new phase of capitalism as they might have been, the orthodox economists seem to have shown little interest in the matter. As late as 1972 the late Harry Johnson – an extremely powerful and lucid, though not imaginative, intellect – predicted an unbroken continuation of world expansion and prosperity until the end of the century on any assumption except that of world war or the collapse of the USA. Few historians would have been so confident.

My argument implies that, divorced from history, economics is a rudderless ship and economists without history have not much idea of where it is sailing to. But I am not suggesting that these defects can be remedied simply be getting some charts, that is by paying more attention to concrete economic realities and historical experience. As a matter of fact, there have always been plenty of economists ready and anxious to keep their eyes open. The trouble is that, if in the mainstream tradition, their theory and method *as such* has not helped them to know where to look and what to look for. The study of economic mechanisms was divorced from that of the social and other factors which condition the behaviour of the agents who comprise such mechanisms. It is a point made long ago in Cambridge by Maurice Dobb.

I am implying a more radical reservation about mainstream economics. So long as it is defined in the fashion of Lionel Robbins purely as a matter of choice – and Samuelson's textbook, the student's bible, still so defines it – it can have only an incidental connection with the actual process of social production which is its ostensible subject, with what Marshall (who failed to live up to his definition) called 'the study of mankind in the ordinary business of life'. It happens to concentrate on activities within this field, but there are plenty of other activities to which the principle of economic choice applies. Divorced from a specific field of reality, economics must become what Ludwig von Mises called 'praxiology', a science, and consequently a set of techniques, for programming; and also, or alternatively, a normative model of how economic man *ought* to act, given ends on which, as a discipline, it has nothing to say.

The second option has nothing to do with science at all. It has led some economists to put on the dog-collar of the (lay) theologian. The first, as already observed, is a major achievement and, as already observed, of immense practical significance. But it is not what either social or natural sciences do. Schumpeter, lucid as always, refused to define its field except as 'an enumeration of the main "fields" now recognized in teaching practice', because it was not, he thought, 'a science in the sense in which acoustics is one, but rather an agglomeration of ill-coordinated and overlapping fields of research'.[9] Fogel unconsciously put his finger on the same weakness, when he praised economics for the 'large library of economic models' on which cliometricians could draw.[10] Libraries have no principle except arbitrary classification. What has been called the 'imperialism' of economics since the 1970s, which multiplies works on the economics of crime, marriage, education, suicide, the environment or whatnot, merely indicates that economics is now regarded as a universal service-discipline, not that it can understand what mankind does in the ordinary business of life, or how its activities change.

And yet economists cannot but be interested in the analysis of empirical material, past or present. But this is just one half of the team pulling what Morishima once called the two-horse carriage of methodology. The other half is primarily based on static models resting on generalized and highly simplified assumptions, whose consequences are then argued through, nowadays mainly in mathematical terms. How are the two to be driven together? Of course a good deal of economics has gone some way towards developing models which derive from economic reality, that is from production in terms of actual inputs and not in terms of utilities; and even from economies divided into sectors each of which has its own socially and hence economically specific mode of action.

Naturally as a historian I am in favour of such historically specific modelling, based on a generalization of empirical reality. A theory that assumes the coexistence of an oligopolistic central sector of the capitalist economy and a competitive margin is obviously preferable to one which assumes a free competitive market throughout. Yet I ask myself whether even this answers the big question about the future, of which historians are always aware, and which even the economists cannot neglect, if only because long-term forward planning is what not only states but big corporations must do all the time – or ought to. Whither is the world moving? What are the tendencies of its dynamic development, irrespective of our capacity to influence them, which, as should be clear, is quite small in the long term. [When this was first written, the global and transnational economy did not yet appear to be as triumphant as it looks in the mid-1990s, and therefore the simple view that the future would consists of an effectively uncontrollable global free-market system did not divert us as yet from actually looking at what it would bring.]

Here precisely lies the value of historically rooted visions of economic development like Marx's or Schumpeter's: both concentrated on the specific internal economic mechanisms of a capitalist economy which move it and impose a direction of it. I am not here discussing whether Marx's more elegant vision is preferable to Schumpeter's, who places both the forces that drive the system – the innovations which drive it forward, the sociological effects which bring it to an end – outside the system. Schumpeter's vision of capitalism as a combination of capitalist and pre-capitalist elements has certainly brought considerable illumination to nineteenth-century historians.

The interest of this kind of approach to historical dynamics does not lie in whether it allows us to test its predictions. Human beings and the complexities of the real world being what they are, prophecy is a hit-and-miss affair. Both in Marx and in Schumpeter it is skewed by ignorance and by their desires, fears and value-judgments. The interest of such approaches lies in the attempt to see future developments in other than linear terms. For even the simplest attempt to do so has a substantial pay-off. The mere recognition by Marx of a secular tendency for free competition to generate economic concentration has been enormously fertile. The mere awareness that the global growth of the economy is not a homogeneous or linear process, governed by the doctrine of comparative costs, produces considerable illumination. The mere recognition that there are long-term economic periodicities which fit in with rather substantial changes in the structure and mood of the economy and society, even if, like Kondratiev waves, we have not the slightest idea how to explain them, would have reduced the confidence of mainstream economists in the 1950s and 1960s.

If economics is not to remain the victim of history, constantly attempting to apply its tool-kit, generally with a time-lag, to yesterday's developments which have become sufficiently visible to dominate the scene today, it must develop or rediscover this historical perspective. For this may have a bearing not only on tomorrow's problems, about which we ought, if possible, to think before we get swamped by them, but also on tomorrow's theory. Let me conclude with a quotation from an exponent of another pure theory. 'When I ask about the significance of Einstein's ideas about curved space–time,' writes Steven Weinberg, 'I do not so much have in mind its applications to general relativity itself, but rather its usefulness in developing the next theories of gravitation. In physics ideas are important always prospectively, in looking towards the future.' I am capable neither of understanding nor of operating the theory of physicists, any more than most of the elaborations of theory in economics. Yet as a historian I am always concerned about the future – whether the future as it has already evolved out of some previous past, or as it is likely to evolve out of the continuum of past and present. I cannot help the feeling that in this respect economists might learn from us as well as from physicists.

CHAPTER 8

Historians and Economists: II

Economists might conceivably agree on the value of history for their discipline, but not historians about the value of economics for theirs. This is partly because history covers a much wider field. As we have seen, it is an obvious drawback of economics as a subject dealing with the real world that it selects out some and only some aspects of human behaviour as 'economic' and leaves the rest to someone else. So long as their subject is defined by exclusion economists can do nothing about this, however aware of their constraints. As Hicks has put it: 'When one becomes conscious of [the] links (which connect the economic story with the things we usually regard as falling outside it) one realizes that recognition is not enough.'[1]

History, on the other hand, cannot decide to leave out *any* aspect of human history *a priori*, though from time to time choosing to concentrate on some and to neglect others. On grounds of convenience or technical necessity, historians will tend to specialize. Some will be diplomatic historians, others ecclesiastical historians, some will confine themselves to seventeenth-century France. However, basically all history aspires to what the French call 'total history'. This is also the case with social history, though it has been traditionally run in tandem with economic history. Unlike the one, the other cannot regard anything as falling outside its potential range. It is safe to say that no economist shares the apparent belief of an ex-editor of the London *Times* that, if Keynes had had different sexual preferences, he would have turned out more like Milton Friedman, still less that his private life has any relevance to the judgment on Keynesian ideas. On the other hand I can easily imagine a social or general historian who might regard both as throwing light on a particular phase of the history of British society.

So even the specialized field of economic history is wider than the conventional field of economics as currently defined. To take Clapham's view, it is valuable chiefly insofar as it can be extended into wider fields. For instance, no economic historian – in my view no historian – can avoid fundamental questions of human social and economic evolution up to the present; why some societies seem to have stopped at some point of this process and others not; why the entire itinerary up to modern industrial society was completed in only one part of the world; and what the mechanisms of these changes, endogenous and/or induced, have been or are. This set of questions automatically integrates history into the wider field of the human and social sciences. However, even if, as Marx held, political economy (in his sense) was the anatomy of civil society, it clearly goes beyond the field of standard economics as usually defined. We can and should use the techniques, modes of argument and models of economics, but we cannot be confined to them.

Some of these models history cannot or need not use except, as it were, as mental controls. I can see little relevance to history, which is what actually happened, in the construction of models of possible or imaginary economies. Econometricians sometimes do not so much test theories as describe what the world would be like if the theories were correct. This is a tempting procedure in the far from infrequent cases when it turns out that in real life the theory does not apply or is untestable. Such exercises, however interesting, concern historians only to the extent the economies so analysed may turn out to be unnoticed real economies, or establish the limits outside which no economy, real or imaginary, could operate.

Similarly it is also possible, and usual, to formulate models so general as to be universally applicable, but at the cost of triviality. Thus it would be possible to demonstrate that the behaviour of Australian aborigines in maximizing utilities (defined in a sufficiently general sense) can be shown to be more rational than that of modern businessmen. This is neither surprising nor interesting. We accept that all members of the class 'economies', from the Bushmen to contemporary Japan, can be assigned to that class because they have certain characteristics in common. However, what interests the historian is what they have *not* in common and why, and how far these differences account for the very different fortunes of peoples who remained hunter-gatherers, and those who eventually developed more complex economies. The statement that Aborigines, or for that matter all social mammals, also confront and solve Robbins' well-known problem of allocating scarce resources among competing uses may be more than a tautology, but in itself it does not help the historian.

Nor does it help them much – though I find it more interesting – to congratulate economic anthropologists on their discovery of 'stone-age affluence'. This reminds us that even the most primitive economies can normally acquire a surplus above that needed for immediate consumption and the reproduction of the group, but it does not tell us why some allocate their available labour time and resources in one way rather than in another. Why, for instance, should traditional Sardinian pastoral communities have periodically organized collective festivals systematically wasting a large part of their modest surplus at the expense of their capacity to save and invest? This choice can certainly be analysed micro-economically in terms of the welfare preferences of individuals. Can we not say that it is preferable for the poor to eat as much meat as they can sometimes, rather than never to eat enough meat? Just so it may be preferable to take one infrequent lump holiday rather than a succession of free days. But this is to overlook the socio-economic function of such festivals, obvious both to anthropologists and historians, which is actually to disperse and redistribute accumulated surpluses in order to prevent the development of excessive economic inequality. They are one of the techniques for maintaining the system of mutual exchange between notionally equal units, which guarantees the permanence of the community. Nor would a rational-individual-choice analysis explain the difference between this pattern of consumption and the one now developing in the Sardinian hinterland as the affluent consumer society penetrates it.

In short, historians must start from Marx's observation that the economy is always historically specific, that production is always 'production at a certain stage of social development, production by social individuals', even if they are also aware, with Marx, that abstraction at a high level of generality – for example 'production in general' – is legitimate. But they must also, like Marx, accept that these generalities, however sophisticated, are insufficient to grasp any real historical stage of production or the nature of its transformation – including our own.

To put the matter more generally, historians need explanations as well as analysis. Economics, perhaps out of justified caution, prefers the latter to the former. What we would like to know is why situation A was followed by situation B and no other. As historians we know that there was always one and only one outcome, though it is important to consider alternative possible outcomes, especially when their absence seems surprising. Why, for instance, did industrial capitalism not develop in China rather than Europe? Even when the outcome is not surprising, it is by no means a waste of time to consider hypothetical alternatives, but for historians the *main* question is why railways were built, not how they might have been dispensed with in the nineteenth century.

Here, once again, the deliberate abstraction, generality and restriction of neo-classical economics limit the use of its kind of economic theory. Consider the problem of slavery, which has been intensively discussed in these terms. It has been argued that the purchase of slaves in nineteenth-century USA was as good an investment as any, and better than manufacturing; that the slave system was flourishing in 1860 and would not soon have been brought to an end for economic reasons; that slave agriculture was not inefficient compared to free agriculture; and that slavery was not incompatible with an industrial system. I am not entering the passionate debate about these propositions, but if the proponents of this view are right,[2] and if their arguments apply to all slave economies of the nineteenth century; and if this type of cost-benefit analysis is sufficient to analyse slave economies: then the causes of the disappearance of slavery must be sought entirely outside economic history. But, if this were so, we should still have to explain why slavery disappeared *everywhere* in the Western world in the nineteenth century. Moreover, even supposing it had been abolished everywhere only by external compulsion, as in the southern states of the USA, we should still have to explain why no functional equivalent was substituted. In fact, in many places it was, in the form of the mass importation of indentured labour, mainly Indian and Chinese, whose situation was not much different from slavery. But indentured labour was also destined to disappear everywhere. Are economic considerations irrelevant to this disappearance also? Furthermore, to return to the USA, the cliometric proof of the efficiency and progress of the slave economy does not explain that obvious anomaly in US economic history, namely that the regional *per capita* income of the southern states did not converge towards the national mean in the same way and to the same extent as the other main regions, anyway before 1950, a phenomenon which cannot be entirely dismissed as the after-effects of the victory of the North in 1865.[3] In short, the projection into the past of current economic analysis throws no light on a large area of the historian's problem. This is no reason to assume that another type of economic analysis – for instance, one less concerned with the rational choice of individual investors and entrepreneurs – would be irrelevant.

This brings me to the question of cliometrics, the school which transforms economic history into retrospective econometrics. It would be absurd to reject quantification and the application of such statistical, mathematical and other tools as are apposite to any part of history. Who cannot count, cannot write history. As August Ludwig von Schlözer, that ornament of eighteenth-century Göttingen, announced even then: statistics are static history, history is statistics in movement. One must welcome the cliometricians' remarkable contribution to measurement in history, and, certainly in the case of Robert Fogel, their impressive ingenuity and originality in the search for, and use of, sources and mathematical techniques. However, their specific characteristic is not this, but to test propositions in economic theory, overwhelmingly of the neo-classical kind.

Their contribution is valuable, but it has so far been predominantly pedagogic. Of course, as Mokyr points out, 'the very definiteness of the new methods has confined them to a narrow range of problems'.[4] Cliometrics has, indeed, suggested or even established a number of revisions of the answers to particular questions of economic history, mainly since the eighteenth century. However, one might say that its chief function has been critical. Observing that traditional economic historians imply propositions from economic theory, often in a confused and inadequately formulated manner, cliometricians have attempted to make these propositions explicit and, insofar as they can be rigorously and meaningfully formulated, to test them by statistical evidence. The first exercise is never superfluous. At any rate, a large part of the literature of economics still seems to consist of this kind of clarification. The second is admirable, to the extent that it can prove widely and uncritically accepted historical statements wrong. Admittedly they can sometimes also be proved wrong by simple counting, with negligible reference to theory. Conversely, of course, statistics may not be adequate to settle the argument definitively. Thus, while 'the New Economic History has reached something of a consensus on the actual course of [British] living standards after Waterloo', namely that it began to rise substantially, the few consumer goods of which we have reliable *per capita* consumption figures for the whole population (tea, sugar, tobacco) show no secular rise before the mid-1840s, and so 'doubt lingers' still over this debate.[5] In any case, insofar as cliometrics forces historians to think clearly and acts as a nonsense detector, it fulfils necessary and valuable functions.

Unlike some other historians I am also ready to welcome its excursions into imaginary or fictional history known as 'counter-factuals', and for the same reasons. All history is full of implicit or explicit counterfactuals. They range from speculations about alternative outcomes, such as Pascal's on Cleopatra's nose, to more specific might-have-beens: what if Lenin had remained stuck in Zurich in 1917? What if Neville Chamberlain had resisted Hitler's demands in 1938, as the German generals who planned a coup against Hitler urged him to? Many of these claim to be real alternatives, that is they assumed that the taking of action A rather than action B would have altered the course of events in a specific manner. The conditions for a sensible discussion of such 'real' counterfactuals have been discussed by Jon Elster in connection with cliometrics.[6] Curiously, traditional economic history is less given to this form of speculation than old-fashioned political history. Both it and economics are, after all, mainly concerned with phenomena which are unlikely to be affected more than momentarily by this type of variation. They are generalizing disciplines.

The function of counterfactuals in cliometrics is therefore not to establish retrospective probabilities, though I am not sure how clear all its practitioners are on this point. To take what has been described as 'the most ambitious attempt at wholesale counterfactualization ever undertaken by a serious historian',[7] Robert Fogel's *Railroads and American Economic Growth*,[8] the American railways *were* built and Fogel has not suggested that somehow they might not have been. His object was to dismantle explanations of the past which gave the railways an imprecise but large contribution to American economic growth, by writing them out of the scenario and then calculating how the economy's needs might have been met by other then available ways – for example, canals. Once again, the major value of this procedure is educational. What, it asks, is implied logically, methodologically and by way of evidence in the attempt to prove that – to return to a traditional counterfactual – the world's history would have been quite different if Cleopatra's nose had been an inch longer? (Actually, I understand it was rather long.) Or by the proposition that free trade was good (or bad) for the nineteenth-century world economy? Historians are much less practised in such questions than economists, whose subject imposes them all the time.

On the other hand, the limitations of cliometrics are severe, even if we leave aside another Nobel Laureate's very general reservation about a purely quantitative economic history, namely that 'we are bound to find, as we go back into the past, that the economic aspects of life are less differentiated from other aspects than they are today'.[9] They are fourfold. In the first place, insofar as it projects upon the past an essentially a-historical theory, its relevance to the larger problems of historical development is unclear or marginal. Economic historians, even cliometric ones, complain of 'the inability of economists to build models which explain big events like the Industrial Revolution'.[10] That is why many economic historians have been reluctant to jump on the cliometric bandwagon. Historians spend all their time dealing with economies which are not in equilibrium, whatever the tendency of market systems to bring the economy rapidly into equilibrium following a shock. It is, after all, the tendency of equilibria to be destabilized which is relevant to the study of historical change and transformation. But economic theory has not concentrated much of its attention on such economies. If we apply equilibrium analysis retrospectively we are in danger of begging the historians' big questions.

Second, the selection of one aspect of economic reality to which such theory can be applied may falsify the picture. We cannot calculate whether building Ely Cathedral or King's College Chapel was, by rational-choice theory, a sensible way of investing money, since a material return on terrestrial capital was not its object. The most we can do – and this is, of course, important – is to estimate the unintended side-effects of this use of social resources (let us beware of calling it anachronistically 'diversion of social resources'). Keynes suggested that they might be treated as a form of job-creating public works, Robert S. Lopez that the larger a city's cathedral, the smaller its trade, and the other way round. Perhaps so. Certainly the economic effects of cathedral building ought legitimately to be analysed in the light of available theory. Yet the cliometrics *directly* relevant to cathedral building would presumably have to estimate, in terms of some kind of eternal-welfare economics, whether, let us say, a donor's salvation was better achieved by contributing to the building of cathedrals or by organizing crusades or some other spiritual activity, which, naturally, also had economic costs and spin-offs. Few of us would rate the value of such an exercise highly. Yet in the fourteenth century the choice of leaving one's fortune to a monastery for the good of one's soul would, to many a merchant, have seemed as good a rational choice as leaving it to one's sons.

Such difficulties apply to much less remote problems. Studies of social investment in nineteenth-century education assume that its social and individual pay-off was essentially economic, that is that it was undertaken *as if* the decision to put resources into universal primary schooling was intended to assist the growth of the economy.

Let us leave aside, for the moment, the often arbitrary assumptions underlying such cliometric calculations (see below). Instituting universal primary education was certainly a substantial use of social resources with economic costs and alternatives forgone, and the economic effects of instituting it were obvious and great, both on individuals and on society. Naturally they can and should be cliometrically analysed. But historians are pretty well united in holding that, for most of nineteenth-century Europe, for the authorities and institutions fostering it, the actual purpose of universal primary education was not economic, unlike that of, say, technical education. It was, in the first place, ideological and political: to instil religion, morality and obedience among the poor, to teach them to accept the existing society contentedly and to bring their children up to do likewise, to turn Auvergnat peasants into good republican Frenchmen and Calabrian peasants into Italians. Whether they did so efficiently, or what better alternative methods were available to achieve these objects, could perhaps, in theory, be investigated by cliometric techniques. But the social costs of primary education in this sense are not to be calculated as though they had been investments in higher productivity for the economy. They were more like the social costs of, say, keeping armies in being. Moreover, insofar as such estimates combine expenditures (real or imputed) on primary education with those on parts of education seen, even then, in terms of economic productivity – for example, technical education – they mix up quite different uses of social resources. In short, cliometric exercises in these fields constantly run the risk of historical unreality.

The third weakness of cliometrics is that it necessarily has to rely not only on real data, often themselves patchy and unreliable, but also and largely on invented or assumed data. On many relevant matters information is lacking even in our well-counted age, as economists know when they have to guess at the size of the informal or 'black' economy today. There are limits even to the very great ingenuity of historians in discovering quantitative data, or in using one set of available data for purposes not intended by its compilers. Most of history remains, in quantitative terms, a zone of darkness and guesswork.

Most of cliometrics therefore takes place in an obscure region which can, as it were, be mapped from the air only by making more or less educated guesses from the shape and configuration of the visible parts of the landscape about the vast stretches of territory which are permanently hidden by cold and fog. Since cliometrics, unlike some traditional history, cannot rely on general impressions but requires (within limits) precise measurement, it must create its data, where they are not available. Some of these may not have existed at all in reality, as in counterfactuals. Even where it is not hypothetical, the information cliometricians need is teased out of such facts as are available and can be made relevant to the purpose in hand, by using relations derived from a theoretical model – that is by a more or less complicated chain of reasoning and assumptions both about the model and about the insufficient data.

From the historians' point of view these assumptions must be realistic or they are junk. If we use the assumption of perfect foresight by businessmen to construct data, the question of its empirical validity is crucial. Altering the assumptions, whether about the model or about the data, can make a substantial difference to both the data and the answers. Suppose, for instance, that we reject, as many economic historians do, the concept of a British 'industrial revolution', on the ground that the aggregate growth of the British economy between 1760 and 1820 was modest, which is another way of saying that the industries dramatically transformed during this period were blanketed by the bulk of the country's more slowly changing, traditionally organized economic activities. As has been pointed out, under these circumstances abrupt changes in the economy *as a whole* are a mathematical impossibility.[11] (An interesting question arises: how far could we demonstrate *any* significant growth during the period if we included in the GNP not only the goods and services entering into market transactions but the vast mass of unpaid and uncounted production of goods and services such as those of women and children within the family?) In short 'measuring aggregate growth rates in the tradition of Kuznets is therefore perhaps not the best strategy in trying to understand the Industrial Revolution, though it has its uses'.[12] Again, by making different assumptions about the indirect economic effects of railway-building (and imputing quantities accordingly) it has been possible to argue that the railways contributed very little or quite a lot to the GNP of a country.

There is a further drawback to these procedures, which constitutes the last of the weaknesses of cliometrics. It risks circularity by arguing from the model to the data, to the extent that these are not independently available. And, of course, it cannot get outside its theory, which is a-historical, and outside its specific model, which is tiresome if that model is beside the point. We cannot prove, as some historians have tried to do, that nothing much was wrong with the

British economy in the late nineteenth century because the business behaviour of British entrepreneurs can be shown to have been highly rational, given the circumstances. The most we can prove by these means is that one explanation of Britain's relative economic decline may be invalid, namely that its entrepreneurs were incompetent money-makers. In short, cliometrics can criticize and modify the history produced by other means, but it does not produce answers of its own. Its function at the cattle-market of history is more like that of the inspector of weights and measures than that of the farmer who breeds the bullocks.

What use, then, can historians make of economic theory? Naturally they can use it as a useful generator of ideas, much as fashion designers are inspired by travelling to Morocco and looking at Berber costumes. This sort of heuristic effect, difficult to define, is not negligible, since we know from the natural sciences that wild analogies and borrowings from outside may be enormously fertile. Why, for instance, should we not analyse the distribution of population in primitive societies according to the kinetic theory of gases? It might (and I understand it actually does) lead to interesting results. We can, of course, also use economic theory eclectically, as and when it seems apposite. But this does not solve the problem.

If theory is to be of more than marginal use to historians (and also, I suggest, in social practice) it has to be specified in ways that bring it closer to social reality. It cannot allow itself, even in its models, to abstract from the actual lumpiness of life, such as the practical difficulties of substitution. The example of agriculture springs to mind. We know, though it has constantly surprised advocates of economic growth, that one form of agrarian structure and productive organization cannot simply be substituted for another within the time-scale required by policy, even when it can be shown to be economically more productive. The world of economic development is divided into countries which have succeeded in backing their industrialization and urbanization with an efficient and highly productive agriculture and those which have not. The economic effects of success or failure are immense: on the whole, the countries with the highest percentage of agricultural population are the ones which have difficulties in feeding themselves, or at any rate their rapidly growing non-farm populations, while the world's food surpluses come, on the whole, from a relatively tiny population in a few advanced countries. But the sort of discussion which is to be found in standard textbooks – Samuelson's comes to mind – throws no light on this problem, because, as Paul Bairoch has pointed out among many others, 'agricultural productivity depends much more on structural factors than industrial productivity', which is why 'failure to understand ... historical differences is all the more serious'.[13] The real problem here has always been, and still remains, not so much how to devise a general recipe for 'agricultural revolution', green or otherwise. Success has usually come, as Milward pointed out, by reform adapted to the specific conditions of regional farming.[14]

In other words, it is quite pointless to argue that nineteenth-century German agriculture would have done better if all of it had followed the pattern of Mecklenburg with less than 36 per cent of land in peasant holdings, or that of Bavaria, with more than 93 per cent in such holdings, even if we could demonstrate conclusively that one pattern was absolutely more efficient than the other. Analysis must start with the coexistence of both, and the difficulties of transforming either into the other. Nor can we turn *a posteriori* analysis into causal explanation.

The truth is that, even in the quite lengthy run, economic choice may be severely limited by institutional and historical constraints. Suppose we accept that the abolition of a traditional peasantry, basically composed of family subsistence units producing a certain surplus, is the best way of achieving an agricultural revolution and further, for the sake of argument, that it can best be replaced by large commercial estates or farms operating with hired labour. There are cases where this has been achieved.[15] However, I can think of at least one Latin American region where rational commercial entrepreneurs tried and failed to carry out this programme effectively, because they simply lacked the power to get rid of a dense peasant population. They were obliged by social realities to adopt semi-feudal methods which they knew to be less than optimal. And since, in spite of Marx, cases of the rapid mass expulsion or expropriation of fairly dense peasant populations are rare before the cruel twentieth century, the historical force of such constraints is not to be underestimated. In analysing both agricultural change and economic growth in general, non-economic factors cannot be divorced from economic ones – certainly not in the short run. To separate them is to abandon the historical, that is the dynamic, analysis of the economy.

As Maurice Dobb argued many years ago:

It seems abundantly clear that the leading questions concerning economic development ... cannot be answered at all unless one goes outside the bounds of that limited traditional type of economic analysis in which realism is so ruthlessly sacrificed to generality, and unless the existing frontier between what it is fashionable to label as 'economic factors' and as 'social factors' is abolished.[16]

I do not wish to imply that bringing in the so-called 'non-economic factors' is incompatible with a rigorous theoretical analysis or, where the questions and data make this suitable, with econometric testing. It does not have to fall into the empiricist bog which swallowed the German historicist economists, though they are entitled to a courteous obituary. But if we do need theoretical models, and these models must be abstract and simplified, at least they should be so within historically specified frameworks.

So far historians have, in general, found help in only two theoretical quarters. The first is that of theorists who are interested in the historic process of economic transformations and regard it as at least in part endogenous. Whether we regard the forces making for change as economic or sociological or political – and the distinction may be arbitrary – they are best seen, with thinkers like Marx and Schumpeter, as products of the development of the system, and therefore as having a bearing on its future development. Other approaches to the 'theory of economic history' pose similar questions, as J. R. Hicks recognizes ('my "theory of history" ... will be a good deal nearer to the kind of thing attempted by Marx').[17] The other source from which historians have at least partly slaked their thirst is among economists who find themselves needing models adjusted to concrete realities for their own purposes. The role of third-world experience is crucial here, for it links theory and concrete realities in a context familiar to both historians and at least some economists.

It seems to me significant that, of the two main variants of growth theory, historians have not been able to do much with those developed from the Harrod–Domar model, which appeals to most economists. They have found themselves on much more familiar and congenial territory with the models which go back beyond neo-classicism to a political economy and Marx, concerned to formulate theories applicable to particular cases, and which take a disaggregated economy as their point of departure, for instance Arthur Lewis' dualist model, sketched out in the 1950s, or Hla Myint's attempt to understand third-world trade. Like historians of pre-industrial European commerce he concludes that the 'comparative cost' model of trade is much less relevant to two-sector transactions than Adam Smith's old 'vent for surplus' model or a so-called 'productivity theory' of trade.[18] This type of approach was devised in order to provide a realistic base for development policies in countries where models based on a theoretically universal market or capitalist economy are too stratospheric for realism. Samuelson rightly traces it back to Marx and Ricardo, though he devotes only one footnote to it. Development economists of this kind and historians speak the same language.

The point about such models, however rough, is that they attempt to simplify an observable social reality which does not fit a purely capitalist or market pattern. Moreover, and for this reason they are of interest to historians, such models are models of *combined* economies. They are about the interaction of two or more games each with its own rules, though no doubt the ensemble could also be treated as a single super-game with all-encompassing rules. Some envisage mainly interactions between games played side by side. Other models, such as Witold Kula's Marxist *Théorie économique du système féodal*,[19] assume that the units of enterprise operate simultaneously in both sectors, playing by both sets of rules, as they are able or obliged to. Kula uses this to analyse the dynamics of the large Polish feudal estates, but since the bulk of the marketable surplus in most pre-capitalist societies probably came from peasants, it applies to them also. Indeed, among peasant specialists there is a vigorous debate on the relation between the non-market and the commodity-producing aspects of the peasant economy.

Historians are familiar with such situations, since any transition from one socio-economic formation to another – say from feudal to capitalist society – must at some stage consist of such a mixture. [The failure to recognize this by the economic gurus of the 'big bang' transformation of communism into capitalism in the former USSR has since plunged a large area of the world's land surface into unnecessary social catastrophe.] We have the option of constructing a single model by abstracting from the peculiarities of the component parts, but at the cost both of sacrificing realism and of sidestepping the general problem of modern economic history, which is how to explain the mutation of the old economy into the permanent high-growth economy of the nineteenth and twentieth centuries. That is what the cliometricians have done. On the other hand we can multiply socially and institutionally specific economic models, such as those the economic anthropologists have derived from Karl Polanyi or from Chayanov's 'peasant economy'. But, without discussing the validity or necessity of this procedure, I think what interests both historians and probably the champions of economic development is the omnipresent *combination*. What has a bearing on the development of capitalism is not that the Hudson's Bay Company for a century bought its furs from the Indians at unchanging prices, because the Indians had a concept of trade but not of the market; nor the fact that the furs were sold on a presumably neo-classical market in London, *but the effects of the combination*.[20] Nor does it matter for our purpose whether we classify such combinations as a mixture of two economic systems or as a complex version of one system.

For historians the interest of such analyses lies in the light they throw on the mechanism of economic transformation in the specific circumstances in which, historically, it took place or failed to take place. This naturally includes the long era before the industrial revolution, which is of course of only peripheral interest to most economists, including development economists. Nevertheless, even for historians the period when this sort of combined development is particularly relevant is during the centuries – and historians continue to argue about the date which marks this turning-point – when all the previously existing economies of the globe came to be, in one way or another, conquered, penetrated, brought into, modified, adapted and eventually assimilated by the originally regional capitalist economy [a fact demonstrated dramatically, since this was first written, by the fall of the socialist economies, which, for several decades after the Russian Revolution, claimed to provide a global economic alternative to capitalism]. This apparent homogenization has tempted social scientists and ideologists to simplify history into a one-step model of 'modernization' and economic development into 'growth'. Few historians succumb to this temptation. We know that the development of the world economy, not to mention any particular part of it, is not just an assembly of the preconditions for 'growth' and then the fluctuating dash forward, the Rostovian Marathon race in which all follow the same track towards the same finishing-post, though starting at different times and running at different speeds. Nor does it depend merely on 'getting economic policy right', that is on the correct application of a timeless 'correct' economic theory, a matter on which, as it so happens, there is no agreement among economists.

Such a reduction of even strictly economic history to a single dimension conceals the non-linearities of – or, if you prefer, the qualitative differences and changing combinations within – the process of capitalist development. The chronology of development cannot be reduced to a curve of variably rising rates of growth. In it observers, however impressionistically, recognize new phases of the system, with characteristics and a *modus operandi* in some ways different from their predecessors, and also the moments which, generally in retrospect, are recognized as secular turning-points within its development – the years after 1848, after 1873 [and, as is now obvious, the early 1970s]. And these, in turn, are relevant – even to economists, politicians and businessmen – because even they want to avoid the traditional weakness of the military, namely that of preparing for the last rather than the next war.

If we want to discover in what direction it is moving, we require a genuine historical analysis of capitalist development rather than a Rostovian listing of 'stages'. Those who want to know in which direction we are going cannot do without the Marxes or Schumpeters who, in their different ways, see that there is a historical direction in capitalist development. And who, even among businessmen, does not need to think about the future of the system?

In undertaking such exercises historians seek models of the historical dynamics of capitalism among the economists, and encounter only the generalities of rational-choice theory, except on the fringes, or perhaps better the frontier, of their discipline. I don't think historians mind that the required theories are not, at present, reducible to mathematical models or exactly quantifiable. Our needs are modest, our expectations less than our hopes, and the time to think of equations is when we have even an approximate idea of all the relevant variables and their possible relations. For the moment it will be enough if such theories are designed to cover the ground we want them to, are not nonsensical and internally inconsistent, are roughly testable against evidence, and are such as to allow us to extend the scope of the theory when this should prove necessary. We would be happy to get help from economists who apply their talents and discipline to questions of socio-economic transformation. We do get some help, but not enough. Perhaps the fact that economics is today more keenly aware of the possible contribution of history than was the case when these lectures were first given is a sign that economists may start applying their minds to historical development again. When they do so, historians must hope that they will do so in the spirit of Marx, Schumpeter and John Hicks rather than in the deliberately restrictive straitjacket of cliometrics.

CHAPTER 9

Partisanship

This paper, which considers the problem of political and ideological bias, was written for and published in Culture, science et développement: Mélanges en l'honneur de Charles Morazé *(Toulouse, 1979), pp. 267–79.*

I

Though there has been a great deal of discussion about the nature, or even the possibility, of objectivity in the social sciences, there has been much less interest in the problem of 'partisanship' in these sciences, including history. 'Partisanship' is one of those words like 'violence' or 'nation' which conceal a variety of meanings beneath an apparently simple and homogeneous surface. It is more often used as a term of disapproval or (much more rarely) praise than defined, and when it is formally defined,[1] definitions tend to be either selective or normative. In fact, the common usages of the term conceal a wide range of meanings, stretching from the unacceptably narrow to the platitudinously broad.

At its broadest it may merely be another way of denying the possibility of a purely objective and value-free science, a proposition from which few historians, social scientists and philosophers would today totally dissent. At the opposite extreme it is the willingness to subordinate the processes and findings of research to the requirements of the researcher's ideological or political commitment and whatever this implies, including their subordination to the ideological or political authorities accepted by him or her: however much these may conflict with what these processes and findings would be without such dictation. More commonly, of course, the researcher internalizes these requirements, which thus become characteristics of science, or rather (since partisanship implies an adversary) of the 'right' science against the 'wrong' science – of women's history as against male chauvinist history, proletarian science as against bourgeois science, and so on.

In fact, there are probably two overlapping spectra of which one expresses the various nuances of the objective political or ideological dimension of the processes and findings of research, and the other, the consequences which may be claimed to derive from this for the historian's subjective behaviour. To put it simply, one is about the partisanship of the facts, the other about that of people.

At one extreme of the first spectrum there is the general, and by now virtually uncontroversial, proposition that there can be no such thing as a purely objective and value-free science; at the other there is the proposition that everything about science, from its procedures to its concrete findings and the theories into which these are grouped, is primarily to be seen as having some specific political (or, more generally, ideological) function or purpose, associated with some specific social or political group or organization. Thus the main significance of the heliocentric astronomy of the sixteenth to the seventeenth century would not be that they were 'more true' than the geocentric ones, but that they provided a legitimation for absolute monarchy ('le roi soleil'). Though this might sound a *reductio ad absurdum* of this position, let us not forget that most of us have on occasion taken a hardly less extreme view when discussing, say, the various aspects of genetics and ethology favoured by National Socialism. The possible truths of various hypotheses in these fields seemed at the time to be much less important than their use for the horrible political purposes of the regime of Adolf Hitler. Even today there are many who refuse to accept research into possible racial differences within the human race or who reject any findings tending to demonstrate inequalities between various human groups, on analogous grounds.

The nuances of the second spectrum range equally widely. At one extreme there is the barely controversial proposition that the scientist, a child of his or her time, reflects the ideological and other preconceptions of his/her milieu and historically or socially specific experiences and interests. At the other there is the view that we must not merely be willing to subordinate our science to the requirements of some organization or authority, but should actively favour this subordination. Except insofar as we make purely psychological statements about scientists, spectrum 2 derives from spectrum 1. Men are or ought to be partisan in their attitude to the sciences, because the sciences are themselves partisan. It is also possible, though no certain, that each position on spectrum 2 corresponds to a position on spectrum 1, and may be regarded as corollary of it. Hence it will be convenient in the following discussion to concentrate on 'partisanship' as a subjective attitude of, or imperative for, historians.

Nevertheless, one important proposition about 'objective' partisanship must first be made. It is that partisanship in science (using the word in the general sense of the German *Wissenschaft*) rests on disagreement not about verified facts, but about their selection and combination, and about what may be inferred from them.[2] It takes for granted non-controversial procedures for verifying or falsifying evidence, and non-controversial procedures of argument about it. Thomas Hobbes' observation that men would suppress or even challenge the theorems of geometry if they conflicted with the political interests of the ruling class may be true, but this kind of partisanship has no place in the sciences.[3] If anyone wishes to argue that the earth is flat or the biblical account of creation literally true, they would be well advised not to become astronomers, geographers or paleontologists. Conversely, those who resist the inclusion of the biblical account of creation into the school textbooks of California as a 'possible hypothesis'[4] do so, not because they may have partisan views (which may be the case), but because they rely on a universal consensus among scientists that it is not only factually wrong, but that no argument in its favour can claim scientific status. It is not, so far as can be seen, 'a possible scientific hypothesis'. To challenge the refutation of the flat-earth thesis, or of the belief that God created the world in seven days, is to challenge what we know as reason and science. There are people who are willing to do so explicitly or by implication. If they should, by some unlikely chance, prove to be right, we as historians, social or other scientists, would be out of a job.

This does not significantly reduce the scope of legitimate scientific disagreement into which partisanship can and does enter. There can be considerable argument about what the facts are, and where they can never be definitively established (as in much of history) argument may continue indefinitely. There may be argument about what they mean. Hypotheses and theories, however universal the consensus which greets them, do not have the non-controversial status of, say, verifiable or falsifiable facts or mathematico-logical propositions. They can be shown to be consistent with the facts, but not necessarily as *uniquely* consistent with the facts. There can be no scientific argument about the fact of evolution, but there can be, even today, about the Darwinian explanation of it, or about any specific version of it. And insofar as the 'fact' itself is trivial, when taken out of the context of the questions we ask about it and the theories we form to link it with other facts, it also remains caught up in the web of possible partisanship. The same is true even of mathematical propositions, which become significant or 'interesting' only by virtue of the links we establish between them and other parts of our intellectual universe.

Nevertheless, and at the risk of being accused of positivism, the non-controversial nature of certain statements and of the means of establishing it must be asserted. Some propositions are 'true' or 'false' beyond reasonable doubt, though the boundaries between reasonable and unreasonable doubt will be drawn differently, within a marginal zone, according to partisan criteria. Thus most traditional scientists would probably require far stronger and more rigorously sifted evidence to establish the existence of various extra-sensory phenomena than they would to accept, for example, the survival of some animal believed to be long extinct; and this because many of them are *a priori* reluctant to accept the existence of such phenomena. Conversely, as the Piltdown forgeries and other examples show, an *a priori* readiness to accept verification of a plausible hypothesis can seriously relax the scientist's own criteria of validation. But this does not seriously undermine the view that the criteria of validation are objective.

Let me translate this into terms relevant to the historian. There can be no legitimate doubt that in the course of the past 200 years the material conditions of the population in the 'advanced' countries of the world have, on average, substantially improved. The fact cannot be seriously disputed, though there may be argument about when this improvement began, and about the rates, fluctuations and divergences of this process. Though in itself neutral, this fact will be widely regarded as having certain ideological and political implications, and insofar as there are historical theories resting on the assumption that it has not taken place, such theories are wrong. If Marx believed in a tendency for capitalism to pauperize the proletariat, it is open to me as a Marxist to do one or more of three things. I can legitimately deny that Marx, at least in his mature years, held a theory of absolute material pauperization or stagnation, in which case I eliminate this element from the theory of 'absolute pauperization' in a way which might enable me to include other elements, hitherto unconsidered, which might offset the improvement (for example, 'insecurity', or mental health, or environmental deterioration). In this case there might be partisan argument of two kinds: about the legitimacy of extending the concept of 'pauperization' in this way, and about the actual measurable movement of the various indices involved, their weighting and combination. Lastly, I may maintain the old argument, but seek to establish that the improvement represents merely a temporary or long-term fluctuation in what can still be held to be a secular downward trend. In this case I am *either* removing the proposition from the range of falsifiability altogether, like those constantly revised predictions of the end of the world which millennial sects engage in, *or* I am laying it open to falsification at some time in the future. Similar considerations apply, if I regard the improvement as a regional phenomenon, which might (or might not) be offset by deterioration in the rest of the world. What I *cannot* do is simply deny the evidence. Nor can I, as a historian, legitimately refuse to accept the criteria of falsifiability, insofar as my views rest on evidence either past, present or future.

In short, for everyone engaged in scientific discourse, statements must be subject to validation by methods and criteria which are, in principle, not subject to partisanship, whatever their ideological consequences, and however motivated. Statements not subject to such validation may nevertheless be important and valuable, but belong to a different order of discourse. They pose extremely interesting and difficult philosophical problems, especially when they are clearly in some sense descriptive (for example, in representative art or criticism 'about' some specific creative work or artist), but cannot be considered here. Nor can we here consider statements of the logico-mathematical type, insofar as they are not (as in theoretical physics) linked to validation by evidence.

II

Let me now turn to the problem of subjective partisanship – omitting, for the sake of simplicity, the question of personal feelings, though these are important in the individual psychology of the scholar. We shall therefore not be concerned with the reluctance of Professor X to give up the theory by which he or she has made, or hopes to make, his or her reputation or to which long polemics have committed him or her. We shall omit the personal feelings about Professor Y whom he or she has always considered a careerist and a charlatan. We shall be concerned with Professor X only as a person motivated by ideological or political views and assumptions shared by others, and carried into research; and more specifically with Professor X as a committed partisan who accepts that commitment may have direct implications for his or her work.

However, we must begin by eliminating the extreme position of partisanship, as put forward and practised in the Stalinist period in the USSR and elsewhere – not necessarily only by Marxists – and reduced *ad absurdum* in the ever changing pages of the *Great Soviet Encyclopedia* of those days. This position assumed (1) a total congruence of political and scientific statements at all times, and therefore (2) a virtual interchangeability of statements in both forms of discourse at all levels,[5] on the ground (3) that no specialized field of scientific discourse or specialized public for such discourses existed. In practice this meant (4) the superiority of political authority (being by definition the repository of science) over scientific statement. It may be pointed out in passing that this position differs from the one, held fairly generally, that there may be imperatives – say moral or political – which are superior to those of scientific statement, and from the one held, for example, in the Catholic Church, that there are truths superior to those of secular science, which may be imposed by authority.

In theory, of course, the unity of science and politics may be maintained as a general proposition, at least by those who believe that politics should be based on a scientific analysis (for example, 'scientific socialism'). That science is inseparable from the rest of society, including the non-scientific public, is also accepted by most people as a general proposition. Yet in practice it is evident that a certain division of labour and functions exists and that the relations between science and politics cannot be those of congruence. The imperatives of politics, however much it may be based on scientific analysis, are not identical with scientific statements, though they may be ideally derivable from them at a greater or lesser remove. The relative autonomy of politics (which includes considerations of expediency, of action, will and decision) precludes not only identity, but even simple analogy between the two spheres. Hence any form of partisanship which holds that whatever is politically required at any moment, must have its equivalent on scientific discourse, can have no theoretical justification. In practice it may also be observed that the existence of authorities, each of which claims the validity of science for its political analysis and consequently imposes certain imperatives on those of its members who engage in scientific discourses, raises the problem of how to decide between such rival scientific claims.[6] To this problem partisanship itself can contribute little except a sense of subjective conviction.

The dilemma of what may be called for the sake of convenience the Zhdanovite version of partisanship, may be illustrated by a non-Marxist example: cartography. Maps are held by cartographers to be factual descriptions (according to various conventions) of aspects of the earth's surface, but by governments and certain political movements to be statements of policy, or at least to have implications for policy. Indeed, this is an undoubted aspect of political maps, and in principle it cannot be denied that, where there is political dispute, the mere fact of drawing, say, a frontier in one place rather than another implies a political decision. Thus, to record the Falkland Islands as a British possession either implies denying the Argentine claim to them, or at least implies that at that moment this claim is regarded as academic. While it existed, to record the country to the east of the German Federal Republic as the German Democratic Republic implied at least a *de facto* recognition of the existence of the GDR as a state within the 1945 frontiers. Yet, however sympathetic the cartographer may be to the claims of Argentina or the Cold War attitudes of the Western states, he or she cannot be expected to conceal the actual situation. It is as absurd to turn countries into uncountries on maps as to turn people into unpersons in history books. Nor did the configuration and character of the GDR change at the moment when the political decision was taken to describe it as such, instead of as a 'Soviet-occupied zone' or a 'Mitteldeutschland', or by some other term which expressed not reality but policy. Insofar as cartographers are not acting under compulsion, they must realize that in describing the Falklands as Argentinian or the GDR as 'Central Germany' they are acting not as geographers but as politicians. They may justify their decision on various grounds, including the philosophical or even the purportedly scientific, but not on geographical ones. Failure to make this distinction would lead not merely to a breakdown in intellectual communication (which is familiar enough) but to the substitution of cartography as a form of programmatic statement to cartography as description, that is to the abolition of cartography.

Fortunately, since we are dealing with a field in which theoretical fantasy has severe practical consequences, programmatic cartography is not allowed to interfere with real maps except marginally and in special fields such as education and propaganda. After all, it would be unwise to suggest to airline pilots that in landing at Kaliningrad they would find themselves in a German state, or before 1989 that in landing in Schoenefeld rather than Tegel their administrative problems would not be rather different.

What may be called Stalinist partisanship[7] though it is not by any means confined to Stalinists or even Marxists – can therefore be excluded from scientific discourse. If scholars and scientists believe that their political commitment requires them to subordinate their science to their commitment, as is perfectly legitimate under certain circumstances, they should admit it, at least to themselves. It is much less dangerous to science, and to a scientifically based political analysis, to know that one is practising *suppressio veri* or even *suggestio falsi* than to convince oneself that lies are, in some complex sense, true. Similarly, if they believe that their political commitment requires them to drop their activity as scholars altogether, which may also be legitimate or even necessary under certain conditions, they should also recognize what they are doing. The historian who becomes editor of a party organ writes his editorials not as a historian but as a political editorialist, though his historical background and interests may show through. This need not prevent him from continuing to practise history at other times. Jaurès produced rather good (partisan) history while leader of the French Socialist Party; but not *while* evolving formulas for conciliation at Party congress.

However, there remains a grey zone between scholarship and political statement, which perhaps affects historians more than others, because they have been used from time immemorial to legitimate the claims (for example dynastic or territorial) of politicians. This is the zone of political advocacy. It would be quite unrealistic to expect scholars to refrain from acting as advocates, especially if (as is often the case) they believe not only that a case ought to be made on the grounds of patriotism or some other political commitment, but that it is actually valid. There will inevitably be Bulgarian, Yugoslav and Greek professors who, even without the urging of governments, parties or churches, are prepared to fight to the last footnote for their interpretation of the Macedonian question. There are, of course, plenty of cases when historians, though personally quite indifferent, may also accept the partisan duty of making some case such as to back their government's claim to a disputed frontier or to write an article on the traditional friendship between the Syldavian and Ruritanian peoples at a time when Syldavia is engaged in improving its diplomatic relations with Ruritania. However, though academics will undoubtedly continue to act as advocates, with more or less conviction, and although the element of advocacy is inseparable from any debate, the difference between it and scientific discussion (however partisan) must be clearly borne in mind.

To put it in its simplest terms, the function of the trial lawyer is not to decide on the guilt or innocence of the client, but to secure his conviction or acquittal; the function of the advertising agency is not to decide on whether the client's product is worth buying, but to sell it. In short, unlike science (however committed) advocacy takes the case to be made as given. The degree of sophistication involved in advocating it is irrelevant to this basic decision. Even where we approve completely of both the case and the manner of advocacy, the distinction remains: Huxley was not Darwin, but 'Darwin's bulldog'. However reluctant to do so in practice, in theory every participant in scientific debate must entertain the possibility of allowing himself to be publicly persuaded by contrary argument or evidence. Of course the very fact that he is known to do so makes him particularly valuable as an advocate, and makes the slide from scientific to partisan advocacy tempting. In liberal, and especially parliamentary, societies, given both to the idealization of the 'independent scientist' and the belief that the truth is likely to emerge from the clash of gladiatorial advocates, this temptation tends to produce more illegitimate partisanship than anything else does. The history of recent debates on poverty and education in the Anglo-Saxon countries bears witness to this.

III

Having established the limits beyond which partisanship ceases to be scientifically legitimate, let me argue the case in favour of legitimate partisanship, both from the point of view of the scientific or scholarly discipline and from that of the cause to which the scholar feels committed.

The latter is somewhat more difficult than the former, since it assumes that the cause will benefit by the scholar's work as a scholar, even if a committed one. But this is plainly not always the case. There are causes such as a belief in Christianity, which not only do not require scientific or scholarly backing, but may actually be weakened by attempts to reformulate faith and dogma in terms which are, by definition, the opposite of both. (Of course most such attempts have been defensive actions against attacks from encroaching secular forces.) This is not to deny the value of Christian commitment as a

stimulus for certain kinds of scholarship, say philological or archae-
ological. But it may be doubted whether this scholarship has ever
strengthened Christianity as a social force. One might at most claim
that it provides esoteric services, perhaps by establishing the correct
translation of sacred texts for those to whom this is of more than
scientific importance, or that it provides the cause with propagandist
arguments or the prestige which scholarship and learning in most
societies still bring to the group with which they are associated. Still,
judgment on such matters is to some extent subjective. No doubt it
is of enormous significance to the Mormons to collect a mass of
genealogical information about ancestors who are, one understands,
by this process in some way brought posthumously closer to the true
faith. For non-Mormons the exercise is interesting and valuable only
because it has incidentally produced one of the most comprehensive
collections of sources for historic demography.

But there are enough political and ideological causes which plainly
benefit from science and scholarship, even if often tempted to develop
pseudo-science and pseudo-scholarship for this purpose. Can it be
denied that nationalist movements have been strengthened by the
devoted scholarly explorations of their people's past, even if the
movements themselves (as distinct from the scholars associated with
them) may find fantasy and forgery just as useful – perhaps more
useful – than sceptical, if committed, enquiry?[8] Moreover, there are
causes – Marxism is prominent among them – which see themselves
specifically as the products of rationalist and scientific analysis, and
consequently must regard the work of scientific enquiry associated
with them as an essential part of their progress, or at any rate not
incompatible with it, except for the frictions between scholarly
research and political expediency, already mentioned above. Any
state requires science for certain purposes. Governments need real
economics (as distinct from apologetics or propaganda) insofar as
they need to manage their economies. Their complaint is not that
economists are insufficiently committed to them, but that, in the
present state of the science, they do not solve the problems they
desperately want them to. There is thus plenty of scope for the
committed scholar to further his cause, without ceasing to be a
scholar.

But how far does he require to have a specific form of commitment
to do so? Is it not, by and large, as irrelevant to a regime whether its
economists are privately conservatives or revolutionaries, so long as
they solve its problems? Would the USSR not have benefited more

from anti-Stalinist biologists who knew their job than from Lysenkoites who did not? (To quote a Chinese communist leader: 'What does it matter if the cats are white or black, so long as they catch mice?') Or, to turn the question round, must not a committed Marxist, to the extent that he is a good expert, expect his findings to be beneficial even to those whom he or she wishes to combat?

The answer to the last question is obviously: to some extent, yes. Nevertheless, the personal partisanship of the scholar is highly relevant, if only because his cause may not be able to draw upon scholars other than the ones committed to it, and because it may be unable to make use of that large part of science – particularly social science – which reflects other kinds of partisanship. The German Social Democratic Party before 1914 could hardly expect help, sympathy or even neutrality from the overwhelming majority of the academics of imperial Germany. It had to rely on 'its own' intellectuals. What is more to the point, partisan intellectuals may be the only ones ready to investigate problems, or subjects which (for ideological or other reasons) the rest of the intellectual community fails to consider. The history of the British labour movement until late in the twentieth century was overwhelmingly in the hands of people who sympathized with it – from Sidney and Beatrice Webb onwards – because hardly any 'orthodox' historians took any serious interest in it until well after the Second World War.

This willingness of partisan scholars and scientists to break new ground leads us to the second part of our argument: the positive value of partisanship for the scientific or scholarly discipline of the partisan scholar. This is undeniable even in some of the natural sciences, though probably marked mainly in those which (like biology) have always had fairly strong ideological associations. We cannot confine this value to any particular kind of partisanship. Modern genetics, for instance, with its constant battle between the advocates of inherited and environmental factors, was undoubtedly in great part a product of an elitist, anti-democratic ideology – from Francis Galton and Karl Pearson onwards.[9] This does not, incidentally, make genetics into an essentially reactionary science, or indeed imply a permanent ideological commitment of this science, some of whose eminent later practitioners were (like J. B. S. Haldane) communists. Indeed in the present phase of the heredity–environment battle, which can be traced back to the First World War, the geneticists have tended to be on the 'left', whereas the main supporters of the 'right' come from among the psychologists.[10] At all events, we have here a field of the unquestioned natural sciences, whose advance has been achieved largely through the political partisanship of its practitioners.

Whatever the case in the natural sciences – which I am not competent to discuss – the argument is unanswerable in the social sciences. It is hard to think of any of the great formative economists who was not deeply committed politically, for the same reason that it is hard to think of any great medical scientist who was not deeply committed to curing human sickness. The social sciences are essentially 'applied sciences' designed, to use Marx's phrase, to change the world and not merely to interpret it (or alternatively to explain why it does not need changing). What is more, even today, at least in the Anglo-Saxon world, the typical economic theorist considers himself less as a producer of 'science' for the use of his or her 'side' (as the anti-fascist scientists did during the last war when they persuaded their governments that nuclear weapons were practicable), but rather as a crusader in his own right – a Keynes or a Friedman – or at least an active and vocal participant in public policy debates. Keynes did not derive his policy from the *General Theory*: he wrote the *General Theory* to provide a sounder basis for, as well as a more powerful means of propagating, his policies. The direct link with policy is less clear among the great sociologists, since in the nature of the subject their general prescriptions are harder to formulate in terms of specific government policies – except perhaps for propagandist (including educational) purposes. Yet the deep political commitment of the founding fathers of sociology hardly needs demonstration, and indeed there have been times when the entire discipline as an academic subject has almost been overwhelmed by the various partisanships of its practitioners. It does not take much effort to make a similar case for other social sciences, including – if we choose to include it – history.

The fact that the development of such sciences has been inseparable from partisanship – that some of them would virtually not have come into existence without it – is not seriously to be denied. The contrary belief, that the scholar is a simple seeker after pure academic truth, which may or may not interest anyone else, probably gained ground partly as a reflection of the sheer numerical growth, and therefore the separation in special institutes, of science and scholarship as a profession, partly as a response to the peculiar and novel social situation of (academic) intellectuals, partly as mystification. At a time when there were no professional economists, it would have made no sense to argue that Quesnay (a doctor), Galiani (a public official),

Adam Smith (a university teacher), Ricardo (a financier) or Malthus (a clergyman) were not essentially political in their intentions. The very fact that the multiplication of professional salaried intellectuals as a social stratum has widened the gap between most of them and the effective economic and political decision-makers would have been enough to strengthen their tendency to see themselves as a class of independent 'experts'.

Moreover, the power of the *status quo* was greatly reinforced if the prevalent teachings of the social sciences were presented, not as politically based and oriented views, but as eternal truths discovered with no purpose other than the pursuit of truth by a class of men, working in certain institutions which guaranteed both impartiality and authority. Imperial German professors, a notoriously partisan group, did not intervene in politics so much as reinforce their side by *ex cathedra* declarations of what was 'unchallengeable'. The intellectual as the member of an occupational category, as the member of a social stratum and as a secular theologian had a substantial incentive to claim that he – more rarely she – stood above the battle. However, for the purpose of the present argument it is neither necessary nor possible to go further into this question.

That sciences in the past, and especially the social sciences, have been inseparable from partisanship does not prove that partisanship is advantageous to them, but only that it is inevitable. The case for the benefits of partisanship must be that it advances science. It can do so, and has done so, insofar as it provides an incentive to change the terms of scientific debate, a mechanism for injecting new topics, new questions and new models of answer ('paradigms', to use Kuhn's convenient term) from outside. There is not much doubt that such fertilization of scientific debate by stimulation and challenge from outside the specific field of research, has been enormously beneficial to scientific advance. Nowadays this is widely recognized, though the outside stimulus is normally conceived as coming from other sciences, and partly for this reason all manner of 'interdisciplinary' contacts and enterprises are encouraged.[11] Nevertheless, in the social sciences, and probably in all sciences believed to have implications for human society (other than perhaps the purely technological), 'outside' is largely, indeed primarily, the experience, ideas and activity of the scientist as a person and as a citizen, a child of his or her times. And partisan scientists are the ones most likely to use their experience 'outside' in their academic work.

This does not necessarily require actual political commitment, or even ideological commitment, though in the nineteenth century and even today strong feelings of hostility to traditional religion have fertilized debates in even the very 'pure' natural sciences. It has played a distinct part in such 'non-political' fields as cosmogony and molecular biology, through the militantly agnostic motivations of some who have revolutionized these fields – for example Hoyle and Francis Crick.[12] For that matter Charles Darwin himself, though reluctant to commit himself in public on the controversial issue of religion, had rather decided opinions on the matter. However, even strong ideological and political commitment has sometimes had a direct influence on the development of theory in the natural sciences. On the left there is the example of A. R. Wallace, co-discoverer with Darwin of natural selection: a lifelong political radical, formed in heterodox Owenite 'Halls of Science' and Chartist 'Mechanics Institutes', and naturally drawn to that 'natural history' which was so attractive to men of a Jacobin spirit. On the right there is the example of Werner Heisenberg.

It would be possible to give numerous examples of how such a political stimulus may operate in the social and historical sciences, but one may suffice. The problem of slavery has recently become a major field for historical analysis and debate. Since this is a subject which arouses strong emotional feelings, it is not surprising that historical partisanship should enter into it, but it is nevertheless striking how large a part it has played in the revival of interest in this field. Of the thirty-three titles since 1940 in the bibliography to the article 'slavery' in the *International Encyclopedia of the Social Sciences* (1968), twelve are the work of authors of Marxist provenance, though many of them are remote from this ideology today. In the vigorous debate on slavery in the USA since 1974 at least two of the leading figures (Fogel and Genovese) were actually militant members of the tiny Communist Party of the USA in the 1950s. One is almost tempted to claim that this contemporary historical debate is a development which sprang from the intra-Marxist discussions of earlier decades.

This does not mean that all political commitment is likely to have such innovating effects on science and scholarship. Much partisan scholarship is trivial, scholastic or, if attached to a body of orthodox doctrine, engaged in proving the predetermined truth of that doctrine. Much of it sets up pseudo-problems of a type reminiscent of theology and then attempts to solve them, perhaps even refusing to consider real ones on doctrinal grounds. There is no point in denying this, even if such practices are not confined to scholars conscious of their own partisanship. Again, there is usually a point beyond which ideological or political commitment, of whatever kind, seriously tempts the scholar to practise what is scientifically illegitimate. The case of the late Professor Cyril Burt is proof of this danger. This eminent psychologist, as has been demonstrated, was so convinced of the insignificance of environmental factors in the formation of human intelligence, that he faked his experimental results to make them more persuasive.[13] Yet the obvious dangers and disadvantages of partisan scholarship hardly need stressing. Its less obvious advantages do.

Today they need to be particularly stressed, because the unprecedented expansion and size of the academic profession and the growing specialization of each discipline and its multiplying subdisciplines tend increasingly to turn academic thought inwards upon itself. The reasons are both sociological and inherent in the development of the sciences themselves. Both combine to push most academics into some small territory within which they are recognized as experts, and outside the boundaries of which only the very rash or the very well established will like to venture. For, as time goes on, they will simply not know enough outside their 'field' to speak with confidence – or even to be familiar with the work done – while the groups of specialists occupying other territories and defending them against incursions by competitors with barricades of esoteric knowledge and special techniques make the raids of relative laymen increasingly dangerous. Specialist journals, newsletters and conferences multiply, and the debates within each field become incomprehensible to those not already inside it, without long preparation and reading which others can rarely find time for except at the expense of their own specialist knowledge. The exhaustive bibliography of the 'literature', increasingly known only to the writers of theses, protects each of these fortresses. Three hundred and eighty or more titles in 1975 warned off the citizens who thought they had something to say about 'social movements, riots and protests' against careless incursions into the field of 'Collective Behaviour', a sub-discipline of sociology now trying to establish itself as a special 'field'.[14]

But if the professionally and technically unqualified intruder is kept out, the insider in turn tends to lose the sense of the wider implications of the subject. A good example, as Lester Thurow of the Massachusetts Institute of Technology has pointed out, is the special field of econometrics, developing mathematical models in economics. These models were originally supposed to test whether a clearly specified theory could be statistically verified, but (largely because they can rarely be) a curious inversion in the relation between theory and data took place:

> Econometrics shifted from being a tool for testing theories to being a tool for exhibiting theories. It became a descriptive language . . . . Good economic theory was stronger than the data – at least in the minds of the economists – and therefore it must be imposed on the data. What started off as a technique for elevating data relative to theory ended up by doing exactly the opposite.

Thus, he argues, econometric equations found no relationship between investment and the movement of interest rates such as was posited by classical economic theory, and no way of establishing such a relationship. They then turned to the intellectually legitimate alternative of designing their equations in such a way that interest rates were mathematically forced to have the right sign. 'The equations did not test the theory, but they described what the world would be like if the theory were correct.' In short, and at the cost of tending to retard the development of economic theory, econometrics was increasingly insulated against the impact of the real world. The incentive to rethink theory, as distinct from developing it in a more sophisticated manner, became weaker.[15] Yet this insulation becomes less noticeable, or even more tolerable, as the number of specialists who appreciate – and indeed practise – the increasingly esoteric intellectual operations of their colleagues has become enormously larger, the time necessarily spent immersed in the literature of the subject immensely greater, notably since 1960. Like the guests of a large hotel, the specialists in a field can supply most of their needs without leaving the building; or through contacts with the outside world mediated through the hotel. There are, after all, probably more economists employed in the academic institutions of the city of Boston and its neighbourhood today than the total number of professional economists in Britain between the publication of the *Wealth of Nations* and Keynes' *General Theory*: and all are kept busy reading and criticizing each other's works. To take only a rather modest and not very rapidly expanding field, that of economic and social history: the membership of the British Economic History Society roughly trebled between 1960 and 1975. Over 25 per cent of all works in the subject published since its foundation in 1925 appeared in 1969–74; 65 per cent of all this literature appeared between 1960 and 1974.[16] By the standards of the 430,000 papers which constituted the stock of the mathematical literature in 1968, the 522,000 papers which embodied the findings of physics in the same year,[17] the 20,000 titles in economic and social history are modest. Yet every worker in the field knows how much of this literature is generated not by problems, but by earlier books and articles; how much more of the life of the economic historian is lived within the increasingly ample and varied equipment of his hotel.

It is in this situation that political partisanship can serve to counteract the increasing tendency to look inwards, in extreme instances the scholiasm, the tendency to develop intellectual ingenuity for its own sake, the self-insulation of the academy. It may indeed fall victim to the same dangers itself, if a sufficiently large 'field' of a self-insulated partisan scholarship develops. There is enough Marxist neo-scholasticism in such fields as philosophy and sociology to provide a salutary warning. Nevertheless, mechanisms for bringing new ideas, new questions, new challenges into the sciences from outside are today more indispensable than ever. Partisanship is a powerful mechanism of this kind, perhaps at present the most powerful in the human sciences. Without it, the development of these sciences would be at risk.

CHAPTER 10

What Do Historians Owe
to Karl Marx?

The following three chapters, which introduce a section on historical contro-versies, deal specifically with Marxism and history. The first two are attempts, with a fifteen-year interval, to assess the impact of Marx on contemporary historians. The present chapter was first written for the symposium 'The Role of Karl Marx in the Development of Contemporary Scientific Thought' held, under the auspices of UNESCO, *in Paris in May 1968. It was published in the resulting volume of the International Social Science Council,* Marx and Contemporary Scientific Thought/Marx et la pensée scientifique contemporaine *(The Hague and Paris, 1969), pp. 197–211, in* Diogenes *64, pp. 37–56, and elsewhere.*

The nineteenth century, that age of bourgeois civilization, has several major intellectual achievements to its credit, but the academic disci-pline of history which grew up in that period is not one of them. Indeed, in all except the techniques of research, it marked a distinct step back from the often ill-documented, speculative and excessively general essays in which those who witnessed the most profoundly revolutionary era – the age of the French and industrial revolutions – attempted to comprehend the transformation of human societies. Academic history, as inspired by the teaching and example of Leopold von Ranke and published in the specialist journals which developed in the latter part of the century, was correct in opposing generalization insufficiently supported by fact, or backed by unreliable fact. On the other hand it concentrated all its efforts on the task of establishing the 'facts' and thus contributed little to history except a set of empirical criteria for evaluating certain kinds of documentary evidence (for example, manuscript records of events involving the conscious decision of influential individuals) and the ancillary techniques necess-ary for this purpose.

It rarely observed that these documents and procedures were

applicable only to a limited range of historical phenomena, because it uncritically accepted certain phenomena as worthy of special study and others not. Thus it did not set out to concentrate on the 'history of events' – indeed in some countries it had a distinct institutional bias – but its methodology lent itself most readily to chronological narrative. It did not by any means confine itself entirely to the history of politics, war, and diplomacy (or, in the simplified but not untypical version taught by schoolmasters relating to kings, battles and treaties), but it undoubtedly tended to assume that this formed the central body of events which concerned the historian. This was history in the singular. Other subjects could, when treated with erudition and method, give rise to various histories, qualified by descriptive epithets (constitutional, economic, ecclesiastical, cultural, the history of art, science or philately, and so on). Their connection with the main body of history was obscure or neglected, except for a few vague speculations about the *Zeitgeist* from which professional historians preferred to abstain.

Philosophically and methodologically academic historians tended to demonstrate an equally striking innocence. It is true that the results of this innocence coincided with what in the natural sciences was a conscious, though controversial, methodology which we can loosely call positivism, but it is doubtful whether many academic historians (outside the Latin countries) knew that they were positivists. In most cases they were merely men who, just as they accepted a given subject-matter (such as politico–military–diplomatic history) and given geographical area (say western and middle Europe) as the most important, also accepted, among other *idées reçues*, those of popularized scientific thought, for example that hypotheses arise automatically from the study of 'facts', that explanation consists of a collection of chains of cause and effect, or the concepts of determinism, evolution and so on. They assumed that, just as scientific erudition could establish the definitive text and succession of the documents which they published in elaborate and invaluable series of volumes, so it would also establish the definite truth of history. Lord Acton's *Cambridge Modern History* was a late but typical example of such beliefs.

Even by the modest standards of the human and social sciences of the nineteenth century, history was therefore an extremely, one might almost say a deliberately, backward discipline. Its contributions to the understanding of human society, past and present, was negligible and accidental. Since the understanding of society requires

142

an understanding of history, alternative and more fruitful ways of exploring the human past had, sooner or later, to be found. The subject of this paper is the contribution of Marxism to this search.

One hundred years after Ranke, Arnaldo Momigliano summed up the changes in historiography under four heads:

(1) Political and religious history had declined sharply, while 'national histories look old-fashioned'. In return there had been a remarkable turn towards social-economic history.

(2) It was no longer usual, or indeed easy, to use 'ideas' as an explanation of history.

(3) The prevalent explanations were now 'in terms of social forces', though this raised in a more acute form than in Ranke's day the question of the relation between the explanation of historical events and explanation of individual actions.

(4) It had now (1954) become difficult to speak of progress or even meaningful development of events in a certain direction.[1]

The last of Momigliano's observations – and we quote him as a reporter of the state of historiography rather than as an analyst – was probably more likely to be made in the 1950s than in earlier or later decades, but the other three observations plainly represent old-established and lasting trends in the anti-Rankean movement within history. From the middle of the nineteenth century, it was noted as long ago as 1910,[2] the attempt had been systematically made to substitute a materialist for an idealist framework in it, thus leading to a decline in political, and the rise of 'economic or sociological', history: no doubt under the increasingly urgent stimulus of the 'social problem' which 'dominated' historiography in the second half of that century.[3] Plainly, it took rather longer to capture the fortresses of university faculties and schools of archives than enthusiastic encyclopaedists supposed. By 1914 the attacking forces had occupied little more than the outlying posts of 'economic history' and historically oriented sociology, and the defenders were not forced into full retreat – though they were by no means routed – until after the Second World War.[4] Nevertheless, the general character and success of the anti-Rankean movement is not in doubt.

The immediate question before us is how far this new orientation has been due to Marxist influence. A second question is in what way Marxist influence continues to contribute to it.

There can be no doubt that the influence of Marxism was from the start very considerable. Broadly speaking, the only other school or current of thought aiming at the reconstruction of history which was influential in the nineteenth century was positivism (whether spelled with a small or large initial letter). Positivism, a belated child of the eighteenth-century Enlightenment, could not win our unstinted admiration in the nineteenth. Its major contribution to history was the introduction of concepts, methods and models from the natural sciences into social investigation and the application to history of such discoveries in the natural sciences as seemed suitable. These were not negligible achievements, but they were limited ones, all the more so as the nearest thing to a model of historical change, a theory of evolution patterned on biology or geology, and drawing both encouragement and example after 1859 from Darwinism, is only a very crude and inadequate guide to history. Consequently the historians inspired by Comte or Spencer have been few, and, like Buckle or even the greater Taine or Lamprecht, their influence on historiography was limited and temporary. The weakness of positivism (or Positivism) was that, in spite of Comte's conviction that sociology was the highest of the sciences, it had little to say about the phenomena that characterize human society, as distinct from those which could be directly derived from the influence of non-social factors, or modelled on the natural sciences. What views it had about the human character of history were speculative, if not metaphysical.

The major impetus for the transformation of history therefore came from historically oriented social sciences (for example the German 'historical school' in economics), but especially from Marx, whose influence was acknowledged to be such that he was often given credit for achievements which he did not himself claim to have originated. Historical materialism was habitually described – sometimes even by Marxists – as 'economic determinism'. Quite apart from disclaiming this phrase, Marx would certainly also have denied that he was the first to stress the importance of the economic basis of historical development, or to write the history of humanity as that of a succession of socio-economic systems. He certainly disclaimed originality in introducing the concept of class and class struggle into history, but in vain. 'Marx ha introdotto nella storiografia il concetto di classe,' wrote the *Enciclopedia Italiana*.

It is not the purpose of this paper to trace the specific contribution of Marxist influence on the transformation of modern historiography. Evidently it differed from one country to another. Thus in France it was relatively small, at least until after the Second World War, because of the remarkably late and slow penetration of Marxist ideas in any field into the intellectual life of that country.[5] Though Marxist influences had by the 1920s penetrated to some extent into the highly political field of the historiography of the French Revolution – but, as the work of Jaurès and Georges Lefebvre shows, in combination with ideas drawn from native traditions of thought – the major reorientation of French historians was led by the *Annales* school, which certainly did not require Marx to draw its attention to the economic and social dimensions of history. (However, the popular identification of an interest in such matters with Marxism is so strong that the *Times Literary Supplement* has only recently[6] put even Fernand Braudel under Marx's influence). Conversely, there are countries in Asia or Latin America in which the transformation, if not the creation, of modern historiography can almost be identified with the penetration of Marxism. So long as it is accepted that, speaking globally, the influence was considerable, we need not pursue the subject further in the present context.

It has been raised, not so much to establish that Marxist influence has played an important part in the modernization of historiography as to illustrate a major difficulty in determining its precise contribution. For, as we have seen, the Marxist influence among historians has been identified with a few relatively simple, if powerful, ideas, which have, in one way or another, been associated with Marx and the movements inspired by his thought, but which are not necessarily Marxist at all, or which, in the form that has been most influential, are not necessarily representative of the mature thought of Marx. We shall call this type of influence 'vulgar-Marxist', and the major problem of analysis is to separate the vulgar-Marxist from the Marxist component in historical analysis.

To give some examples. It seems clear that 'vulgar-Marxism' embraced in the main the following elements:

(1) The 'economic interpretation of history', that is the belief that 'the economic factor is the fundamental factor on which the others are dependent' (to use R. Stammler's phrase); and more specifically, on which phenomena hitherto not regarded as having much connection with economic matters, depended. To this extent it overlapped with

(2) The model of 'basis and superstructure' (used most widely to explain the history of ideas). In spite of Marx and Engels' own warnings and the sophisticated observations of some early Marxists such as

Labriola, this model was usually interpreted as a simple relation of dominance and dependence between the 'economic base' and the 'superstructure', mediated at most by

(3) 'Class interest and the class struggle'. One has the impression that a number of vulgar-Marxist historians did not read much beyond the first page of the Communist Manifesto, and the phrase that 'the [written] history of all hitherto existing societies is the history of class struggles'.

(4) 'Historical laws and historical inevitability'. It was believed, correctly, that Marx insisted on a systematic and necessary development of human society in history, from which the contingent was largely excluded, at all events at the level of generalization about long-term movements. Hence the constant preoccupation of early Marxist writers on history with such problems as the role of the individual or of accident in history. On the other hand this could be, and largely was, interpreted as a rigid and imposed regularity, for example in the succession of socio-economic formations, or even a mechanical determinism which sometimes came close to suggesting that there were no alternatives in history.

(5) Specific subjects of historical investigations derived from Marx's own interests, for instance in the history of capitalist development and industrialization, but also sometimes from more or less casual remarks.

(6) Specific subjects of investigation derived not so much from Marx as from the interest of the movements associated with his theory, for example in the agitations of the oppressed classes (peasants, workers), or in revolutions.

(7) Various observations about the nature and limits of historiography, derived mainly from no. 2 and serving to explain the motives and methods of historians who claimed to be nothing but impartial searchers after truth, and prided themselves on establishing simply *wie es eigentlich gewesen.*

It will at once be obvious that this represented, at best, a selection from Marx's views about history and at worst (as quite often with Kautsky) an assimilation of them to contemporary non-Marxist – for example evolutionist and positivistic – views. It will also be evident that some of it represented not Marx at all, but the sort of interests which would naturally be developed by any historian associated with popular, working-class and revolutionary movements, and which would have been developed even without the intervention of Marx, such as a preoccupation with earlier examples of social struggle and socialist ideology. Thus in the case of Kautsky's early monograph on Thomas Moore, there is nothing particularly Marxist about the choice of the subject, and its treatment is vulgar-Marxist.

Yet this selection of elements from, or associated with, Marxism, was not arbitrary. Items 1–4 and 7 in the brief survey of vulgar-Marxism made above represented concentrated charges of intellectual explosive, designed to blow up crucial parts of the fortifications of traditional history, and as such they were immensely powerful – perhaps more powerful than less simplified versions of historical materialism would have been, and certainly powerful enough in their capacity to let light into hitherto dark places, to keep historians satisfied for a considerable time. It is difficult to recapture the amazement felt by an intelligent and learned social scientist at the end of the nineteenth century, when encountering the following Marxist observations about the past: 'That the very Reformation is ascribed to an economical cause, that the length of the Thirty Years War was due to economic causes, the Crusades to feudal land-hunger, the evolution of the family to economic causes, and that Descartes' view of animals as machines can be brought into relation with the growth of the Manufacturing system.'[7] Yet those of us who recall our first encounters with historical materialism may still bear witness to the immense liberating force of such simple discoveries.

However, if it was thus natural, and perhaps necessary, for the initial impact of Marxism to take a simplified form, the actual selection of elements from Marx also represented a historical choice. Thus a few remarks by Marx in the *Capital* on the relation between Protestantism and capitalism were immensely influential, presumably because the problem of the social basis of ideology in general, and of the nature of religious orthodoxies in particular, was a subject of immediate and intense interest.[8] On the other hand some of the works in which Marx himself came closest to writing as a historian, such as the magnificent *Eighteenth Brumaire*, did not stimulate historians until very much later, presumably because the problems on which they throw most light, say of class-consciousness and the peasantry, seemed of less immediate interest.

The bulk of what we regard as the Marxist influence on historiography has certainly been vulgar-Marxist in the sense described above. It consists of the general emphasis on the economic and social factors in history which have been dominant since the end of the Second World War in all but a minority of countries (for example, until recently West Germany and the United States), and which continue to gain ground. We must repeat that this trend, though undoubtedly in the main the product of Marxist influence, has no special connection with Marx's thought.

The major impact which Marx's own specific ideas have had in history and the social sciences in general is almost certainly that of the theory of 'basis and superstructure', that is to say of his model of a society composed of different 'levels' which interact. Marx's own hierarchy of levels or mode of their interaction (insofar as he has provided one)[9] need not be accepted for the general model to be valuable. It has, indeed, been very widely welcomed as a valuable contribution even by non-Marxists. Marx's specific model of historical development – including the role of class conflicts, the succession of socio-economic formations and the mechanism of transition from one to the other – has remained much more controversial, even in some instances among Marxists. It is right that it should be debated, and in particular that the usual criteria of historical verification should be applied to it. It is inevitable that some parts of it, which are based on insufficient or misleading evidence, should be abandoned, for instance in the field of the study of Oriental societies, where Marx combines profound insight with mistaken assumptions, say about the internal stability of some such societies. Nevertheless it is the contention of this paper that the chief value of Marx for historians today lies in his statements about history, as distinct from his statements about society in general.

The Marxist (and vulgar-Marxist) influence which has hitherto been most effective is part of a general tendency to transform history into one of the social sciences, a tendency resisted by some with more or less sophistication, but which has unquestionably been the prevailing one in the twentieth century. The major contribution of Marxism to this tendency in the past has been the critique of positivism, that is of the attempts to assimilate the study of the social sciences to that of the natural ones, or the human to the non-human. This implies the recognition of societies as systems of relations between human beings, of which the relations entered into for the purpose of production and reproduction are primary for Marx. It also implies the analysis of the structure and functioning of these systems as entities maintaining themselves, in their relations both with the outside environment – non-human and human – and in their internal relationships. Marxism is far from the only structural–functionalist theory of society, though it has good claims to be the first of them, but it differs from most others in two respects. It insists, first, on a hierarchy of social phenomena (such as 'basis' and 'superstructure'), and second, on the existence within any society of internal tensions ('contradictions') which counteract the tendency of the system to maintain itself as a going concern.[10]

The importance of these peculiarities of Marxism is in the field of history, for it is they which allow it to explain – unlike other structural–functional models of society – why and how societies change and transform themselves: in other words, the facts of social evolution.[11] The immense strength of Marx has always lain in his insistence on both the existence of social structure and its historicity, or in other words its internal dynamic of change. Today, when the existence of social systems is generally accepted, but at the cost of their a-historical, if not anti-historical analysis, Marx's emphasis on history as a necessary dimension is perhaps more essential than ever.

This implies two specific critiques of theories prevalent in the social sciences today.

The first is the critique of the mechanism which dominates so much of the social sciences, especially in the United States, and draws its strength both from the remarkable fruitfulness of sophisticated mechanical models in the present phase of scientific advance and from the search for methods of achieving social change which do not imply social revolution. One may perhaps add that the wealth of money and of certain new technologies suitable for use in the social field, which are now available in the richest of the industrial countries, makes this type of 'social engineering' and the theories on which it is based very attractive in such countries. Such theories are essentially exercises in 'problem-solving'. Theoretically, they are extremely primitive, probably cruder than most corresponding theories in the nineteenth century. Thus many social scientists, either consciously or *de facto*, reduce the process of history to a single change from 'traditional' to 'modern' or 'industrial' society, the 'modern' being defined in terms of the advanced industrial countries, or even of the mid-twentieth-century United States, the 'traditional' as that which lacks 'modernity'. Operationally this single large step can be sub-divided into smaller steps, such as those of Rostow's Stages of Economic Growth. These models eliminate most of history in order to concentrate on one small, though admittedly vital, span of it, and grossly oversimplify the mechanisms of historical change even with this small span of time. They affect historians chiefly because the size and prestige of the social sciences which develop such models encourage historical researchers to embark on projects which are influenced by them. It is, or should be, quite evident that they can provide no adequate model of historical change, but their present popularity makes it important that Marxists should constantly remind us of this.

The second is the critique of structural–functional theories which, if vastly more sophisticated, are in some respects even more sterile inasmuch as they may deny historicity altogether, or transform it into something else. Such views are more influential even within the range of influence of Marxism, because they appear to provide a means of liberating it from the characteristic evolutionism of the nineteenth century, with which it was so often combined, though at the cost of also liberating it from the concept of 'progress' which was also characteristic of nineteenth-century thought, including Marx's. But why should we wish to do so?[12] Marx himself certainly would not have wished to do so: he offered to dedicate the second volume of *Capital* to Darwin, and would hardly have disagreed with Engels' famous phrase at his graveside, which praised him for discovering the law of evolution in human history, as Darwin had done in organic nature. (He would certainly not have wished to dissociate progress from evolution, and indeed specifically blamed Darwin for making it into its merely accidental byproduct.)[13]

The fundamental question in history implies the discovery of a mechanism for both the differentiation of various human social groups and the transformation of one kind of society into another, or the failure to do so. In certain respects, which Marxists and common sense regard as crucial, such as the control of man over nature, it certainly implies unidirectional change or progress, at least over a sufficiently long time-span. So long as we do not suppose that the mechanisms of such social development are the same as or similar to those of biological evolution, there seems to be no good reason for not using the term 'evolution' for it.

The argument is, of course, more than terminological. It conceals two kinds of disagreements: about the value-judgment on different types of societies, or in other words the possibility of ranking them in any kind of hierarchical order, and about the mechanisms of change. Structural–functionalisms have tended to shy away from ranking societies into 'higher' and 'lower', partly because of the welcome refusal of social anthropologists to accept the claim of the 'civilized' to rule the 'barbarian' because of their alleged superiority in social evolution, and partly because, by the formal criteria of function, there is indeed no such hierarchy. The Eskimo solve the problems of their existence as a social group[14] as successfully in their own way as the white inhabitants of Alaska – some would be tempted to say, more successfully. Under certain conditions and on certain assumptions, magical thinking may be as logical in its way as scientific thinking and as adequate for its purpose. And so on.

These observations are valid, though they are not very useful insofar as the historian, or any other social scientist, wishes to explain the specific content of a system rather than its general structure.[15] But in any case they are irrelevant to the question of evolutionary change, if not indeed tautologous. Human societies must, if they are to persist, be capable of managing themselves successfully, and therefore all existing ones must be functionally adequate; if not, they would have become extinct, as the Shakers did for want of a system of sexual procreation or outside recruitment. To compare societies in respect of their system of internal relations between members is inevitably to compare like with like. It is when we compare them in respect of their capacity to control outside nature that the differences leap to the eye.

The second disagreement is more fundamental. Most versions of structural–functional analysis are synchronic, and the more elaborate and sophisticated they are the more they are confined to social statics, into which, if the subject interests the thinker, some dynamizing element has to be introduced.[16] Whether this can be done satisfactorily is a matter of debate even among structuralists. That *the same analysis* cannot be used to explain both function and historic change seems widely accepted. The point here is not that it is illegitimate to develop separate analysis models for the static and the dynamic, such as Marx's schemas of simple and extended reproduction, but that historical enquiry makes it desirable for these different models to be connected. The simplest course for the structuralist is to omit change, and leave history to someone else, or even, like some of the earlier British social anthropologists, virtually to deny its relevance. However, since it exists, structuralism must find ways of explaining it.

These ways must either, I suggest, bring it closer to Marxism, or lead to a denial of evolutionary change. Lévi-Strauss' approach (and that of Althusser) seem to me to do the latter. Here historical change becomes simply the permutation and combination of certain 'elements' (analogous, to quote Lévi-Strauss, to genes in genetics), which in the sufficiently long term, may be expected to combine in different patterns and, if sufficiently limited, to exhaust the possible combinations.[17] History is, as it were, the process of playing through all the variants in an end-game of chess. But in what order? The theory here provides us with no guide.

Yet this is precisely the specific problem of historical evolution. It is of course true that Marx envisaged such a combination and recombination of elements or 'forms' as Althusser stresses, and in this as other respects was a structuralist *avant la lettre*; or, more precisely, a thinker from whom a Lévi-Strauss (by his own admission) could, in part at least, borrow the term.[18] It is important to remind ourselves of an aspect of Marx's thought which earlier traditions of Marxism undoubtedly neglected, with a few exceptions (among which, curiously, must be numbered some of the developments of Soviet Marxism in the Stalin period, though these were not wholly aware of the implications of what they were doing). It is even more important to remind ourselves that the analysis of the elements and their possible combinations provides (as in genetics) a salutary control on evolutionary theories, by establishing what is theoretically possible and impossible. It is also possible – though this question must remain open – that such an analysis could lend greater precision to the definition of the various social 'levels' (basis and superstructure) and their relationships, as Althusser suggests.[19] What it does not do is to explain why twentieth-century Britain is a very different place from neolithic Britain, or the succession of socio-economic formations, or the mechanism of the transitions from one to the other, or, for that matter, why Marx devoted so much of his life to answering such questions.

If such questions are to be answered, both the peculiarities which distinguish Marxism from other structural–functional theories are necessary: the model of levels, of which that of the social relations of production are primary, and the existence of internal contradictions within systems, of which class conflict is merely a special case.

The hierarchy of levels is necessary to explain why history has a *direction*. It is the growing emancipation of man from nature and his growing capacity to control it which make history as a whole (though not every area and period within it) 'oriented and irreversible', to quote Lévi-Strauss once again. A hierarchy of levels not arising on the base of the social relations of production would not necessarily have this characteristic. Moreover, since the process and progress of man's control over nature involves changes not merely in the forces of production (for example new techniques) but in the social relations of production, it implies a certain order in the succession of socio-economic systems. (It does not imply the acceptance of the list of formations given in the Preface to the *Critique of Political Economy*, as chronologically successive, which Marx probably did not believe them to be, and still less a theory of universal unilinear evolution. However, it does imply that certain social phenomena cannot be conceived as appearing in history earlier than others, such as economies possessing the town–country dichotomy before those which lack it.) And for the same reason it implies that this succession of systems cannot be ordered simply in one dimension technological (lower technologies preceding higher) or economic (*Geldwirtschaft* succeeding *Naturalwirtschaft*) but must also be ordered in terms of their social systems.[20] For it is an essential characteristic of Marx's historical thought that it is neither 'sociological' nor 'economic' but both simultaneously. The social relations of production and reproduction (that is, social organization in its broadest sense) and the material forces of production cannot be divorced.

Given this 'orientation' of historical development, the internal contradictions of socio-economic systems provide the mechanism for change which becomes development. (Without it, it might be argued that they would produce merely cyclical fluctuation, an endless process of destabilizing and restabilizing; and, of course, such changes as might arise from the contacts and conflicts of different societies.) The point about such internal contradictions is that they cannot be defined simply as 'dysfunctional' except on the assumption that stability and permanence are the norm, and change the exception; or even on the more naive assumption, frequent in the vulgar social sciences, that a specific system is the model to which all change aspires.[21] It is rather that, as is now recognized much more widely than before among social anthropologists, a structural model envisaging only the maintenance of a system is inadequate. It is the simultaneous existence of stabilizing and disruptive elements which such a model must reflect. And it is this which the Marxist model – though not the vulgar-Marxist versions of it – has been based on.

Such a dual (dialectical) model is difficult to set up and use, for in practice the temptation is great to operate it, according to taste or occasion, either as a model of stable functionalism or as one of revolutionary change, whereas the interesting thing about it is that it is both. It is equally important that internal tensions may sometimes be reabsorbed into a self-stabilizing model by feeding them back as functional stabilizers, and that sometimes they cannot. Class conflict can be regulated through a sort of safety-valve, as in so many riots of urban plebeians in pre-industrial cities, or institutionalized as 'rituals of rebellion' (to use Max Gluckman's illuminating phrase) or in other ways; but sometimes it cannot. The state will normally legitimize the social order by controlling class conflict within a stable framework of institutions and values, ostensibly standing above and outside them (the remote king as 'fountain of justice'), and in doing so perpetuate a society which would otherwise be riven asunder by its internal tensions. This is indeed the classical Marxist theory of its origin and function, as expounded in *Origin of the Family*.[22] Yet there are situations when it loses this function and – even in the minds of its subject – this capacity to legitimate and appears merely as, to use the phrase of Thomas More, 'a conspiracy of the rich for their own benefit', if not indeed the direct cause of the miseries of the poor.

This contradictory nature of the model can be obscured by pointing to the undoubted existence of *separate* phenomena within society representing regulated stability and subversion: social groups which can allegedly be integrated into feudal society, such as 'merchant capital', and these which cannot, such as an 'industrial bourgeoisie', or social movements which are purely 'reformist' and those which are consciously 'revolutionary'. But though such separations exist, and, where they do, indicate a certain stage in the development of the society's internal contradictions (which are *not*, for Marx, exclusively those of class conflict),[23] it is equally significant that the same phenomena may, according to the situation, change their functions – movements for the restoration of the old regulated order of class society turning (as with some peasant movements) into social revolutions, consciously revolutionary parties being absorbed into the *status quo*.[24]

Difficult though it may be, social scientists of various kinds (including, we may note, animal ecologists, especially students of population dynamics and animal social behaviour) have begun to approach the construction of models of equilibria based on tension or conflict, and in doing so draw nearer to Marxism and further away from the older models of sociology which regarded the problem of order as logically prior to that of change and emphasized the integrative and normative elements in social life. At the same time it must be admitted that Marx's own model must be made more explicit than it is in his writings, that it may require elaboration and development, and that certain vestiges of the nineteenth-century positivism, more evident in Engels' formulations than in Marx's own thought, must be cleared out of the way.

We are then still left with the *specific* historical problems of the nature and succession of socio-economic formations, and the mechanisms of their internal development and interaction. These are fields in which discussion has been intensive since Marx,[25] not least in the past decades, and in some respects the advance upon Marx has been most striking.[26] Here also recent analysis has confirmed the brilliance and profundity of Marx's general approach and vision, though it has also drawn attention to the gaps in his treatment, particularly of pre-capitalist periods. However, these themes can hardly be discussed even in the most cursory form except in terms of concrete historical knowledge, that is they cannot be discussed in the context of the present colloquium. Short of such a discussion I can only assert my conviction that Marx's approach is still the only one which enables us to explain the entire span of human history, and forms the most fruitful starting-point for modern discussion.

None of this is particularly new, though some of the texts which contain the most mature reflections of Marx on historical subjects did not become effectively available until the 1950s, notably the *Grundrisse* of 1857–8. Moreover, the diminishing returns on the application of vulgar-Marxist models have in recent decades led to a substantial sophistication of Marxist historiography.[27] Indeed, one of the most characteristic features of contemporary Western Marxist historiography is the critique of the simple, mechanical schemata of an economic-determinist type.

However, whether or not Marxist historians have advanced substantially beyond Marx, their contribution today has a new importance, because of the changes which are at present taking place in the social sciences. Whereas the major function of historical materialism in the first half-century after Engels' death was to bring history closer to the social sciences, while avoiding the oversimplifications of positivism, it is today facing the rapid historization of the social sciences themselves. For want of any help from academic historiography, these have increasingly begun to improvise their own – applying their own characteristic procedures to the study of the past, with results which are often technically sophisticated, but, as has been pointed out, based on models of historic change in some respects even cruder than those of the nineteenth century.[28] Here the value of Marx's historical materialism is great, though it is natural that historically minded social scientists may find themselves less in need of Marx's insistence on the importance of economic and social elements in history than did the historians of the early twentieth century; and conversely might find themselves more stimulated by aspects of Marx's theory which did not make a great impact on historians in the immediately post-Marxian generations.

Whether this explains the undoubted prominence of Marxian ideas in the discussion of certain fields of historically oriented social science today, is another question.[29] The unusual prominence at present of Marxist historians, or of historians trained in the Marxist school, is certainly in large part due to the radicalization of intellectuals and students in the past decade, the impact of the revolutions in the third world, the break-up of Marxist orthodoxies inimical to original scientific work, and even to so simple a factor as the succession of generations. For the Marxists who reached the point of publishing widely read books and occupying senior positions in academic life in the 1950s were often only the radicalized students of the 1930s or 1940s, reaching the normal peak of their careers. Nevertheless, as we celebrate the 150th anniversary of Marx's birth and the centenary of the *Capital*, we cannot but note – with satisfaction if we are Marxists – the coincidence of a significant influence of Marxism in the field of historiography, and a significant number of historians inspired by Marx or demonstrating, in their work, the effects of training in the Marxist schools.

CHAPTER 11

Marx and History

This lecture was given at the Marx Centenary Conference organized by the Republic of San Marino in 1983, and printed in New Left Review *143 (February 1984), pp. 39–50.*

We are here to discuss themes and problems of the Marxist conception of history a hundred years after the death of Marx. This is not a ritual of centenary celebration, but it is important to begin by reminding ourselves of the unique role of Marx in historiography. I will simply do so by three illustrations. My first is autobiographical. When I was a student in Cambridge in the 1930s, many of the ablest young men and women joined the Communist Party. But as this was a very brilliant era in the history of a very distinguished university, many of them were profoundly influenced by the great names at whose feet we sat. Among the young communists there we used to joke: the communist philosophers were Wittgensteinians, the communist economists were Keynesians, the communist students of literature were disciples of F. R. Leavis. And the historians? They were Marxists, because there was no historian that we knew of at Cambridge or elsewhere – and we did hear and know of some great ones, such as Marc Bloch – who could compete with Marx, as a master and an inspiration. My second illustration is similar. Thirty years later, in 1969, Sir John Hicks, Nobel Laureate, published his *Theory of Economic History*. He wrote: 'Most of those [who wish to fit into place the general course of history] would use the Marxian categories, or some modified version of them, since there is so little in the way of an alternative version that is available. It does, nevertheless, remain extraordinary that one hundred years after *Das Kapital* ... so little else should have emerged.'[1] My third illustration comes from Fernand Braudel's splendid *Capitalism and Material Life* – a work whose very title provides a link with Marx. In that noble work Marx is referred to more often than any other author, even than any *French* author. Such a tribute from a country not given to underestimate its national thinkers is impressive in itself.

This influence of Marx on the writing of history is not a self-evident development. For although the materialist conception of history is the core of Marxism, and although everything Marx wrote is impregnated with history, he himself did not write much history as historians understand it. In this respect Engels was more of a historian, writing more works which could be reasonably classified as 'history' in libraries. Of course Marx studied history and was extremely erudite. But he wrote no work with 'History' in the title except a series of polemical anti-Tsarist articles later published as *The Secret Diplomatic History of the Eighteenth Century*, which is one of the least valuable of his works. What we call Marx's historical writings consist almost exclusively of current political analysis and journalistic comment, combined with a degree of historical background. His current political analyses, such as *Class Struggles in France* and *The Eighteenth Brumaire of Louis Bonaparte*, are truly remarkable. His voluminous journalistic writings, though of uneven interest, contain analyses of the greatest interest -- one thinks of his articles on India -- and they are in any case examples of how Marx applied his method to concrete problems both of history and of a period which has since become history. But they were not written as history, as people who pursue the study of the past understand it. Finally, Marx's study of capitalism contains an enormous amount of historical material, historical illustration and other matter relevant to the historian.

The bulk of Marx's historical work is thus integrated into his theoretical and political writings. All these consider historical developments in a more or less long-term framework, involving the whole span of human development. They must be read together with his writings which focus on short periods or particular topics and problems, or on the detailed history of events. Nevertheless, no complete synthesis of the actual process of historical development can be found in Marx; nor can even *Capital* be treated as 'a history of capitalism until 1867'.

There are three reasons, two minor and one major, why this is so -- and why Marxist historians are therefore not merely commenting on Marx but doing what he himself did not do. First, as we know, Marx had great difficulty in bringing his literary projects to completion. Second, his views continued to evolve until his death, though within a framework established in the middle of the 1840s. Third, and most important, in his mature works Marx deliberately studied history in reverse order, taking developed capitalism as his starting-point. 'Man' was the clue to the anatomy of the 'ape'. This is not, of course, an anti-historical procedure. It implies that the past cannot be understood exclusively or primarily in its own terms: not only because it is part of a historical process, but also because that historical process alone has enabled us to analyse and understand things about that process and the past.

Take the concept of *labour*, central to the materialist conception of history. Before capitalism – or before Adam Smith, as Marx says more specifically – the concept of labour-in-general, as distinct from particular kinds of labour which are qualitatively different and incom-parable, was not available. Yet if we are to understand human history, in a global, long-term sense, as the progressively more effective utilization and transformation of nature by mankind, then the concept of social labour in general is essential. Marx's approach still remains debatable, in that it cannot tell us whether future analysis, on the basis of future historical development, will not make comparable analytical discoveries that enable thinkers to reinterpret human history in terms of some other central analytical concept. This is a potential gap in the analysis, even though we do not think that such a hypothetical future development is likely to abandon the centrality of Marx's analysis of labour, at least for certain obviously crucial aspects of human history. My point is not to call Marx into question, but simply to show that his approach must leave out, as not immediately relevant to his purpose, much of what historians are interested to know – for example, many aspects of the transition from feudalism to capitalism. These were left to later Marxists, although it is true that Friedrich Engels, always more interested in 'what actually happened', did concern himself more with such matters.

Marx's influence on historians, and not only Marxist historians, is nevertheless based both upon his general theory (the materialist conception of history), with its sketches of, or hints at, the general shape of human historical development from primitive communalism to capitalism, and upon his concrete observations relating to particular aspects, periods and problems of the past. I do not want to say much about the latter, even though they have been extremely influential and can still be enormously stimulating and illuminating. The first volume of *Capital* contains three or four fairly marginal references to Protestantism, yet the entire debate on the relationship between religion in general, and Protestantism in particular, and the capitalist mode of production derives from them. Similarly, *Capital* has one footnote on Descartes linking his views (animals as machines, real as opposed to speculative, philosophy as a means of mastering nature and perfecting human life) with the 'manufacturing period' and raising the question why the early economists preferred Hobbes and Bacon as their philosophers, and later ones Locke. (For his part, Dudley North believed that Descartes' method had 'begun to free political economy from its old superstitions'.)[2] In the 1890s this was already used by non-Marxists as an example of Marx's remarkable originality, and even today it would provide seminar material for at least a semester. However, nobody at this meeting will need to be convinced of Marx's genius or the range of his knowledge and interests; and it should be appreciated that much of his writing about particular aspects of the past inevitably reflects the historical knowledge available in his lifetime.

The materialist conception of history is worth discussing at greater length because it is today controverted or criticized not only by non-Marxists and anti-Marxists, but also within Marxism. For generations it was the least questioned part of Marxism and was regarded, rightly in my view, as its core. Developed in the course of Marx's and Engels' critique of German philosophy and ideology, it is essentially directed against the belief that 'ideas, thoughts, concepts produce, determine and dominate men, their material conditions and real life'.[3] From 1846 this conception remained essentially the same. It can be summarized in a single sentence, repeated with variations: 'It is not consciousness that determines life, but life that determines consciousness.'[4] It is already elaborated in *The German Ideology*:

> This conception of history thus relies on expounding the real process of production – starting from the material production of life itself – and comprehending the form of intercourse connected with and created by this mode of production, i.e., civil society in its various stages, as the basis of all history; describing it in its action as the state, and also explaining how all the different theoretical products and forms of consciousness, religion, philosophy, morality, etc., etc., arise from it, and tracing the process of their formation from that basis; thus the whole thing can, of course, be depicted in its totality (and therefore, too, the reciprocal action of these various aspects on one another).[5]

We should note in passing that for Marx and Engels the 'real process of production' is not simply the 'material production of life itself' but something broader. To use Eric Wolf's just formulation, it is 'the

160

complex set of mutually dependent relations among nature, work, social labour and social organization'.[6] We should also note that humans produce with both hand and head.[7]

This conception is not history but a guide to history, a programme of research. To quote *The German Ideology* again:

> Where speculation ends, where real life starts, there consequently begins real, positive science, the expounding of the practical activity, of the practical process of human development. ... When reality is described, self-sufficient philosophy [*die selbständige Philosophie*] loses its medium of existence. At the best its place can only be taken by a summing-up of the most general results, abstractions which are derived from the observation of the historical development of men. These abstractions in themselves, divorced from real history, have no value whatsoever. They can only serve to facilitate the arrangement of historical material, to indicate the sequence of its separate strata. But they by no means afford a recipe or schema, as does philosophy, for neatly trimming the epochs of history.[8]

The fullest formulation comes in the 1859 Preface to *A Contribution to the Critique of Political Economy*. It has to be asked, of course, whether one can reject it and remain a Marxist. However, it is perfectly clear that this ultra-concise formulation requires elaboration: the ambiguity of its terms has aroused debate about what precisely are 'forces' and 'social relations' of production, what constitutes the 'economic base', the 'superstructure' and so on. It is also perfectly clear from the beginning that, since human beings have consciousness, the materialist conception of history is the *basis* of historical explanation but not historical explanation itself. History is not like ecology: human beings decide and think about what happens. It is not quite so clear whether it is determinist in the sense of allowing us to discover what will inevitably happen, as distinct from the general procedures of historical transformation. For it is only in retrospect that the question of historical inevitability can be firmly settled, and even then only as tautology: what happened was inevitable because nothing else happened; therefore, what else might have happened is academic.

Marx wanted to prove *a priori* that a certain historical result, communism, was the inevitable result of historical development. But it is by no means clear that this can be shown by scientific historical analysis. What was apparent, from the very beginning, was that historical materialism was not *economic* determinism: not all non-economic phenomena in history can be derived from specific economic phenomena, and particular events or dates are not determined in this sense. Even the most rigid proponents of historical materialism devoted lengthy discussions to the role of accident and the individual in history (Plekhanov); and, whatever philosophical criticisms can be made of his formulations, Engels was quite unambiguous on this point in his late letters to Bloch, Schmidt, Starkenburg and others. Marx himself, in such specific texts as *The Eighteenth Brumaire* and his journalism of the 1850s, leaves us in no doubt that his view was basically the same.

In reality, the crucial argument about the materialist conception of history has concerned the fundamental relationship between social being and consciousness. This has centred not so much on philosophical considerations (such as 'idealism' versus 'materialism') or even moral–political questions ('what is the role of "free will" and conscious human action?', 'if the situation is not ripe, how can we act?'), as on empirical problems of comparative history and social anthropology. One typical argument would be that it is impossible to distinguish social relations of production from ideas and concepts (that is base from superstructure), partly because this is itself a retrospective historical distinction, and partly because social relations of production are structured by culture and concepts which cannot be reduced to them. Another objection would be that since a given mode of production is compatible with n types of concepts, these cannot be explained by reduction to the 'base'. Thus we know of societies which have the same material base but widely varying ways of structuring their social relations, ideology and other superstructural features. To this extent men's views of the universe determine the forms of their social existence, at least as much as the latter determine the former. What determines these views must therefore be analysed quite differently: for example, following Lévi-Strauss, as a set of variations on a limited number of intellectual concepts.

Let us leave aside the question of whether Marx abstracts from culture. (My own view is that in his actual historical writings he is the very opposite of an economic reductionist.) The basic fact remains that analysis of any society, at any moment of historical development, must begin with analysis of its mode of production: that is to say, of (a) the technical–economic form of 'the metabolism between man and nature' (Marx), the way in which man adapts to and transforms nature by labour; and b) the social arrangements by which labour is mobilized, deployed and allocated.

This is so today. If we wish to understand anything about Britain or Italy in the late twentieth century, we must obviously begin with the massive transformations in the mode of production that took place in the 1950s and 1960s. In the case of the most primitive societies, kinship organization and the system of ideas (of which kinship organization is, among other things, an aspect) will depend on whether we are dealing with a food-gathering or a food-production economy. For instance, as Wolf has pointed out,[9] in a food-gathering economy resources are widely available for anyone with the ability to obtain them, and in a food-producing economy (agricultural or pastoral) access to these resources is restricted. It has to be defined, not only here and now but across generations.

Now, although the concept of base and superstructure is essential in defining a set of analytical priorities, the materialist conception of history faces another, more serious criticism. For Marx holds not just that the mode of production is primary and that the superstructure must in some sense conform to 'the essential distinctions among human beings' which it entails (that is the social relations of production), but also that there is an inevitable evolutionary trend for the material productive forces of society to develop, and thus to come into contradiction with the existing productive relationships and their relatively inflexible superstructural expressions, which then have to give way. As G. A. Cohen has argued, then, this evolutionary trend is, in the broadest sense, technological.

The problem is not so much why such a trend should exist, since, over the history of the world as a whole, it unquestionably has existed up to the present time. The real problem is that this trend is patently not universal. Although we can explain away many cases of societies which do not exhibit such a trend, or in which it seems to stop at a certain point, this is not enough. We may well posit a general trend to progress from food-gathering to food-production (where this is not made impossible or unnecessary for ecological reasons), but we cannot do so for the modern developments of technology and industrialization, which have conquered the world from one and only one regional base.

This seems to create a Catch-22 situation. *Either* there is not a general tendency for the material forces of production of society to develop, or to develop beyond a certain point – in which case the development of Western capitalism has to be explained without primary reference to such a general tendency, and the materialist conception of history can at best be used to explain a special case. (I note in passing that to abandon the view that men are constantly acting in a way which tends to increase their control over nature is both unrealistic and productive of considerable historical and other complications.) *Or else* there is such a general historical tendency – in which case we have to explain why it has not operated everywhere, or even why in many cases (such as China) it has clearly been effectively counteracted. It would seem that nothing other than the strength, inertia or some other force of the social structure and superstructure over the material base could have held up the movement of that material base.

In my view this does not create an insuperable problem for the materialist conception of history as a way of interpreting the world. Marx himself, who was far from being a unilinearist, offered an explanation of why some societies evolved from classical antiquity through feudalism to capitalism, and also of why other societies (a vast body which he roughly grouped under the Asiatic mode of production) did not. However, it does create a very difficult problem for the materialist conception of history as a way of *changing* the world. The core of Marx's argument in this respect is that revolution must come because the forces of production have reached, or must reach, a point at which they are incompatible with the 'capitalist integument' of relations of production. But if it can be shown that in other societies there has been no trend for the material forces to grow, or that their growth has been controlled, sidetracked or otherwise prevented by the force of social organization and superstructure from causing revolution in the sense of the 1859 Preface, then why should not the same occur in bourgeois society? It may, of course, be possible and even relatively easy to formulate a more modest historical case for the necessity or perhaps inevitability of the transformation from capitalism to socialism. But we would then lose two things which were important to Karl Marx and certainly to his followers (myself included): (a) the sense that the triumph of socialism is the logical end of all historical evolution to date; and (b) the sense that it marks the end of 'prehistory' in that it cannot and will not be an 'antagonistic' society.

This does not affect the value of the concept of a 'mode of production', which the Preface defines as 'the aggregate of the productive relationships which constitute the economic structure of a society and form the mode of production of the material means of existence'. Whatever the social relations of production are, and whatever other functions in society they may have, the mode of production constitutes the structure which determines what form the growth of the productive forces and the distribution of the surplus will take, how society can or cannot change its structures, and how, at suitable moments, the transition to another mode of production can or will take place. It also establishes the range of superstructural possibilities. In short, the mode of production is the base of our understanding of the variety of human societies and their interactions, as well as of their historical dynamics.

The mode of production is not identical with a society: 'society' is a system of human relations, or, to be more precise, of relations between human groups. The 'mode of production' (MOP) concept serves to identify the forces guiding the alignment of these groups – which can be done variously in different societies, within a certain range. Do the MOPS form a series of evolutionary stages, ordered chronologically or otherwise? There seems to be little doubt that Marx himself saw them as forming a series in which man's growing emancipation from, and control over, nature affected both the forces and the relations of production. According to this set of criteria, the various MOPS could be thought to be ranged in ascending order. But while some MOPS clearly cannot be thought as prior to others (for example those requiring commodity production or steam engines as prior to those that do not), Marx's list of MOPS is not intended to form a unilinear chronological succession. In fact, it is a matter of observation that at all but the (hypothetical) earliest stages of human development a variety of MOPS have coexisted and interacted.

A mode of production embodies both a particular programme of production (a way of producing on the basis of a particular technology and productive division of labour) and 'a specific, historically occurring set of social relations through which labour is deployed to wrest energy from nature by means of tools, skills, organization and knowledge' at a given phase of their development, and through which the socially produced surplus is circulated, distributed and used for accumulation or some other purpose. A Marxist history must consider both functions.

Here lies the weakness of a highly original and important book by the anthropologist Eric Wolf: *Europe and the Peoples without History.* This attempts to show how the global expansion and triumph of capitalism have affected the pre-capitalist societies it has integrated into its world system; and how capitalism has in turn been modified and shaped through being embedded, in some sense, within a plurality of modes of production. It is a book about connections rather than causes, although connections may turn out to be essential to the analysis of causes. It brilliantly sets out a way of grasping 'the strategic features of ... [the] variability' of different societies – that is the manners in which they could and could not be modified by contact with capitalism. It also, incidentally, provides an illuminating guide to the relations between MOPS and the societies within them and their ideologies or 'cultures'.[10] What it does not do – or, indeed, set out to do – is to explain the movements of the material base and division of labour, and hence the transformations of the MOPS.

Wolf operates with three broad MOPS or 'families' of MOPS: the 'kin-ordered' mode, the 'tributary' mode and the 'capitalist mode'. But while he allows for the change from hunting and food-collecting societies to producing societies within the kin-ordered mode, his 'tributary' mode is a vast continuum of systems which includes both what Marx called 'feudal' and what he called 'Asiatic'. In all these, surplus is essentially appropriated by ruling groups which exert political and military force. There is much to be said for this broad classification, borrowed from Samir Amin, but its drawback is that the 'tributary' mode clearly includes societies at widely differing stages of productive capacity: from Western feudal lords in the Dark Ages to the Chinese Empire; from economies without cities to urbanized ones. Only peripherally, however, does the analysis touch on the essential problem of why, how and when one variant of the tributary mode generated developed capitalism.

In short, the analysis of modes of production must be based on study of the available material forces of production: study, that is, both of technology and its organization, and of economics. For let us not forget that in the same Preface whose later passage is so often quoted, Marx argued that political economy was the anatomy of civil society. Nevertheless, in one respect the traditional analysis of MOPS and their transformation must be developed – and recent Marxist work has, in fact, done so. The actual transformation of one mode into another has often been seen in causal and unilinear terms: within each mode, it is argued, there is a 'basic contradiction' which generates the dynamic and the forces that will lead to its transformation. It is far from clear that this is Marx's own view – except for capitalism – and it certainly leads to great difficulties and endless debates, particularly in connection with the passage from Western feudalism to capitalism.

It seems more useful to make the following two assumptions. First, that the basic elements within a mode of production which tend to destabilize it imply the potentiality rather than the certainty of transformation, but that, depending on the structure of the mode, they also set certain limits to the kind of transformation that is possible. Second, that the mechanisms leading to the transformation of one mode into another may not be exclusively internal to that mode, but may arise from the conjunction and interaction of differently structured societies. In this sense all development is *mixed* development. Instead of looking only for the specific regional conditions which led to the formation of, say, the peculiar system of classical antiquity in the Mediterranean, or to the transformation of feudalism into capitalism within the manors and cities of western Europe, we ought to look at the various paths which led to the junctions and crossroads at which, at a certain stage of development, these areas found themselves.

This approach – which seems to me perfectly in the spirit of Marx, and for which, if required, some textual authority may be found – makes it easier to explain the coexistence of societies which progress further on the road to capitalism and those which, until penetrated and conquered by capitalism, failed to develop in that way. But it also draws attention to the fact, of which historians of capitalism are increasingly aware, that the evolution of this system is itself a mixed evolution: that it builds on pre-existing materials, utilizing, adapting but also being shaped by them. Recent research on the formation and development of the working classes has illustrated this point. In fact one reason why the past twenty-five years in world history have seen such profound social transformations is that such pre-capitalist elements, hitherto essential parts of the operation of capitalism, have finally become too eroded by capitalist development to play the vital role they once did. I am thinking here, of course, of the family.

Let me now return to the illustrations of Marx's unique significance for historians which I gave at the start of this talk. Marx remains the essential base of any adequate study of history, because – so far – he alone has attempted to formulate a methodological approach to history as a whole, and to envisage and explain the entire process of human social evolution. In this respect he is superior to Max Weber, his only real rival as a theoretical influence on historians, and in many respects an important supplement and corrective. A history based on Marx is conceivable without Weberian additions, but Weberian history is inconceivable except insofar as it takes Marx, or at least the Marxist *Fragestellung*, as its starting-point. To investigate the process of human social evolution means asking Marx's type of questions, if not accepting all his answers. The same is true if we wish to answer the second great question implicit in the first: that is, why this evolution has not been even and unilinear, but extra-ordinarily uneven and combined. The only alternative answers which have been suggested are in terms of biological evolution (for example sociobiology), but these are plainly inadequate. Marx did not say the last word – far from it – but he did say the first word, and we are still obliged to continue the discourse he inaugurated.

The subject of this talk is Marx and history, and it is not my function here to anticipate discussion on what the major themes are or ought to be for Marxist historians today. But I would not wish to conclude without drawing attention to two themes which seem to me to require urgent attention. The first I have already mentioned: it is the mixed and combined nature of the development of any society or social system, its interaction with other systems and with the past. It is, if you wish, the elaboration of Marx's famous dictum that men make their own history but not as they choose, 'under circumstances directly found, given and transmitted from the past'. The second is class and class struggle.

We know that both concepts are essential to Marx, at least in the discussion of the history of capitalism, but we also know that the concepts are poorly defined in his writings and have led to much debate. A great deal of traditional Marxist historiography has failed to think them out, and has therefore landed in difficulties. Let me give just one example. What is a 'bourgeois revolution'? Can we think of a 'bourgeois revolution' as being 'made' by a bourgeoisie, as being the objective of a bourgeoisie's struggle for power against an old regime or ruling class which stands in the way of the institution of a bourgeois society? Or *when* can we think of it in this way? The present critique of Marxist interpretations of the English and French revolutions has been effective, largely because it has shown that such a traditional image of the bourgeoisie and bourgeois revolution is inadequate. We should have known this. As Marxists, or indeed as realistic observers of history, we will not follow the critics in denying the existence of such revolutions, or in denying that the seventeenth-century English revolutions and the French Revolution did mark fundamental changes and 'bourgeois' reorientations of their societies. But we shall have to think more precisely about what we mean.

How, then, can we summarize Marx's impact on the writing of history a hundred years after his death? We may make four essential points.

(1) Marx's influence in non-socialist countries is undoubtedly greater among historians today than ever before in my own lifetime – and my memory goes back fifty years – and probably than ever before since his death. (The situation in countries officially committed to his ideas is obviously not comparable.) This needs to be said, because at this moment there is a fairly widespread move away from Marx among intellectuals, particularly in France and Italy. The fact is that his influence may be seen not only in the number of historians who claim to be Marxist, though this is very large, and in the number who acknowledge his significance for history (such as Braudel in France, the Bielefeld school in Germany), but also in the large number of ex-Marxist historians, often eminent, who keep Marx's name before the world (such as Postan). Furthermore, there are many elements which, fifty years ago, were stressed chiefly by Marxists and have now become parts of mainstream history. True, this has not only been due to Karl Marx, but Marxism probably has been the main influence in 'modernizing' the writing of history.

(2) As it is written and discussed today, at least in most countries, Marxist history takes Marx as its starting-point and not at its point of arrival. I do not mean that it necessarily disagrees with Marx's texts, although it is prepared to do so where these are factually wrong or obsolete. This is clearly so in the case of his views on Oriental societies and the 'Asiatic mode of production', brilliant and profound though his insights so often were, and also of his views on primitive societies and their evolution. As a recent book on Marxism and anthropology by a Marxist anthropologist has pointed out: 'Marx and Engels's knowledge of primitive societies was quite insufficient as a basis for modern anthropology.'[11] Nor do I mean that it necessarily wishes to revise or abandon the main lines of the materialist conception of history, although it is prepared to consider these critically where necessary. I, for one, do not want to abandon the materialist conception of history. But Marxist history, in its most fruitful versions, now uses his methods rather than commenting on his texts – except where these are clearly worth commenting on. We try to do what Marx himself did not as yet do.

(3) Marxist history is today plural. A single 'correct' interpretation of history is not a legacy that Marx left us: it became part of the heritage of Marxism, particularly from 1930 or thereabouts, but this is no longer accepted or acceptable, at least where people have a choice in the matter. This pluralism has its disadvantages. They are more obvious among people who theorize about history than among

169

those who write it, but they are visible even among the latter. Nevertheless, whether we think these disadvantages are greater or smaller than the advantages, the pluralism of Marxist work today is an inescapable fact. Indeed, there is nothing wrong with it. Science is a dialogue between different views based upon a common method. It only ceases to be science when there is no method for deciding which of the contending views is wrong or less fruitful. Unfortunately this is often the case in history, but by no means only in Marxist history.

(4) Marxist history today is not, and cannot be, isolated from the remainder of historical thinking and research. This is a double-sided statement. On the one hand, Marxists no longer reject – except as the source of raw material for their work – the writings of historians who do not claim to be Marxists, or indeed who are anti-Marxist. If they are good history, they have to be taken account of. This does not stop us, however, from criticizing and waging ideological battle against even good historians who act as ideologists. On the other hand, Marxism has so transformed the mainstream of history that it is today often impossible to tell whether a particular work has been written by a Marxist or a non-Marxist, unless the author advertises his or her ideological position. This is not a cause for regret. I would like to look forward to a time when nobody asks whether authors are Marxist or not, because Marxists could then be satisfied with the transformation of history achieved through Marx's ideas. But we are far from such a utopian condition: the ideological and political, class and liberation struggles of the twentieth century are such that it is even unthinkable. For the foreseeable future, we shall have to defend Marx and Marxism in and out of history, against those who attack them on political and ideological grounds. In doing so, we shall also defend history, and man's capacity to understand how the world has come to be what it is today, and how mankind can advance to a better future.

CHAPTER 12

All Peoples Have a History

This is a fuller discussion of the important study by Eric Wolf, Europe and the Peoples without History, *utilized in the preceding chapter. It was published in the* Times Literary Supplement, *28 October 1983.*

The celebrated discovery by Andersen's child that the Emperor wore no clothes implied another proposition: he should have been wearing some. But of what kind? It does not take more than a layman's common sense to observe, in the teeth of fashionable historiographical scepticism, that the social sciences and history itself need 'a history that could account for the ways in which the social system of the modern world came into being, and that would strive to make analytic sense of all societies, including our own'. It takes a considerable effort by a sophisticated intellect, great lucidity of mind, not to mention a lot of reading and courage, to sketch the ways in which such a history could be constructed, taking the entire development of the globe since about 1400 as an illustration. Eric Wolf's new book sets out to do no less.

Wolf is unusually well qualified for the task. Unlike most Anglo-American anthropologists, he is known not so much for 'his' tribe or region, as for his subject: people in agriculture. His title book on *Peasants* (1966) is much the finest introduction there is to the subject, and he is known to a wider public for a study of the peasant element in the revolutions of our time, *Peasant Wars of the Twentieth Century*. He has published not only on his own area of Spanish Central America, on estates, plantations and peasants, but on the origins of Islam and the formation of nations. He is the co-author of *The Hidden Frontier* (1974) a superb historico-anthropological study of two neighbouring but ethnically different Tyrolean communities, which is essential reading for students of modern nationality. Not surprisingly, he has long been associated with the first modern interdisciplinary journal of its kind, *Comparative Studies in Society and History*.

The anthropological tradition against which Wolf rebels is that which treats human societies (that is, in practice the micro-populations which have been the subject of field-work and monographs) as self-contained, self-reproducing and ideally self-stabilizing systems. But, he argues, no tribe or community is or has ever been an island, and the world, a totality of interconnected processes or system, is not and never has been a sum of self-contained human groups and cultures. What appears as unchanging and self-replicating is not only the result of coping with the constant, complex process of internal and external tensions, but is often the product of historical change. What happened to the Amazonian Mundurucú, who changed from patrilocality and patriliny to the unusual combination of matrilocality and patrilineal reckoning, under the impact of the Brazilian rubber boom, had probably happened to many a 'tribe' encountered by nineteenth-century ethnographers and regarded as a 'primitive' pre-historic or a-historic survival, like some collective human coelacanth. There are no people without history or who can be understood without it. Their history, like ours, is incomprehensible outside its setting in a wider world (which has become coterminous with the inhabited globe) and, certainly, in the past half-millennium it cannot be understood except through the intersections of different types of social organization, each modified by interaction with the others.

This approach has the advantage for historians concerned to present history in global terms that it gives them a genuine jus-tification for their endeavours, which are usually undertaken on no better grounds than those which lead shops to describe their goods in Arabic or Japanese, or which reflect the image of contemporary politics (those of the doubly misdescribed 'United Nations') and the contemporary, and evidently global, economy. It also reduces arguments for or against Eurocentrism to irrelevancy. That the forces which transformed the world since the fifteenth century were geographically European, is patent. How much space should be occupied in a textbook of modern world history by this or that non-European region is a relatively trivial question, except in the classrooms of the states of those regions, or for their cultural diplo-mats. The point is that history consists of the interaction of variously structured (and geographically distributed) social entities, which mutually reshape each other. Europe and non-Europe can no more be separated than Ibn Khaldun's Beduin and sedentaries: each is the other's history.

In fact, Wolf argues, the geographical form of interaction is merely a special aspect of a more general pattern. The history of the working classes in industrial society poses exactly the same problems as that of the impact of capitalism on notionally traditional societies 'supposedly arrested on some timeless plateau of evolution'. 'In fact, the two branches of history are but one.' Or, in even more general terms, whether a society exports or imports capitalism, belongs to 'core' or 'periphery', it has developed and evolves out of a plurality of social orderings. In this sense macrocosm and microcosm in history are one.

How is this intermingling of orders to be analysed? The major merit of Wolf's book does not lie in his ability critically to synthesize the literature about the world since 1400, registered in forty-five pages of bibliography. Others can do as much, at the inevitable risk of exposure to the flanking fire of specialist snipers. It lies in the attempt to provide a way of grasping the 'strategic features of ... [the] variability' in the 'different social systems and cultural understandings' which European capitalism encountered in its expansion and consequently 'the central processes at work in the interaction of Europeans with the majority of the world's population.'

The test of a book such as this is therefore not whether we accept its actual reading of the historical record, or the authorities whose findings Wolf accepts, modifies or reinterprets. It would not be significantly less interesting if, say, the notion of 'long waves' of capitalist development which he accepts proved untenable, or if it turns out that his sources on the Mundurucú are mistaken. The question is rather whether his analytical approach is superior to others.

This is inevitably a question about a Marxian approach to history, since Wolf clearly gives a central place to two basically Marxian concepts: production as 'the complex of mutually dependent relations among nature, social labor and social organization' and culture, or systems of ideas, seen as occurring 'within the determinate compass of a mode of production deployed to render nature amenable to human use'. 'Mind' for him does not 'follow an independent course of its own'. For the purposes of his book the long-term evolution of humanity, or the possible sequence of social formations, are irrelevant and remain undiscussed, except for remarks incidental to his argument. He is not concerned with the famous 'contradiction' between the developing material productive forces of society and the existing productive relationships, except insofar as structural tensions of this kind within any of the 'modes of production' and those arising out of the interaction between various modes, may or may not bear on his problem. Marxian ideas are here employed primarily to explain the 'global interactions of human aggregates' in the past half-millenium, though they are evidently intended also to explain them for any other period.

Wolf's particular positions in the lively international Marxist debates about theory and history will not be of major concern to non-specialists, any more than his specific disagreements with various schools of anthropologists. The lengthy bibliographical notes, in which he discusses his sources and obligations, throw some light on these matters. One might merely note that his main interest lies not in causal connections but in variability and combination. Hence the central importance for his analysis of various 'modes of production', that is, of the 'social mobilization, deployment and allocation of labor'. For their value is precisely that the mode of production 'used comparatively ... calls attention to major variations in political-economic arrangements and allows us to visualize their effects' as well as to understand the 'variable and shifting supports' of the development of global capitalism, which 'were often embedded in different modes of production'.

Three broad 'modes' of this kind are directly relevant to his purpose, which, very sensibly, shows no interest in exhaustive classification and – one might add – is incompatible with evolutionary unilinearity: a 'capitalist mode', a 'tributary mode' and a 'kin-ordered mode'. None are identical with the notion of a 'society', for this belongs to a different level of abstraction and has a different explanatory scope. One may add that Wolf holds that each mode tends to generate its own types of 'culture' or symbolic universes which, in their various versions, generalize the 'essential distinctions among human beings' that each mode entails.

His analytical model of the 'capitalist mode' is more or less classically Marxian. The 'tributary mode' is a continuum of systems in which tribute is extracted from producers by political and military means, ranging from systems of highly concentrated to those of extremely diffused power, and varying in the ways in which tribute is collected, circulated and distributed. The 'feudalism' and 'Asiatic mode of production' of classic Marxist debate are regarded as among the possible variants of a mode in which surpluses are essentially extracted non-economically. The larger fields constituted by the political and commercial interaction of tributary societies, Wolf holds, have their counterpart in 'civilizations' or zones of ideology with a prevalent model of the cosmic order, which tends to pivot on a hegemonic tributary society central to each zone.

The historical dynamics of such societies were, at least in the old world, closely bound up with the ebb and flow of pastoral-nomadic populations – acutely analysed – but also 'with the widening and narrowing of surplus transfer through overland trade'. For, with rather rare exceptions (for example where all the surplus is consumed *in situ* or, as perhaps among the Inca, where commerce is virtually absent), the distribution of the surplus normally depends partly on buying and selling, and special groups engaged in these activities. This and the mercantile activity integral to the tributary mode requires control, if the commercialization of the goods and services on which tributary power rests is not to risk 'reshuffling social priorities' away from political or military rulers. In certain circumstances, as within medieval Europe and later, when Western merchants, backed by independent power, impinged on non-European societies, such control becomes difficult. Yet, against Weber and 'world-market' Marxists like Frank and Wallerstein, Wolf insists on the basic symbiosis of trade and precapitalist modes. Capitalism becomes dominant only with industrialization. So long as production was dominated by tribute or kin, mercantile activity does not automatically lead to capitalism, though it might tend in this direction by making direct producers dependent on the market, as in 'proto-industry' or, indirectly, by extending slavery. In Wolf's view, 'slave labor has never constituted a major independent mode of production, but it has played a subsidiary role in providing labor under all modes', notably, for capitalism, during its expansion overseas.

Kinship, in the 'kin-ordered mode', is seen neither as essentially a device for the social regulation of biological descent, nor as a system of symbolical constructs (though it is obviously both also), but as a way of ordering social labour and access to it. The ways of establishing such rights and claims vary widely, but are clearly simpler where resources are widely distributed and available to any able-bodied person (as in food-collecting 'bands') than where they are restricted, as is the case when nature is transformed by plant or animal cultivation.

This second situation implies not only a rather more complex social division of labour, but 'a transgenerational corpus of claims and counterclaims to social labor' through real or fictitious pedigrees, and the elements of an unequal politico-social order which threatens to burst the bounds of kinship. It can be contained so long as there is no other mechanism, for aggregating or mobilizing labour apart from the particular relations set up by kinship, that is, so long as alliances and oppositions are not between *classes* of people and the potential rulers cannot call upon outside resources. It would seem that the kin-ordered mode turns into class society, and with it into societies possessing states, either by the transformation of 'chiefly' lineages into a ruling class, especially when such aristocracies 'bud off to conquer and rule foreign populations', or when kin-ordered groups enter into relations with tributary or capitalist societies, which may offer chiefs external resources and hence 'a possible following outside of kinship and unencumbered by it'. Hence, Wolf argues, the notorious readiness of chiefs to collaborate with European slave-hunters and fur-traders.

Neither 'Europe' nor the 'people without history' in their various versions of pre-capitalist modes would have developed in quite the way each did without the others. Yet if the relationship is two-sided, it is also plainly asymmetrical. Wolf has little except nuances to add to the large literature on European expansion and its significance for the development of capitalism. What will be unfamiliar to most readers, especially those brought up on conventional history, is his treatment of the non-European societies and their adaptation under the impact of capitalist penetration. The initial survey of the world in 1400 can be strongly recommended. It is not only an excellent introduction for the layman – not least for its sense of human geography – but an illuminating and critical analysis, not without original interpretations especially on India, of the strength and weakness of pastoral nomad societies, Indian caste structure, East and South-east Asia, as well as, at understandably greater length, pre-Columbian America.

Much of what Wolf says about the transformation of society under the impact of European trade and conquest will be new to anyone who has not followed the striking recent advances in ethno-history and the history of Africa and Indo-America. Virtually all of it is exciting. The sheer historical novelty of apparently 'primitive' cultural configurations such as those of the Plains Indians (adopted 'in the course of a few brief years' by pedestrian hunter-gatherers and pastoralists making use of the Euro-imported horse and gun); the effect of the European fur trade on the economy, politics and culture of Huron, Iroquois and Cree; and the different effects of the Russian fur trade in Asia and America: these will open quite novel perspectives for most of us. Wolf's own expertise on Latin America naturally stands him in good stead. His anthropological colleagues will no doubt soon show whether they accept his 'historisations' of some of the peoples who were the subject of several of the more celebrated monographs in the literature of their subject.

The major strength of Wolf's book – his concentration on inter-action, intermingling and mutual modification – is at the same time its major weakness, since it tends to take for granted the nature of the dynamism which has brought the world from pre-history to the late twentieth century. This is a book about connections rather than causes. Or rather, the author has re-thought the problems of the genesis and development of capitalism less fundamentally than those of the interconnections essential to it. No doubt this is a task more suited to historians than anthropologists. His account of capitalist development is a useful contribution to a debate, not by any means confined to Marxists, which has recently regained much vigour, and is valuable chiefly for clearly pointing to questions which are usually unrecognized, such as why the work-force of capitalism should have developed as 'free labour' and not in some other form. Wolf's most interesting contribution to the debate lies closest to his major concern. It is his insistence on the continuous 'processes by which new working classes are simultaneously created and segmented', as the labour force is recruited 'from a wide variety of social and cultural backgrounds and [inserted] ... into variable political and economic hierarchies'. Today, 'within an ever more integrated world, we witness the growth of ever more diverse proletarian diasporas'. This, the final sentence of a very impressive book, forms a characteristically suggestive and open-ended conclusion to it.

Europe and the People without History is the work of a powerful theoretical intelligence, but one informed by a lived sense of social realities. Behind Wolf's analysis, subdued in style but expressed with a notable gift for concise and lucid exposition, there lies a personal and intellectual trajectory which has taken the author from Vienna and the North Bohemian working-class communities devastated by the Great Slump, to the United States and the plantations and peasants of the third world. Like all good anthropologists he is a 'participant observer' – in this case of the world history which is his subject. This book could only have been written by a 'son of the shaking earth', to quote the title of one of Wolf's own works. It is an important book, which will be widely discussed. The centenary year of Marx's death is not over yet, but it may be doubted whether a more original work exemplifying the living influence of that great thinker will have been published in the course of it.

CHAPTER 13

British History and the
Annales: A Note

In 1978 Immanuel Wallerstein founded a 'Fernand Braudel Center' at the State University of New York at Binghamton and, on the occasion of Braudel's own visit to the university, organized a colloquium on the influence of this great historian and the journal Annales: Economies, Sociétés, Civilisations, *which he inherited from its founders, Marc Bloch and Lucien Febvre. My comments on the influence of French history in Britain are reprinted from* Review 1 *(Winter–Spring 1978), pp. 157–62. They provide a bridge between the preceding and the following chapters.*

I want to add a footnote or two on the reception of *Annales* in Britain.

The first observation I would like to make is that what has been influential in England, insofar as we can talk of influence, is not so much *Annales* specifically as what might be called the French *nouvelle vague* in history. *Annales* is a part of this and, of course, increasingly a very important part, thanks to the triple significance of Fernand Braudel. First, he was influential as the author of a great book which – and here I think I disagree with Peter Burke – was read with great excitement by many of us, almost from the time it appeared, and has been influential in ways which are not very easy to define. Secondly, from a certain period on, he made his mark on us as director of *Annales* itself. And thirdly, and perhaps most importantly, he is the man who built the VIe *Section* of the Ecole Pratique, which is now the School of Higher Studies in the Social Sciences, into the main powerhouse and centre of the French social sciences during the period of a generation. In doing so, he gradually integrated most of what I have just called the *nouvelle vague* in French history, and associated it with, brought it into the ambit of, *Annales* and this group.

I don't say this simply in order to express – which I would like to do in passing – my personal appreciation of Fernand Braudel, and my appreciation of long years of friendship with him, but as an explanation of why we are talking of the impact of the *Annales*, whereas in fact we are dealing with the impact of a wider phenomenon in French history. For instance, we have heard that, in Poland, Labrousse and Braudel and people like that were mentioned in the same breath. In the eyes of the Poles, there was not any very clear distinction between them. This is also true on the whole in England. In some ways, it was Labrousse as much as Marc Bloch and more than Lucien Febvre; it was Georges Lefebvre as much as Braudel. They were all regarded by us as part of a French school which we admired, and which many of us in England thought of as the most interesting thing in historiography. But of course increasingly this historiography became concentrated in, focused on, *Annales*.

That's one point. There is a second. I think Peter Burke slightly exaggerates the lateness of the reception of *Annales* and the main French historians in Britain. I think some of us, at least at Cambridge, were told to read *Annales* as early as the 1930s. What is more, when Marc Bloch came and talked to us in Cambridge – I can still remember this as the great moment it then seemed and was – he was presented to us as the greatest living medievalist, quite rightly I think. Perhaps this was due specifically to a local phenomenon, the existence in Cambridge of Michael Postan, who then held the chair of economic history, a man of unusually cosmopolitan sympathies and wide knowledge. But it was also due to another phenomenon which has been mentioned by people at this conference before, namely the curious confluence, via economic history, of Marxism and the French school. It was on the ground of economic and social history, which was of course the banner heading of the original *Annales*, that we met. The young Marxists in those days found that the only part of official history that made any kind of sense to them, or at least that they could use, was economic history, or economic and social history. It was therefore through this that the junction was made.

May I further add that it is through economic history, or economic and social history, that the influence, the direct influence and relationship of the *Annales* group and British history, has been chiefly conducted, until the generation of Peter Burke. In some ways the organization of economic history in the world, through the organization of the International Economic History Congresses and Association, was for long an Anglo-French condominium, and the French were represented in it very largely by precisely the people with whom the English economic historians of any kind found it easiest to collaborate, that is Fernand Braudel and his colleagues, disciples, and pupils.

I mention this in passing, but I would also like to mention another thing briefly in passing, the curious fact also referred to by earlier speakers, that there had been a relationship between *Annales* and the Marxists. As Peter Burke says, in general the Marxists thought of themselves as fighting on the same side as *Annales*, even though there were times, for instance in France in the 1950s, when those of us outside France were being criticized by our comrades in the more sectarian parts of the French Communist Party for collaborating with reactionaries. Curiously enough, however, this was never a major feeling in Britain. And this is strange because, historically speaking, Marxists have been more likely to separate themselves from non-Marxist schools, and to point out how they were different from these and why the others were wrong, than to find themselves converging with them or at any rate working parallel with them. And yet, as K. Pomian mentioned and as Peter Burke confirmed, and people like Rodney Hilton and myself and others can also confirm, the relationship between the Marxist left in various countries and the *Annales* has been, for reasons which are perhaps worth investigating, a great deal more friendly and co-operative. It is for this reason perhaps that, when we founded *Past and Present*, we certainly in our first number referred to *Annales*; not that I think in other respects we were notably influenced by *Annales*. We were trying a different kind of exercise, and yet we greatly respected and wished to show our respect for this great predecessor in what you might call 'opposition history', anti-establishment history. Of course, by the time we were founded they were no longer anti-establishment; they had conquered. But that is another matter.

Yet there is I think a more concrete reason why *Annales* and its group exercised some quite significant influence or at least stimulation in Britain, perhaps more so than Peter Burke is prepared to acknowledge. In the years after the war, the French seem to me to have been the one country in which there was a consistent, systematic effort to explore what we now know – Wallerstein will be the first to agree – to be a crucial period in the development of the modern world, namely the economy of the sixteenth and seventeenth centuries. Of course, Braudel's great book is not merely a monument to his concern; he also, in a sense, dramatized it. But he was not the only one. There were a large number of other people in France who were also concerned with it – I am thinking of things like Pierre Vilar's famous article at the time, 'Le Temps de Quichotte', which in a different way was also concerned with the similar problem of the sixteenth century, the crisis, the change to the seventeenth century. And there is no doubt that it was in and through *Annales* that this concentration of French historical (if you prefer, intellectual) energies, this historical phase, found its most significant and concentrated expression. This was due no doubt to the sixteenth-century interests both of Febvre and of Braudel.

This was a comparatively new thing. The original *Annales* in the 1930s did not have this particular interest at the centre of their preoccupations. And the reason why it emerged is perhaps worth investigation. I know why it emerged among the Marxists. It clearly emerged in the very early fifties in the course of discussions about Maurice Dobb's *Studies in the Development of Capitalism*. The famous Sweezy–Dobb debate was essentially about the question exactly where we stood between the fifteenth and eighteenth centuries, what the significance of this period was in the development of the modern-world economy. And many of us found ourselves, while exploring this difficult problem, drawn naturally towards people in France who had, from a different point of view – and I hope Fernand Braudel will forgive me if I underline the fact that he is not a Marxist – begun to be concerned with it. I found myself personally drawn briefly into an excursion from my own century into the seventeenth-century crisis, and looking back at my articles I find an enormous number of references to *Annales*, to articles in *Annales*, to people from *Annales*, to Braudel, to Meuvret, to people of this kind. Where else at that time would one have got the references? And indeed, when the matter was discussed at the time, I remember Hugh Trevor-Roper saying this isn't new at all. The French have been doing this all the time.

Well, he was right. The French had been doing it all the time and the mention of Trevor-Roper shows that concern about this problem was not confined simply to one school of British historians but affected several. Why? Here again it seems to me, looking back, we can see that the sixteenth–seventeenth centuries are a crucial period in the development of the modern world, but why at this stage we developed this concentration on the period remains a subject of some obscurity. Certainly, in the early years of *Past and Present*, we found that of the articles that were submitted to us by far the greater number dealt with the sixteenth and seventeenth centuries. It was, so to speak, a hot issue at that time. And I think it is through preoccupation with this problem, which in the obscure way in which scholarly disciplines and sciences operate, had moved into the centre of concern, at least among people who had economic and social long-term interests, that a certain junction between Marxism and *Annales* was made.

So much for excursions back into history and memory about the reception of *Annales* in Britain. Let me now say a few words about what *Annales* is doing now, about what it is or rather ought to be doing. It is not our business to tell *Annales* what they ought to do. I don't really want to say very much about the present crisis in *Annales*. I think it is not too much to call it one. Revel mentioned it in one form, Peter Burke mentioned it when he talked about *Annales* speaking not one language but several languages, between which there is not always complete mutual intelligibility. At all events, it seems to me that this great journal is at the moment going through a mid-life crisis, but the exact nature of this crisis is something which can perhaps be discussed elsewhere.

Rather, I want to say something in connection with Peter Burke's very interesting, and I think very useful, references to the problem of the history of mentalities. It doesn't really matter what you call the subject. We call it the history of mentalities once again to show our debt to the French who have been systematically preoccupied with it, though I do not believe this means that French historians have practised it more than other historians. Certainly, in spite of the enormous value of the contributions from people associated with *Annales*, I don't believe that in England people practising the history of 'mentalities' have owed very much directly to the *Annales*, except in the field of the Middle Ages, where it seems to me Bloch is clearly fundamental. I would say, for instance, that even some of the people in France who are most successful, at least for the more recent period, in this field do not belong to the *Annales* group, though gradually they have drawn closer to *Annales*. Vovelle is a man who is clearly now, so to speak, integrated, but who did not begin in or near *Annales* at all. And neither did Agulhon, whose name I think should be mentioned. This is as it should be. I think one of the great strengths of the *Annales* school is precisely that it has been big enough to receive anybody who makes such original contributions. Certainly in England, Georges Lefebvre's *La Grande Peur* was disproportionately significant in attracting the attention of those of us who practised the history of the common people, grassroots history, to the problem of mentalities.

But in addition to these foreign influences, there have been important local or, if you like, international ones. There has been Marx and

Marxism, including Gramsci. First, it has underlined the absolutely essential connection between the world of ideas and feelings and the economic base, if you like, the way in which people get their living in production. Secondly, after all the Marxist model of base and superstructure, whatever you may think of it, implies a consideration of superstructure as well as a base, that is, the importance of ideas. It is not widely recognized that in the discussion of the seventeenth-century English Revolution it was Marxists like Christopher Hill who constantly insisted against pure economic determinists on the importance of Puritanism, as something that people believed in, and not simply a kind of froth on the top of class structures or economic movements.

Again, Marxism has insisted on the point that Peter Burke has made, namely the crucial importance of class structure, of authority, of the varied interests of rulers and ruled and the relations between them in the field of ideas as well. In addition to this Marxist element, I think there is the double influence to which Peter Burke has referred. First, we have a home-grown tradition of the study of culture in a quasi-anthropological sense, as represented by people like Raymond Williams or even Edward Thompson, in their writings on nineteenth-century culture, both high and medium. They have generalized this into a history of mentalities. But, more specifically, there is the importance of social anthropology. Peter Burke mentioned this. In Britain, social anthropology has been the crucial discipline in the social sciences, at least the only one which some historians, myself included, have found consistently interesting, and from which we have consistently been able to draw benefit. Not just Evans-Pritchard, but all sorts of people, Max Gluckman and his group, all sorts of social anthropologists, who have in a sense taught us or stimulated us, even though I think very few historians have taken over the social anthropological models wholesale. Indeed we have often criticized them, and still do, for their lack of understanding of historical evolution. Nevertheless, the concept of a society and its interactions, including its mental interactions, is one we have found enormously stimulating.

And this brings me to my final point. Perhaps it is because of this, shall we say, social anthropological bias (in the British sense) that I myself feel that the future of the studies of mentality is different from the ones that have been practised by at least some of our French colleagues. It isn't simply the study of the otherness of the mentality which Peter Burke mentioned. You don't have to be a believer in the

Lévy–Bruhl duality to think that people in the sixteenth century really did apparently think quite differently. This discovery of otherness is important. It is important to see, for instance, how different the sense of time was in the pre-industrial period as Edward Thompson and others have tried to show, to discover how different the sense of history was, as Moses Finley has tried to point out in analysing the classics. This is very important, and until we have discovered this we can't really do very much with the past.

Much less useful, I think however, is the search for deep structures and particularly the search for *la conscience*. I may be entirely heterodox, but I don't think historians have an awful lot to learn from Freud, who was a bad historian, whenever he actually wrote anything about history. I have no opinions about Freud's psychology, but I regard the belated discovery of Freud in France some forty years after the rest of the world as by no means an unqualified plus. It seems to me it is a minus, insofar as it diverts attention into the unconscious or deep structures from, I won't say conscious, but anyway logical cohesion. It neglects system. It seems to me the problem of mentalities is not simply that of discovering that people are different, and how they are different, and making readers *feel* the difference, as Richard Cobb does so well. It is to find a logical connection between various forms of behaviour, of thinking and feeling, to see them as being mutually consistent. It is, if you like, to see why it makes sense, let us say, for people to believe about famous robbers that they are invisible and invulnerable, even though they obviously are not. We must see such beliefs not purely as an emotional reaction but as part of a coherent system of beliefs about society, about the role of those who believe, and the role of those about whom the beliefs are held. Take, for instance, the question of peasants. Why do peasants demand land, why do peasants demand only land to which they believe they have certain types of legal or moral claims? What is the nature of these claims? Why do they not listen to people who ask them to demand land on other grounds, such as, for instance, the grounds put forward by modern political radicals? Why is it that they simultaneously appear to hold arguments for land or for justice which appear to us to be incompatible? It is not because they are stupid. It is not because they don't know any better. There ought to be some cohesion.

I think the programme, for the history of mentalities, is not so much discovery as analysis. What I would like to do is not simply, like Edward Thompson, to save the stockinger and the peasant, but also the nobleman and the king of the past, from the condescension of modern historians who think they know better, who think they know what is logical and theoretical argument. What I would like to do and what I think we ought to do is to see mentality as a problem not of historical empathy or archaeology or, if you like, of social psychology, but of the discovery of the internal logical cohesion of systems of thought and behaviour which fit in with the way in which people live in society in their particular class and in their particular situation of the class struggle, against those above or, if you like, below them. I would like to restore to men of the past, and especially the poor of the past, the gift of theory. Like the hero of Molière, they have been talking prose all the time. Only whereas the man in Molière didn't know it himself, I think they have always known it, but we have not. And I think we ought to.

CHAPTER 14

On the Revival of Narrative

This paper was a critical contribution to a debate launched, like many others in history, by Lawrence Stone, my long-time colleague on the board of the review Past and Present, *on the revival of narrative history. It was published in no. 86 of that journal (February 1980), pp. 2–8.*

Lawrence Stone believes that there is a revival of 'narrative history' because there has been a decline in the history devoted to asking 'the big *why* questions', the generalizing 'scientific history'. This in turn he thinks is due to disillusionment with the essentially economic determinist models of historical explanation, Marxist or otherwise, which have tended to dominate in the post-war years; to the declining ideological commitment of Western intellectuals; contemporary experience which has reminded us that political action and decision can shape history; and the failure of 'quantitative history' (another claimant to 'scientific' status) to deliver the goods.[1] Two questions are involved in this argument, which I have brutally oversimplified: what has been happening in historiography, and how are these developments to be explained? Since it is common ground that in history the 'facts' are always selected, shaped and perhaps distorted by the historian who observes them, there is an element of *parti pris*, not to say intellectual autobiography, in Stone's treatment of both questions, as there is in my comments on it.

I think we may accept that the twenty years following the Second World War saw a sharp decline in political and religious history, in the use of 'ideas' as an explanation of history, and a remarkable turn to socio-economic history and to historical explanation in terms of 'social forces', as Momigliano noted as early as 1954.[2] Whether or not we call them 'economic-determinist', these currents of historiography became influential, in some cases dominant, in the main Western centres of historiography, not to mention, for other reasons, the Eastern ones. We may also accept that in recent years there has been considerable diversification, and a marked revival of interest in themes which were rather more marginal to the main concerns of the historical outsiders who in those years became historical insiders, though such themes were never neglected. After all, Braudel wrote about Philip II as well as the Mediterranean, and Le Roy Ladurie's monograph on *Le Carnaval de Romans* of 1580 is anticipated by a much briefer, but most perceptive, account of the same episode in his *Les Paysans du Languedoc*.[3] If Marxist historians of the 1970s write entire books on the role of radical–national myths, such as the Welsh Madoc legend, Christopher Hill at least wrote a seminal article on the myth of the Norman Yoke in the early 1950s.[4] Still, there probably has been a change.

Whether this amounts to a revival of 'narrative history' as defined by Stone (basically chronological ordering of the material in 'a single coherent story, albeit with sub-plots' and a concentration 'on man not circumstances') is difficult to determine, since Stone deliberately eschews a quantitative survey and concentrates on 'a very tiny, but disproportionately prominent, section of the historical profession as a whole'.[5] Nevertheless there is evidence that the old historical avant-garde no longer rejects, despises and combats the old-fashioned 'history of events' or even biographical history, as some of it used to. Fernand Braudel himself has given unstinted praise to a notably traditional exercise in popular narrative history, Claude Manceron's attempt to present the origins of the French Revolution through a series of overlapping biographies of contemporaries, great and small.[6] On the other hand the historical minority whose supposedly changed interests Stone surveys has not in fact changed over to practising narrative history. If we leave aside deliberate historiographical conservatives or neo-conservatives such as the British 'antiquarian empiricists', there is very little simple narrative history among the works Stone cites or refers to. For almost all of them the event, the individual, even the recapture of some mood or way of thinking of the past, are not ends in themselves, but the means of illuminating some wider question, which goes far beyond the particular story and its characters.

In short those historians who continue to believe in the possibility of generalizing about human societies and their development continue to be interested in 'the big *why* questions', though they may sometimes focus on different ones from those on which they concentrated twenty or thirty years ago. There is really no evidence that such historians – the ones Stone is mainly concerned with – have abandoned 'the attempt to produce a coherent ... explanation of change in the past'.[7] Whether they (or we) also regard their attempt as 'scientific' will no doubt depend on our definition of 'science', but we need not enter this dispute about labels. Moreover I very much doubt whether such historians feel that they are 'forced back upon the principle of indeterminacy',[8] any more than Marx felt his writings about Louis Napoleon to be incompatible with the materialist conception of history.

No doubt there are historians who have abandoned such attempts, and certainly there are some who combat them, perhaps with a zeal increased by ideological commitment. (Whether or not Marxism has declined intellectually, it is hard to detect much muting of ideological controversy among Western historians, though the participants and the specific issues may not be the same as twenty years ago.) Probably neo-conservative history has gained ground, at any rate in Britain, both in the form of the 'young antiquarian empiricists' who 'write detailed political narratives which implicitly deny that there is any deep-seated meaning to history except the accidental whims of fortune and personality',[9] and in the form of works like Theodore Zeldin's (and Richard Cobb's) remarkable plunges into those strata of the past, to which 'almost every aspect of traditional history' is irrelevant, including the answering of questions.[10] So, probably, has what might be called anti-intellectual leftist history. But this, except very tangentially, is not what Stone is concerned with.

How then are we to account for the shifts in historical subject-matter and interests, insofar as they have occurred or are occurring?

One element in them, it may be suggested, reflects the remarkable widening of the field of history in the past twenty years, typified by the rise of 'social history', that shapeless container for everything from changes in human physique to symbol and ritual, and above all for the lives of *all* people from beggars to emperors. As Braudel has observed, this 'histoire obscure de tout le monde' is 'the history towards which, in different ways, all historiography tends at present'.[11] This is not the place to speculate on the reasons for this vast extension of the field, which certainly does not necessarily conflict with the attempt to produce a coherent explanation of the past. It does, however, increase the technical difficulty of writing history. How are these complexities to be presented? It is not surprising that historians experiment with different forms of such presentation, including notably those that borrow from the ancient techniques of literature (which has made its own stabs at displaying *la comédie humaine*), and also from the modern audiovisual media, in which all but the oldest of us are saturated. What Stone calls the *pointilliste* techniques are, at least in part, attempts to solve such technical problems of presentation.

Such experiments are particularly necessary for that part of history which cannot be subsumed under 'analysis' (or the rejection of analysis) and which Stone rather neglects, namely synthesis. The problem of fitting together the various manifestations of human thought and action at a specific period is neither new nor unrecognized. No history of Jacobean England is satisfactory which omits Bacon or treats him exclusively as a lawyer, a politician, or a figure in the history of science or of literature. Moreover even the most conventional historians recognize it, even when their solutions (a chapter or two on science, literature, education or whatnot appended to the main body of politico-institutional text) are unsatisfactory. Yet the wider the range of human activities which is accepted as the legitimate concern of the historian, the more clearly understood the necessity of establishing systematic connections between them, the greater the difficulty of achieving a synthesis. This is, naturally, far more than a technical problem of presentation, yet it is that also. Even those who continue to be guided in their analysis by something like the 'three-tiered hierarchical' model of base and superstructures, which Stone rejects,[12] may find it an inadequate guide to presentation, though probably a less inadequate guide than straight chronological narrative.

Leaving aside the problems of presentation and synthesis, two more substantial reasons for a change may also be suggested. The first is the very success of the 'new historians' in the post-war decades. This was achieved by a deliberate methodological simplification, the concentration on what were seen as the socio-economic base and determinants of history, at the expense of – sometimes, as in the French battle against the 'history of events', in direct confrontation with – traditional narrative history. While there were some extreme economic reductionists, and others who dismissed people and events as negligible ripples on the *longue durée* of *structure* and *conjoncture*, such extremism was not universally shared either in *Annales* or among the Marxists who – especially in Britain – never lost interest in events or culture, nor regarded 'superstructure' as always and entirely dependent on 'base'. Yet the very triumph of works like those of Braudel, Goubert and Le Roy Ladurie, which Stone underlines, not only left 'new' historians free to concentrate on those aspects of history hitherto deliberately set aside, but advanced their place on the 'new historians' agenda. As an eminent *Annalist*, Le Goff, pointed out several years ago, 'political history was gradually to return in force by borrowing the methods, spirit and theoretical approach of the very social sciences which had pushed it into the background'.[13] The new history of men and minds, ideas and events may be seen as complementing rather than as supplanting the analysis of socio-economic structures and trends.

But once historians turn to such items on their agenda, they may prefer to approach their 'coherent explanation of change in the past' as it were ecologically rather than as geologists. They may prefer to start with the study of a 'situation' which embodies and exemplifies the stratified structure of a society but concentrates the mind on the complexities and interconnections of real history, rather than with the study of the structure itself, especially if for this they can rely partly on earlier work. This, as Stone recognizes, lies at the root of some historians' admiration for works like Clifford Geertz's 'close reading' of a Balinese cock-fight.[14] It implies no necessary choice between monocausality and multicausality, and certainly no conflict between a model in which some historical determinants are seen as more powerful than others, and the recognition of interconnections, both vertical and horizontal. A 'situation' may be a convenient point of departure, as in Ginzburg's study of popular ideology through the case of a single village atheist in the sixteenth century or a single group of Friulian peasants accused of witchcraft.[15] These topics could also be approached in other ways. It may be a necessary point of departure in other cases, as in Agulhon's beautiful study of how, at a particular time and place, French villagers converted from Catholic traditionalism to militant republicanism.[16] At all events, for certain purposes historians are likely to choose it as a starting-point.

There is thus no necessary contradiction between Le Roy Ladurie's *Les Paysans du Languedoc* and his *Montaillou*, any more than between Duby's general works on feudal society and his monograph on the battle of Bouvines, or between E. P. Thompson's *The Making of the English Working Class* and his *Whigs and Hunters*.[17] There is nothing new in choosing to see the world via a microscope rather than a telescope. So long as we accept that we are studying the same cosmos, the choice between microcosm and macrocosm is a matter of selecting the appropriate technique. It is significant that more historians find the microscope useful at present, but this does not necessarily mean that they reject telescopes as out of date. Even the historians of *mentalité*, that vague catch-all term which Stone, perhaps wisely, does not try to clarify, do not exclusively or predominantly avoid the broad view. This at least is a lesson they have learned from the anthropologists.

Do these observations account for Stone's 'broad cluster of changes in the nature of historical discourse'?[18] Perhaps not. However, they demonstrate that it is possible to explain much of what he surveys as the continuation of past historical enterprises by other means, instead of as proofs of their bankruptcy. One would not wish to deny that some historians regard them as bankrupt or undesirable and wish to change their discourse in consequence, for various reasons, some of them intellectually dubious, some to be taken seriously. Clearly some historians have shifted from 'circumstances' to 'men' (including women), or have discovered that a simple base-super-structure model and economic history are not enough, or – since the pay-off from such approaches has been very substantial – are no longer enough. Some may well have convinced themselves that there is an incompatibility between their 'scientific' and 'literary' functions. But it is not necessary to analyse the present fashions in history entirely as a rejection of the past, and insofar as they cannot be entirely analysed in such terms, it will not do.

We are all anxious to discover where historians are going. Stone's essay is to be welcomed as an attempt to do so. Nevertheless it is not satisfactory. In spite of his disclaimer the essay does combine the charting of 'observed changes in historical fashion' with 'value judgements about what are good, and what are less good, modes of historical writing',[19] especially about the latter. I think this is a pity, not because I happen to disagree with him about 'the principle of indeterminacy' and historical generalization, but because, if the argument is wrong, a diagnosis of the 'changes in historical discourse' made in terms of this argument must also be inadequate. One is tempted, like the mythical Irishman, asked by the traveller for the way to Ballynahinch, to stop, ponder and reply: 'If I were you, I wouldn't start from here at all.'

CHAPTER 15

Postmodernism in the Forest

In this chapter I have used the fascinating and important research of Richard Price into the Saramaka of Suriname to enquire into the historical utility of some of the currently fashionable 'postmodernist' approaches. This review of Price's Alabi's World *was published in the* New York Review of Books, *6 December 1990, pp. 46–8, under the title 'Escaped Slaves of the Forest'.*

Shortly after settling in the conquered New World, Spaniards began to use the word *cimarrón*, of debated etymology, to describe imported European domestic animals that had escaped from control and reverted to natural freedom. For obvious reasons the term was also applied in slave societies to escaped slaves living in freedom outside the world of the masters. It was translated into other masters' languages as *marrons* or *maroons*. That the same word should also be applied by the Caribbean buccaneers to sailors expelled from their community and forced to live the life of nature marooned on some island suggests that freedom was not seen as a bed of roses.

Maroon life, whether in the form of (most temporary) individual fugitives (*petit marronage*) or larger communities of escaped slaves (*grand marronage*), inevitably accompanied slave plantation society. One cannot say that its history has been neglected – certainly not in Brazil or Jamaica – but there is no doubt that our knowledge of it has advanced enormously in the past twenty years. The 'new social history' of the 1960s and 1970s could hardly fail to overlook a subject so obviously appealing to the technical and political interests of so many of its practitioners: one that combined social protest and the study of grassroots anonymity, black liberation and anti-imperialism or at least third world concerns, and seemed ideally suited to exemplify that liaison between history and social anthropology which was then producing such exciting results. And the new interest in maroon history could not but point in the direction of Suriname.

For in Suriname, formerly a Dutch colony on the Guyana coast, now a disappointing independent statelet, six ancient maroon communities still make up 10 per cent of the population of a small and extraordinary mixed country. This is remarkable. For maroon communities had trouble surviving, even though the last genuine individual slave fugitive lived long enough to recount his autobiography to a Cuban writer in the 1960s.[1] Since slaves were most likely to abscond shortly after arriving from Africa, free maroon communities beyond the range of colonial society were most easily established in the early stages of such societies, in the sixteenth and seventeenth centuries. The greatest of the Brazilian *quilombos*, Palmares, was at its height in the 1690s, shortly before its fall after sixty years of warfare. Even where colonial powers were obliged to make treaties recognizing maroon independence, as happened from time to time in a number of countries, they rarely lasted. It is doubtful whether outside Suriname any free black communities exist today that have not ceased to regard as binding the mid-eighteenth-century treaties recognizing their freedom.

Richard Price, whose *Maroon Societies*, together with a chapter of Eugene Genovese's *From Rebellion to Revolution* provides the most convenient introduction to the subject,[2] is at present the leading authority on *marronage* in general and on the Suriname maroons ('bush Negroes'), or rather on one of their communities, the Saramakas, to whom he has devoted many years of research. He has already written extensively about them, notably in his path-breaking *First Time: The Historical Vision of an Afro-American People*,[3] an account of the Saramakas' establishment and war of independence, based on written records and on their own orally transmitted 'strongly linear, causal sense of history', which is central to their identity and, incidentally, makes them fascinating to historians. *Alabi's World* takes the story up after independence, as Saramaka society settled down, and it does so in the form of a 'life and times' of one Alabi (1740–1820), who was supreme chief of his people for almost forty years. However, it contains enough introductory matter about the origins of the Suriname maroons to put readers into the picture; for, as the Saramakas say, 'If we forget the deeds of our ancestors, how can we hope to avoid being returned to white folks' slavery?'

Price has chosen a subject equally important to historians and social anthropologists, quite apart from the heroism of the maroons' struggles. For maroon societies raise fundamental questions. How do casual collections of fugitives of widely different origins, possessing nothing in common but the experience of transportation in slave ships and of plantation slavery, come to form structured communities? How, one might say more generally, are societies founded from scratch? What are the relations between the societies of ex-slaves rejecting bondage and the dominant society on whose margins they live, in a curious kind of symbiosis, for, as Price has pointed out elsewhere,[4] *marronage* was not a simple flight, a reversion to peasant life in the wilderness, but also, in a curious way, 'a kind of westernization.' What exactly did or could such refugee communities – at least in the days when most of their members were African-born – derive from the old continent? For if maroon communities struck observers as African in feeling – and perhaps, a historic novelty, as *conscious* of a common Africanness, as they could not possibly have been in the old world – specific African models and precedents for their institutions are not readily traceable.

Unfortunately the author, though keenly aware of questions such as these, has not tried to answer them directly. His fascinating but puzzling book is really about cultural collisions, confrontations, and dialogues of the deaf, not least between Richard Price's views about how history should be written and those of more traditional historians and anthropologists.

Since the main character of this book, Alabi, eventually became a Christian, while the essence of being a Saramaka was the rejection, or at least the non-acceptance, of white people's values, Christianity among them, the collision of cultures must be at the core of a book about him. Christians are still a small minority among Suriname's 'bush Negroes'. Since much, indeed most, of Price's information about eighteenth-century maroon life comes from the bulky correspondence of the Moravian missionaries who were the only whites in constant contact with the Saramakas, two kinds of cultural misunderstanding are also central to it: that of the Moravian Brethren and sisters whose failure to understand what was going on around them seems to have been monumental, and that of modern researchers to whom the world view of eighteenth-century pietistic zealots such as the Moravians, with their sensual, almost erotic, cult of Christ's wounds, is almost certainly less comprehensible than that of the ex-slaves. Trying (however unsuccessfully) to understand 'their' chosen people is what all field anthropologists are supposed to do; but the commonest reaction of the most rational moderns to the lunatic fringes of Western religions is still apt to be a mix of fascinated pity and repulsion.

However, cultural uncertainty is also built into Price's book in a third way. In recent years anthropology-ethnography and, to a rather smaller extent, history have been convulsed and undermined (under such general headings as 'post-modernism') by doubts about the possibility of objective knowledge or unified interpretation, that is to say, about the legitimacy of research as hitherto understood. The various and conflicting justifications of such a retreat are both epistemological and political as well as social (is anthropology 'an ethnocentric attempt to incorporate others' or 'part of Western hegemonic practice,' not to mention male domination?)[5] but they are all rather troublesome to the practitioner of these disciplines. Admittedly, when the native hue of resolution is sicklied o'er by the pale cast of thought, talk can still amply replace action, as *Hamlet* proves and as what has been called 'the literary turn of anthropology' confirms.[6] But 'a self-styled ethnographic historian' or ethno-historian like Richard Price is still obliged to do the job he assigns himself.

For, however much we apply the fashionable and question-begging terms of literary creation to ethnography or history, 'the grounding act of fiction in any project of ethnographic writing is the construction of a whole that guarantees the facticity of fact.'[7] In short, it isn't and can't be fiction. And insofar as any attempt at anthropological description accepts the 'facticity of fact' it can't even totally avoid the awful accusation of 'positivism'.

But does not *any* 'whole' amount to 'the imposition of some arbitrary order'? Price makes it clear that he shares the horror of such an order that many of his fellow anthropologists now follow. He therefore 'eschew[s] modern Western categories, such as religion, politics, economics, art, or kinship as organizing principles' and, to the regret of readers and colleagues, he refuses even to compile an index 'that encourages consultation along such ethnological lines', in the belief that this practice plays 'a pernicious obfuscating role in intercultural understanding'. He apparently considers two principles of organizing the material to be safe: chronological narrative, especially in the linear form of biography, and a sort of polyphony, in which the various voices of the sources speak side by side with the author's, each distinguished, in this instance, by a separate typeface. Could relativism or the abdication of authorial authority (Western, imperialist, male, capitalist, or whatever) go further?

The result is certainly a splendid effort to recover the past of the kind of people, inarticulate and usually undocumented as individuals, which is usually beyond recovery. It is also the presentation of an extremely moving experience: that of a people whose identity even today, as they work on the French space station or for Alcoa, rests on memories of an armed struggle against outsiders two or three centuries ago, which they are still prepared to resume. But how helpful is it as history or anthropology, rather than as the raw material for both? And how far does it meet the postmodern requirements Price himself seems so concerned about?

Inevitably the planned polyphony turns out to be an accompanied aria. There is only one voice and one conception: the author's. Among his sources the Dutch 'postholders', colonial officials charged with dealing with the free 'bush Negroes' of the forest, do not speak for themselves at all. They are here cited primarily for events and dates suited to the author's narrative, and for their frequently expressed frustration. We are left in the dark about the strategies of planters and authorities, although it is not hard to guess that, since it was impossible to stop the slaves from escaping into the rain forest in a continental plantation society, the logical policy, sooner or later, was to recognize the independence of maroon communities in the hinterland by treaty, in return for a promise to return subsequent refugees, paid for by bounty and by free deliveries ('tribute') of coastal goods which bound the maroon economy to the colony. We gather that such a policy was followed and that leaders of the maroon community were sought out and persuaded to make agreements. How did the settlers in the colony think this worked? We are again left in the dark. Were they perhaps satisfied, while also bitterly complaining about the failure of maroons to comply, that the arrangement actually cut down slave escapes? Did it do so? We are not told.

Again, while the Moravian Brethren speak for themselves at considerable length, their voluble letters serve the author overwhelmingly as an old-fashioned ethnographic source. Their merit is to have been in the field two centuries ago, but, unlike Price, who can correct them, they did not understand what they were observing. The contemporary Saramakas, of course, speak for themselves literally, since the author has spoken to them and recorded their own attempts to describe the past through the stories passed on to them; Price also transmits some of past writings of Saramakas themselves. But it is safe to say that these words would tell the uninstructed reader very little by themselves, without the setting and commentary that the author supplies. For, even if we suppose that the texts would be readily understood by Saramakas, they are not our kind of 'historical writing', and, in any case, it is the nature of writing about other cultures that it has to explain what needs no explanation at home.

The only voice that really speaks to us is Richard Price's.

However, the nature of his project is far from clear, apart from the fashionable insistence on fieldwork anthropology as self-analysis ('though I cast this book in a biographical rather than an auto-biographical mode') and the admirable intention to remind us that his people's struggles, and ours, are by no means over. On the one hand *Alabi's World* 'is intended as, among other things, an eth-nography of early Afro-American life'. On the other, Price shares the view that 'the primary aim of historical analysis is the recovery ... of the lived reality of people in their past,' an aim which does not exhaust historical analysis for many of us and a statement devoid of meaning unless there is prior agreement on what bits of an infinite 'lived reality' we are talking about.

That, of course, is precisely the difficulty of a history-cum-social anthropology that abandons the old belief in the procedures and vocations of both disciplines, inadequate as they may be *sub specie aeternitatis*, especially for the sort of intellectual models that have swept literature departments. It becomes very difficult to give both intellectual and expository or literary structure to one's writings, quite apart from the risk that one's subject will be deconstructed into fragments united only by the common experience of an incom-municable identity crisis.[8]

This difficulty is illustrated by the author's decision to divide his book into a main text and an extensive and in itself unstructured 'Notes and Commentaries section which is nearly as long as the main text.' It is safe to say this second section contains 90 per cent of what would interest most old-style historians and possibly anthropologists. Apart from passing references in the text it is here alone that we discover how the groups and clans that make up Saramaka society came into being, 'deriving their respective common identity from a combination of putative plantation origins and putative matrilineal kinship.' This matrilineal system apparently developed in maroon societies in the post-slave era in ways that remain obscure, but Price's notes delve into the question why certain women (sometimes late arrivers) were retrospectively chosen as founders of new clans. The notes, but not the text, also investigate the necessary syncretism of a society in which a young Saramaka, even in the mid-eighteenth century, might have 'great grandparents who hailed from as many as eight different African groups' and the coexistence of African rites of different origin shared to some extent by all Saramakas but maintained by special groups of adepts. Here we find information about demography, settlement, distribution, and even the, under the circumstances, natural, Saramaka way of referring to their territory in linear terms: 'upstream', 'downstream', 'in-land', 'toward the river'.

The notes alone give us more than oblique information about how the Saramakas gained a living in the rain forest, what crops they grew, what they hunted (thirty-three species according to the Moravians) and refused on certain ritual occasions to hunt (twenty-five of them). And to what extent they traded, what they sold and what they bought (peanuts, canoes, lumber, and rice against salt, sugar, household goods, tools, ornaments, and illegal guns). It seems odd that such obvious aspects of 'lived reality' are only treated as part of the learned apparatus.

Again, only in the notes can we discover something about the maroons' complex and ambiguous relations with the Indians, from whom they learned so much about how to live in the hinterland, and a variety of other matters which the author thinks 'would have unbalanced the narrative/descriptive alternance of the main text'. This procedure may indeed be 'textually richer than any that has yet been attempted', but it undoubtedly complicates the reading of what looks like a major contribution to a major subject.

As for the text, some readers may ask themselves what (other than plain curiosity about remote and exotic places) can sustain them through the elaborate biography of a man who was, by the author's own account, at best a not very enterprising or influential chief of some four thousand Guyanese backwoods-men in unexciting times. For the author, of course, the story is important, not because he has spent twenty years on Saramaka affairs, but rather because only thus can he demonstrate the extraordinary historical memory of this community, a corpus of oral knowledge preserved, partly in ritual secrecy, which allows them to recall in detail people, events, and connections of the eighteenth century. Price's comparison of sources shows this beyond doubt, thus providing a scholarly rationale for his procedure.

But if it satisfies the author, does it help the reader 'to penetrate existential words different from his own and to evoke their texture'? This is not clear. Central to any attempt at an understanding across cultures and centuries is the maroons' attitude to slavery and nonslavery. (According to my count a word translated by Price as 'freedom' occurs only once in all the Saramaka texts quoted, which are said to amount to 80 per cent of all the relevant written material for the period.) The question is complex and obscure. Our assumptions and theirs have only one point of contact: both probably agree on the status of white owners' slaves as pieces of living property like cattle ('chattel') at the unrestricted disposal of their owners. Even here it is not clear whether maroons, who sometimes themselves picked what whites described as 'slaves' and certainly sometimes hunted and returned plantation runaways, regarded all chattel slavery as always theoretically unacceptable, or only rejected some situations of absolute dependency, for example those in which the owner by excessive cruelty, or in some other way, transgressed the limits of what was tacitly accepted as the 'moral economy' of power over people. However, though this book naturally contains many references to the subject, I cannot see that it is possible for even the attentive reader to get a sense from Price's narrative of how Saramakas saw such matters as slavery and the ownership of people and land. It just cannot be done by the mode of exposition he has chosen.

But it has often been done, as a matter of course, for periods and societies at least as remote as the Saramakas, by analytical medieval historians, from F. W. Maitland to Georges Duby, unaware of the requirements of postmodernism, but perfectly conscious that the past is another country where things are done differently, that we must understand it even though the best interpreters still remain biased strangers. To judge by the sensitivity and quality of his research, Price is fully capable of following in their footsteps when not hampered by a project better suited to deconstruction than to construction.

What *Alabi's World* can convey vividly, however, is misunderstanding. How and why forest blacks could not get it in their heads that all whites were not very rich. How Christianity became entirely unconvincing once the Saramakas applied their practical-minded, instrumental view of spiritual forces to it. A person who had not sinned, they concluded, obviously did not need Christ, who had been resurrected because of men's sins. Anyway, if one were a sinner, the gods would have done something about it long ago. 'The people here pray every day. Won't their god be angry because they burden him so?' Observing the Moravians with a sound sense of statistics, they noted that 'Christians get sicker more often.' It was not a convincing argument for Jesus.

Voltaire (who, incidentally, denounced the torture of slaves in Suriname) would not have understood much of Saramaka affairs, but in this respect he would have applauded them. As, indeed, did other observers of the era of reason and enlightenment, always on the lookout for proof of the eighteenth-century German poet's 'See, we savages are better human beings after all' ('*Seht wir Wilden sind doch bess're Menschen*').

> It is a great pleasure [wrote an ex-missionary] to see a people who are so content with their fate. They enjoy the fruits of their labour and are unacquainted with the poison of hatred.

Well, things were more complicated than that, but after making the acquaintance, through *Alabi's World*, of these independent, self-confident, relaxed and proud men and women at ease with the world, one can see what he meant.

Let us, however, spare a final thought for those whose strange 'lived reality' *is* evoked successfully by Price's technique: the Moravians. They came to the benighted heathen in conditions which often seemed 'a foretaste of what hell must be like'. Unprepared for the forest, inexperienced, they suffered and died like flies – honest, uncomprehending German tailors, shoemakers or linen weavers in unsuitable European costumes, who could be expected to last a few months or weeks, preaching Jesus the Crucified with Blood and Wounds, among the scorpions and jaguars, before contentedly going home to Him. They were entirely dependent on the maroons, who did not like them as whites, made fun of them and occasionally persecuted them. They played music, and were uncomfortable when the blacks danced to it. They failed in all their endeavours except the heroic task of compiling Brother Schumann's Saramaka–German dictionary in nine pain-wracked months. Their successors are still there and still the Saramakas' only road to reading and writing.

They remain as hard for us to understand as they were for the forest maroons. But let us not withhold admiration for men and women who, in their own way, knew what their lives were for.

CHAPTER 16

On History from Below

This was originally written as a contribution to the 1985 Festschrift *honouring my friend, comrade and collaborator, the late George Rudé. It was published in Frederick Krantz (ed.),* History from Below: Studies in Popular Protest and Popular Ideology *(Oxford, 1988), pp. 13–28. The text was first given as a lecture at Concordia University, Montreal, where Rudé taught.*

Grassroots history, history seen from below or the history of the common people, of which George Rudé was a distinguished pioneer, no longer needs commercials. However, it may still benefit from some reflections on its technical problems, which are both difficult and interesting, probably more so than those of traditional academic history. To reflect on some of them is the purpose of this paper.

But before turning to my main subject let me ask why grassroots history is so recent a fashion – that is why most of the history written by contemporary chroniclers and subsequent scholars from the beginning of literacy until, say, the end of the nineteenth century, tells us so little about the great majority of the inhabitants of the countries or states it was recording, why Brecht's question 'Who built Thebes of the Seven Gates' is a typically twentieth-century question. The answer takes us into both the nature of politics – which was until recently the characteristic subject of history – and the motivations of historians.

Most history in the past was written for the glorification of, and perhaps for the practical use of, rulers. Indeed certain kinds of it still have this function. Those fat neo-Victorian biographies of politicians which have recently become the fashion again are certainly not read by the masses. Who reads them, apart from a handful of professional historians and a sprinkling of students who have to look into them for essays, is not clear. I have been gravely puzzled by those alleged best-seller lists which always seem to contain the latest blockbuster of this type. But certainly politicians gobble them up like popcorn, at least if they are literate. This is natural enough. Not only are they about people like themselves, and activities like the ones they are engaged in, but they are about eminent practitioners of their own trade, from which – if the books are good – they can learn something. Roy Jenkins still sees himself living in the same universe as Asquith, just as Harold Macmillan certainly saw people like Salisbury or Melbourne as in some sense contemporaries.

Now the practical business of ruling-class politics could, for most of history until the latter part of the nineteenth century and in most places, normally be carried on without more than an occasional reference to the mass of the subject population. They could be taken for granted, except in very exceptional circumstances – such as great social revolutions or insurrections. This does not mean either that they were contented or that they didn't have to be taken into account. It merely means that the terms of the relationship were arranged in such a way as to keep discontent within acceptable bounds, that is in such a way that the activities of the poor did not normally threaten the social order. Furthermore, mostly they were fixed at a level below that on which the top people's politics operated – for instance, locally and not nationally. Conversely, the ordinary people accepted their subalternity most of this time, and mostly confined their struggles, such as they were, to fighting those oppressors with whom they had immediate contact. If there is one safe generalization about the normal relation between peasants and kings or emperors in the period before the nineteenth century, it is that they regarded the king or emperor as by definition just. If he only knew what the landowning gentry were up to – or more likely a particular named nobleman – he would stop them or him oppressing the peasants. So in a sense he was outside their world of politics and they were outside his.

There are naturally exceptions to this generalization. I am inclined to believe that China is the main one, for that is a country in which, even in the days of the Celestial Empire, peasant risings were not occasional freak phenomena like earthquakes or pestilences, but phenomena which could be, were and were expected to be capable of overthrowing dynasties. But by and large they were not. Grassroots history therefore becomes relevant to, or part of, the sort of history that was written traditionally – the history of major political decisions and events – only from the moment when the ordinary people become a constant factor in the making of such decisions and events. Not only at times of exceptional popular mobilization, such as revolutions, but at all or most times. By and large this did not begin to happen until the era of the great revolutions at the end of the eighteenth century. But in practice of course it did not become significant until much later. Outside the USA even the typical institutions of bourgeois democracy – that is elections by general male suffrage (the women's vote is an even later development) – were exceptional until the late nineteenth century. The economy of mass consumption is, in Europe at least, a phenomenon of this century. And the two characteristic techniques for discovering people's opinions – market research by sampling, and its offspring, the public opinion poll – are quite implausibly young by historical standards. In effect they were products of the 1930s.

The history of the common people as a special field of study therefore begins with the history of mass movements in the eighteenth century. I suppose Michelet is the first great practitioner of grassroots history: the Great French Revolution is at the core of his writing. And ever since, the history of the French Revolution, especially since Jacobinism was revitalized by socialism and the Enlightenment by Marxism, has been the proving-ground of this kind of history. If there is a single historian who anticipates most of the themes of contemporary work, it is Georges Lefebvre, whose *Great Fear*, translated into English after forty years, is still remarkably up to date. To put it more generally: it was the French tradition of historiography as a whole, steeped in the history not of the French ruling class but of the French *people*, which established most of the themes and even the methods of grassroots history, Marc Bloch as well as Georges Lefebvre. But the field really began to flourish in other countries only after the Second World War. In fact its real advance only began in the middle 1950s, when it became possible for Marxism to make its full contribution to it.

For the Marxist, or more generally the socialist, interest in grassroots history developed with the growth of the labour movement. And though this provided a very powerful incentive to study the history of the common man – especially the working class – it also imposed some quite effective blinkers on the socialist historians. They were naturally tempted to study not just any common people, but the common people who could be regarded as ancestors of the movement: not workers as such so much as Chartists, trade unionists, Labour militants. And they were also tempted – equally naturally – to suppose that the history of the movements and organizations which led the workers' struggle, and therefore in a real sense 'represented' the workers, could replace the history of the common people themselves. But this is not so. The history of the Irish revolution of 1916–21 is not identical with the history of the IRA, the Citizen Army, the Irish Transport Workers Union or the Sinn Fein. You have only to read Sean O'Casey's great plays about Dublin slum life during this period to see how much else there was at the grassroots. Not until the 1950s did the left begin to emancipate itself from the narrow approach.

Whatever its origins and initial difficulties, grassroots history has now taken off. And in looking back upon the history of ordinary people, we are not merely trying to give it a retrospective political significance which it did not always have, we are trying more generally to explore an unknown dimension of the past. And this brings me to the technical problems of doing so.

Every kind of history has its technical problems, but most of these assume that there is a body of ready-made source-material whose interpretation raises these problems. The classical discipline of historical scholarship, as developed in the nineteenth century by German and other professors, made this assumption which, as it happens, fitted in very conveniently with the prevailing fashion of scientific positivism. This sort of scholarly problem is still dominant in a few very old-fashioned branches of learning such as literary history. To study Dante, one has to become very sophisticated in interpreting manuscripts and in working out what can go wrong when manuscripts are copied from each other, because the text of Dante depends on the collation of medieval manuscripts. To study Shakespeare, who left no manuscripts but a lot of corrupt printed editions, means becoming a sort of Sherlock Holmes of the early seventeenth-century printing trade. But in neither case is there much doubt about the main body of the subject we are studying, namely the works of Dante or Shakespeare.

Now grassroots history differs from such subjects, and indeed from most of traditional history, inasmuch as there simply is not a ready-made body of material about it. It is true that sometimes we are lucky. One of the reasons why so much modern grassroots history has emerged from the study of the French Revolution is that this great event in history combines two characteristics which rarely occur together before that date. In the first place, being a major revolution, it suddenly brought into activity and public notice enormous numbers of the sort of people who previously attracted very little attention outside their family and neighbours. And in the second place it documented them by means of a vast and laborious bureaucracy, classifying and filing them for the benefit of the historian in the national and departmental archives of France. The historians of the French Revolution, from Georges Lefebvre to Richard Cobb, have vividly described the pleasures and troubles of travelling through the French countryside in search of the Frenchmen of the 1790s – but chiefly the pleasures, for once the scholar arrived at Angoulême or Montpellier, and got the right archival series, practically every dusty packet of ancient paper – beautifully legible, unlike the crabbed hands of the sixteenth or seventeenth centuries – contained nuggets of gold. Historians of the French Revolution happen to be lucky – luckier than British ones, for instance.

In most cases the grassroots historian finds only what he is looking for, not what is already waiting for him. Most sources for grassroots history have only been recognized as sources because someone has asked a question and then prospected desperately around for some way – any way – of answering it. We cannot be positivists, believing that the questions and the answers arise naturally out of the study of the material. There is generally no material until our questions have revealed it. Take the now flourishing discipline of historical demography, which rests on the fact that the births, marriages and deaths of people were recorded in parish registers from, more or less, the sixteenth century. This was long known, and many of these registers were actually reprinted for the convenience of the genealogists, who were the only people to take much of an interest in them. But once the social historians got going on them, and techniques for analysing them were developed, it turned out that tremendous discoveries could be made. We can now discover how far people in the seventeenth century practised birth control, how far they suffered famine or other catastrophes, what their life expectancy was at various periods, how likely men and women were to remarry, how early or late they married and so on – all questions about which, until the 1950s, we could only speculate for the pre-census periods.

It is true that, once our questions have revealed new sources of material, these themselves raise considerable technical problems: sometimes too much so, sometimes not enough. Much of the time of historical demographers has been taken up simply with the increasingly complex technicalities of their analysis, which is why much of what they publish is at present interesting only for other historical demographers. The time-lag between research and result is unusually long. We must learn that a lot of grassroots history doesn't produce quick results, but requires elaborate, time-consuming and expensive processing. It is not like picking up diamonds in a river-bed, more like modern diamond or gold-mining which requires heavy capital investment and high technology.

On the other hand some kinds of grassroots material have not yet stimulated enough methodological thinking. Oral history is a good example. Thanks to the tape-recorder a lot of this is now practised. And most taped memories seem sufficiently interesting, or have sufficient sentimental appeal, to be their own reward. But in my opinion we shall never make adequate use of oral history until we work out what can go wrong in memory with as much care as we now know what can go wrong in transmitting manuscripts by manual copying. The anthropologists and African historians have begun to do so for the inter-generational transmission of facts by word of mouth. For instance we know over what number of generations certain kinds of information can be transmitted more or less accurately (for example genealogies) and that the transmission of historical events is always likely to lead to chronological telescoping. To quote a personal example, the memory of the Labourers' Rising of 1830, as preserved in and around Tisbury, Wiltshire, today, remembers as contemporary things which happened in 1817 and in 1830.

But most oral history today is personal memory, which is a remarkably slippery medium for preserving facts. The point is that memory is not so much a recording as a selective mechanism, and the selection is, within limits, constantly changing. What I remember of my life as a Cambridge undergraduate is different today from what it was when I was thirty or forty-five. And unless I have worked it up into conventional form for the purpose of boring people (we are all familiar with those who do this with their wartime experiences), it is likely to be different tomorrow or next year. At the moment our criteria for judging oral sources are almost entirely instinctive or non-existent. It either sounds right or it doesn't. Of course we can also check it against some verifiable independent source and approve it because it can be confirmed by such a source. But this doesn't get us nearer the crucial problem, which is to know what we can believe when there is nothing to check it against.

The methodology of oral history is not simply important for checking the reliability of the tapes of old ladies' and gentlemen's reminiscences. One significant aspect of grassroots history is what ordinary people remember of big events as distinct from what their betters think they should remember, or what historians can establish as having happened; and insofar as they turn memory into myth, how such myths are formed. What did the British people actually feel in the summer of 1940? The records of the Ministry of Information present a somewhat different picture from what most of us now believe. How can we reconstruct either the original feelings or the formation of the myth? Can we separate them? These are not insignificant questions. My own view is that they require not merely the collection and interpretation of tapes of retrospective questionnaires, but experiments – if necessary in conjunction with psychologists. There is plenty of the methodological, hypothetical and what is more arbitrary involved here. The curve of support for the Liberal–Social Democratic Alliance, indicted by monthly questions about how people would vote if a general election were held tomorrow, indicates nothing about their political behaviour except how they answer this particular question and the assumption that voting intention is the crucial variable in politics. It is not based on any model of how people actually make up their minds about politics, and it does not investigate their political behaviour, but their present view about one particular political act in hypothetical circumstances. But if we discover the equivalent of retrospective opinion polls, we are investigating what people actually thought or actually did.

Sometimes this can be done by actually discovering their opinions. For instance Hanak analysed opinions about the First World War in the different nationalities of the Habsburg Empire by working through the censored letters from and to soldiers at the front, and Kula in Poland has published a collection of letters from emigrant relatives to Polish peasants in the late nineteenth century intercepted by the Tsarist police. But this is rare, because for most of the past people were generally illiterate anyway. Much more commonly we infer their thoughts from their actions. In other words we base our historical work on Lenin's realistic discovery that voting with one's feet can be as effective a way of expressing one's opinion as voting in the ballot box. Sometimes, of course, we are halfway between opinion and action. Thus Marc Ferro investigated the attitude of different groups to war and revolution in Russia by analysing the telegrams and resolutions sent to Petrograd in the first weeks of the February Revolution – that is before public meetings, workers', peasants' or soldiers' councils or whatever had acquired party labels or character. To send a resolution to the capital is political action – though at the beginning of a great revolution it is likely to occur more frequently than at other times. But the content of the telegram is opinion, and the differences between say workers', peasants' and soldiers' opinions is significant. Thus peasants 'demanded' much more often than they petitioned. They were more opposed to the war than workers, who were also less self-confident. Soldiers were not at this point opposing the war at all, but complaining about officers. And so on.

But the prettiest sources are the ones which simply record actions which *must imply* certain opinions. They are almost always the result of searching for some way – any way – of asking a question already in the historian's mind. Also, they are generally quite conclusive. Suppose, for instance, you want to discover what difference the French Revolution made to monarchist sentiment in France. Marc Bloch, investigating the belief that the kings of France and England could work miracles, which was widespread for many centuries, points out that at the coronation of Louis xvi in 1774 2,400 sufferers from scrofula came forward to be cured of the 'king's evil' by the royal touch. But when Charles x revived the ancient ceremonial of coronation at Rheims in 1825, and was reluctantly persuaded to revive the ceremony of royal healing also, a mere 120 people turned up. Between the last pre-revolutionary king and 1825 the Shakespearean belief that 'there's some divinity doth hedge a king' had virtually disappeared in France. There is no arguing with such a finding.

The decline of traditional religious beliefs and the rise of secular ones has similarly been investigated by analysing wills and funeral inscriptions. For though Dr Johnson said that in writing lapidary inscriptions a man is not on oath, it is even more true that he or she is more likely to express their real religious views in such a context than at other times. And not only these. Vovelle has illustrated very prettily the decline in eighteenth-century Provence of the belief in a stratified hierarchical society by counting the frequency of the testamentary formula 'to be buried according to his or her rank and condition'. It declines steadily and quite markedly throughout the century. But – interestingly enough – not more steeply than, say, the invocation of the Virgin Mary in Provençal wills.

Suppose we look for other ways of discovering changes in attitude towards traditional religion, and decide to turn from burial to baptism. In Catholic countries the saints provide the main body of given names. Actually, they only do so overwhelmingly from the time of the Counter-Reformation on, so that this index can also tell us something about the evangelization or re-evangelization of the common people in the period of Reform and Counter-Reform. But purely secular names become common in some parts in the nineteenth century, and sometimes deliberately non-Christian, or even anti-Christian, names.

A Florentine colleague got his children to do a small bit of research on Tuscan telephone directories to check up on the frequency of first names taken either from deliberately secular sources – say Italian opera and literature (for instance, Spartaco). It turns out that this correlates particularly well with the areas of former anarchist influence – more so than with those of socialist influence. So we can infer – what is also probable on other grounds – that anarchism was more than a mere political movement, and tended to have some of the characteristics of an active conversion, a change in the entire way of life of its militants. It is possible that the social and ideological history of personal names has been investigated in England (other than by that gentleman who annually keeps track of the names in the *Times* announcements), but if so I have not come across these studies. I suspect there aren't any, at least by historians.

So, with more or less ingenuity, what the poet called the simple annals of the poor – the bare records of, or connected with, birth, marriage and death – can yield surprising quantities of information. And everyone can try his or her own hand at the historian's game of discovering ways of not merely speculating about what songs the sirens sang (Sir Thomas Browne), but actually finding some indirect records of those songs. A lot of grassroots history is like the trace of the ancient plough. It might seem gone for good with the men who ploughed the field many centuries ago. But every aerial photographer knows that, in a certain light, and seen at a certain angle, the shadows of long-forgotten ridge and furrow can still be seen.

Nevertheless, mere ingenuity doesn't take us far enough. What we need, both to make sense of what the inarticulate thought and to verify or falsify our hypotheses about it, is a coherent picture, or, if you prefer the term, a model. For our problem is not so much to discover one good source. Even the best of such sources – let's say the demographic ones about births, marriages and deaths – only illuminate certain areas of what people did, felt and thought. What we must normally do is to put together a wide variety of often fragmentary information: and to do that we must, if you'll excuse the phrase, construct the jigsaw puzzle ourselves, that is work out how such information *ought* to fit together. This is another way of repeating what I've already stressed, namely that the grassroots historian cannot be an old-fashioned positivist. He must in a way know what he is looking for and, only if he does, can he recognize whether what he finds fits in with his hypothesis or not; and if it doesn't, try to think of another model.

How do we construct our models? Of course, there is an element – a rather strong element – of knowledge, of experience, of simply having a sufficiently wide and concrete acquaintance with the actual subject. This enables us to eliminate obviously useless hypotheses. To quote an absurd illustration. An African candidate in the London external BA once answered a question about the industrial revolution in Lancashire by saying the cotton industry developed there because Lancashire is so suitable for growing cotton. We happen to know that it isn't, and therefore think the answer absurd, though it might not seem so in Calabar. But there are plenty of answers which are equally absurd, and could be avoided by equally elementary information. For instance, if we do not happen to know that in the nineteenth century the term 'artisan' in Britain was used almost exclusively to describe a skilled wage-worker, and the term 'peasant' generally meant a farm-labourer, we might make some substantial howlers about nineteenth-century British social structure. Such howlers have been made – continental translators persistently translate the term 'journeyman' as 'day-labourer' – and who knows how many discussions about seventeenth-century society are hamstrung by our ignorance of what exactly the common meaning or meanings of the term 'servant' or 'yeoman' was. There simply are things one has to know about the past, which is why most sociologists make bad historians: they don't want to take the time to find out.

We also need imagination – preferably in conjunction with information – in order to avoid the greatest danger of the historian, anachronism. Practically all popular treatments of Victorian sexuality suffer from a failure to understand that our own sexual attitudes are simply not the same as those of other periods. It is plain wrong to assume that the Victorians – all except a small and rather atypical minority – had the same attitudes to sex as we have, only they suppressed it or concealed it. But it is fairly hard to make the imaginative effort to understand this, all the more so since sex seems to be something fairly unchanging and we all think we are expert on it.

But knowledge and imagination alone are not enough. What we need to construct, or to reconstruct, is ideally speaking a coherent, preferably a consistent, *system* of behaviour or thought – and one which can be, in some senses, inferred once we know the basic social assumptions, parameters and tasks of the situation, but before we know very much about that situation. Let me give you an example. When communities of Indian peasants in Peru occupied the land to which they felt they were entitled, notably in the early 1960s, they almost invariably proceeded in a highly standardized manner: the whole community would assemble, with wives, children, cattle and implements to the accompaniment of drums, horns and other musical instruments. At a certain time – generally at dawn – they would all cross the line, tear down the fences, advance to the limit of the territory they claimed, immediately start building little huts as near the new line as possible, and begin to pasture the cattle and dig the land. Curiously enough, other land-occupations by peasants in different times and places – for instance in southern Italy – took exactly the same form. Why? In other words, on what assumptions does this highly standardized, and obviously not culturally determined, behaviour make sense?

Suppose we say: first the occupation has to be collective, (a) because the land belongs to the community and (b) because all members of the community must be involved to minimize victimization and to prevent the community being disrupted by arguments between those who stuck out their necks and those who didn't. For, after all, they are breaking the law and unless there is a successful revolution they will certainly be punished – even if their demands are actually conceded. Can we verify this? Well, there is considerable supporting evidence about the importance of minimizing victimization. Thus in Japanese peasant risings before the Meiji restoration, a lot of villages were conventionally 'coerced' into joining the rising, meaning that their village authorities were provided with an official cover for participation. Lefebvre made similar points about French villages in 1789. If everybody can say 'I'm sorry, but I had no option but to join,' it is likely that the authorities in turn will have an official excuse for limiting the punishment which they feel obliged to mete out for rebellion. For of course they have to live with the peasants just as the peasants have to live with them. The fact that one lot rules and the other is subaltern doesn't mean that the rulers need take no account of the ruled.

Very well. Now what is the most familiar way of mobilizing the entire community? It is the village *fiesta* or its equivalent – the combination of collective ritual and collective entertainment. And of course a land-occupation is both: it is bound to be a very serious and ceremonial affair, reclaiming land which belongs to the village, but it is also probably the most exciting thing that has happened to the village in a long time. So it is natural that there should be an element of the village fair about the rising. Hence the music – which also serves to mobilize and rally the people. Can we verify this? Well, time and again we have evidence in such peasant mobilizations of the people – especially the young people – putting on their Sunday best; and we certainly have evidence in regions of heavy drinking, that a certain number of pints are being sunk.

Why do they invade at dawn? Presumably for sound military reasons – to catch the other side napping and to give themselves at least some daylight by which to settle in. But why do they settle in with huts, animals and implements, instead of just waiting to repel the landlords or the police? Actually, they hardly ever try seriously to repel the police or the army, for the good reason that they know very well they can't, being too weak. Peasants are more realistic than many of the ultra-left insurrectionaries. They know perfectly well who is going to kill whom if it comes to a confrontation. And what is more important, they know who can't run away. They know that revolutions can happen, but they also know that their success doesn't depend on them in their specific village. So mass land-occupations are normally by way of being a try-on. Generally there is something in the political situation which has percolated to the villages and convinced them that times are a-changing: the normal strategy of passivity can perhaps be replaced by activity. If they are right, nobody will come to throw them off the land. If they are wrong, the sensible thing is to retreat and wait for the next suitable moment. But they must nevertheless not only lay claim to the land but actually live on it and *labour* it, because their right to it is not like bourgeois property right, but more like Lockean property right in the state of nature: it depends on mixing one's own labour with the resources of nature. Can we verify this? Well yes, we know quite a lot from nineteenth-century Russia about peasants' belief in the so-called 'labour principle'. And we can actually see the argument in action: in the Cilento, south of Naples, before the 1848 revolution 'every Christmas Day the peasants went out onto the lands to which they laid claim in order to carry out agricultural labours, thus seeking to maintain the ideal principle of possession of their rights'. If you don't work the land, you cannot justly own it.

I could give you other examples. Indeed I've tried this sort of construction – which, I confess, I think I learned from the social anthropologists – on other problems: for instance, on the problem of social banditry, another phenomenon which lends itself to this type of analysis, because it is highly standardized.

It implies three analytical steps: first, we have to identify what the doctors would call the syndrome – namely all the 'symptoms' or bits of the jigsaw puzzle which have to be fitted together, or at least enough of them to go on with. Second, we have to construct a model which makes sense of all these forms of behaviour, that is to discover a set of assumptions which would make the combination of these different kinds of behaviour consistent with one another according to some scheme of rationality. Third, we must then discover whether there is independent evidence to confirm these guesses.

Now the trickiest part of this is the first, since it rests on a mixture of the historian's prior knowledge, his theories about society, sometimes his hunch, instinct or introspection, and he is generally not really clear in his own mind about how he makes his initial selection. At least I've not been, even though I try hard to be conscious of what I'm doing. For instance, on what grounds does one pick out a variety of disparate social phenomena, generally treated as curious footnotes to history, and classify them together as members of a family of 'primitive rebellion' – of what you might call pre-political politics: banditry, urban riots, certain kinds of secret societies, certain kinds of millennial and other sects and so on? When I first did so I did not really know. Why do I notice, among the numerous other things I could notice (some of which I obviously don't), the significance of clothes in peasant movements; clothes as a symbol of the class struggle, as in the Sicilian hostility between the 'caps' and the 'hats', or in the Bolivian peasant risings in which the Indians occupying the cities force the city people to take off their trousers and wear peasant (that is Indian) costume? Clothes as symbols of rebellion itself, as when the farm-labourers of 1830 put on Sunday best to march to the gentry with their demands, thus indicating that they are not in the normal state of oppression which equals labour but in the state of freedom which equals holiday and play? (Remember that even in the early labour movement the concept of the strike and the holiday are not clearly separated: miners 'play' when they are on strike, and the Chartist plans for a general strike of 1839 were plans for a 'National Holiday.') I don't know, and this ignorance is dangerous, for it may make me unaware of introducing my own contemporary assumptions into the model, or of omitting something important.

The second phase of the analysis is also tricky, since we may simply be placing an arbitrary construction on the facts. Still, insofar as the model is capable of testing – unlike many beautiful models, such as, say, a lot of structuralist ones – this is not too troublesome. More troublesome is a certain vagueness about what one is trying to prove. For to assume that a certain kind of behaviour makes sense on certain assumptions is not to claim that it is sensible, that is rationally justifiable. The great danger of this procedure – and the one to which a lot of field anthropologists have succumbed – is to equate all behaviour as equally 'rational'. Now some of it is. For instance, the behaviour of the good Soldier Schweik, who, of course, had been certified as a *bona fide* halfwit by the military authorities, was anything but halfwitted. It was undoubtedly the most effective form of self-defence for someone in his position. Time and again, in studying the political behaviour of peasants in a state of oppression, we discover the practical value of stupidity and a refusal to accept any innovation: the great asset of peasants is that there are many things you simply can't make them do, and by and large no change is what suits a traditional peasantry best. (But, of course, let us not forget that many of these peasants don't just play at being dense, they really *are* dense.) Sometimes the behaviour was rational under some circumstances, but is no longer rational under changed circumstances. But there are also plenty of kinds of behaviour which are not rational at all, in the sense that they are effective means of achieving definable practical ends, but are merely comprehensible. This is obviously the case with the revival of beliefs in astrology, witchcraft, various fringe religions and irrational beliefs in the West today, or with certain forms of violent behaviour, such as – to take the most common example – the madness which seizes so many people once they get into a car. The grassroots historian does not, or at least he ought not to, abdicate his judgment.

What is the object of all these exercises? It is not simply to discover the past but *to explain it*, and in doing so to provide a link with the present. There is an enormous temptation in history simply to uncover what has hitherto been unknown, and to enjoy what we find. And since so much of the lives, and even more of the thoughts, of the common people have been quite unknown, this temptation is all the greater in grassroots history, all the more so since many of us identify ourselves with the unknown common men and women – the even more unknown women – of the past. I don't wish to discourage this. But curiosity, sentiment and the pleasures of antiquarianism are not enough. The best of such grassroots history makes wonderful reading, but that is all. What we want to know is *why*, as well as *what*. To discover that in seventeenth-century Puritan villages in Somerset, or in Victorian Poor Law Unions in Wiltshire, girls with illegitimate children were not treated as sinners or as 'unrespectable' if they genuinely had reason to believe that the father of the child had intended to marry them, is interesting, and provides food for reflection. But what we really want to know is why such beliefs were held, how they fitted in with the rest of the value-system of those communities (or of the larger society of which these formed a part), and why they changed or didn't change.

The link with the present is also obvious, for the process of understanding it has much in common with the process of understanding the past, quite apart from the fact that understanding how the past has turned into the present helps us understand the present, and presumably something of the future. Much about the behaviour of people *of all classes* today is, in fact, as unknown and undocumented as was much of the lives of the common people in the past. Sociologists and others who monitor developments in everyday life are constantly trailing behind their quarry. And even when we are aware of what we are doing as members of our society and age, we may not be conscious of the role which our acts and beliefs play in creating the image of what we would all wish to regard as an orderly social cosmos – even those who regard themselves as being outside of it – or in expressing our attempt to come to terms with its changes. Much of what is written, said and acted out today about family relationships clearly belongs to the realm of symptoms rather than diagnosis.

And as in the past one of our tasks is to uncover the lives and thoughts of common people and to rescue them from Edward Thompson's 'enormous condescension of posterity', so our problem at present is also to strip away the equally presumptuous assumptions of those who think they know both what the facts and what the solutions are, and who seek to impose them on the people. We must discover what people really want of a good or even a tolerable society, and, what is by no means the same – because they may not actually know – what they *need* from such a society. That is not easy, partly because it is difficult to get rid of prevailing assumptions about how society should work, some of which (such as most liberal ones) are very unhelpful guides, and partly because we do not know actually what makes a society work in real life: even a bad and unjust society. So far in the twentieth century all countries I know have failed to solve by deliberate planning a problem which, for many centuries, appeared to pose no great difficulties for humanity, namely how to construct a working city which should also be a human community. That should give us pause.

Grassroots historians spend much of their time finding out how societies work and when they do not work, as well as how they change. They cannot help doing this, since their subject, ordinary people, make up the bulk of any society. They start out with the enormous advantage of knowing that they are largely ignorant of either the facts or the answers to their problems. They also have the substantial advantage of historians over social scientists who turn to history, of knowing how little we know of the past, how important it is to find out, and what hard work in a specialized discipline is needed for the purpose. They also have a third advantage. They know that what people wanted and needed was not always what their betters, or those who were cleverer and more influential, thought they ought to have. These are modest enough claims for our trade. But modesty is not a negligible virtue. It is important to remind ourselves from time to time that we don't know all the answers about society and that the process of discovering them is not simple. Those who plan and manage society now are perhaps unlikely to listen. Those who want to change society and eventually to plan its development ought also to listen. If some of them will, it will be due partly to the work of historians like George Rudé.

CHAPTER 17

The Curious History of Europe

This is the English version of a lecture on Europe and its history given in German, under the auspices of the Fischer Taschenbuch Verlag, which launched its new series Europäische Geschichte *on the occasion of the annual congress of German historians (Munich, 1996). A version of the German lecture was published by* Die Zeit *on 4 October 1996. The (longer) English version is published here for the first time.*

Can continents have a history as continents? Let us not confuse politics, history and geography, especially not in the case of these shapes on the page of atlases, which are not natural geographical units, but merely human names for parts of the global land-mass. Moreover, it has been clear from the beginning, that is to say ever since antiquity when the continents of the Old World were first baptized, that these names were intended to have more than a mere geographical significance.

Consider Asia. Since 1980, if I am not mistaken, the census of the USA has granted its inhabitants the option of describing themselves as 'Asian-Americans', a classification presumably by analogy with 'African-Americans', the term by which black Americans currently prefer to be described. Presumably an Asian-American is an American born in Asia or descended from Asians. But what is the sense in classifying immigrants from Turkey under the same heading as those from Cambodia, Korea, the Philippines or Pakistan, not to mention the unquestionably Asian territory of Israel, though its inhabitants do not like to be reminded of this geographical fact? In practice these groups have nothing in common.

If we look more closely at the category 'Asian', it tells us more about us than about maps. For instance, it throws some light on the American, or more generally 'Western', attitudes towards those parts of humanity originating in the regions once known as the 'East' or the 'Orient'. Western observers, and later conquerors, rulers, settlers and entrepreneurs, looked for a common denominator for populations which were plainly unable to stand up to them, but equally plainly belonged to established, ancient cultures and political entities worthy of respect, or at least serious consideration by eighteenth- and nineteenth-century standards. They were not, in the then current terms, 'savages', or 'barbarians', but belonged in a different category, namely that of 'Orientals', whose characteristics as such accounted, among other things, for their inferiority to the West. The influential book *Orientalism* by the Palestinian Edward Said has excellently caught the typical tone of European arrogance about the 'Orient', even though it rather underestimates the complexity of Western attitudes in this field.[1]

On the other hand 'Asian' today has a second and geographically more restricted meaning. When Lee Kwan Yew of Singapore announces an 'Asian way' and an 'Asian economic model', a theme happily taken up by Western management experts and ideologists, we are not concerned with Asia as a whole, but with the economic effects of the geographically localized heritage of Confucius. In short, we are continuing the old debate, launched by Marx and developed by Max Weber, on the influence of particular religions and ideologies on economic development. It used to be Protestantism which fuelled the engine of capitalism. Today Calvin is out and Confucius is in, both because the Protestant virtues are not very traceable in Western capitalism and because the economic triumphs of East Asia have occurred in countries marked by the Confucian heritage – China, Japan, Korea, Taiwan, Hong Kong, Singapore, Vietnam – or carried by a Chinese entrepreneurial diaspora. As it happens, Asia today contains the headquarters of all the major world faiths with the exception of Christianity, including what remains of communism, but the non-Confucian culture-regions of the continent are irrelevant to the current fashion in the Weberian debate. They do not belong in *this* Asia.

Nor, of course, does the Western prolongation of Asia known as Europe. Geographically, as everyone knows, it has no eastern borders, and the continent therefore exists *exclusively* as an intellectual construct. Even the cartographic dividing-line of the traditional school atlases – Ural Mountains, Ural river, Caspian Sea, Caucasus, so much more easily remembered in the German mnemonic than in other languages – is based on a political decision. As Bronislaw Geremek has recently reminded us[2] when V. Tatishchev in the eighteenth century nominated the Ural Mountains as the divider between Europe and Asia, he consciously wished to break with the stereotype which assigned the Moscow state and its heirs to Asia. 'It required the decision of a geographer and historian, and the acceptance of a convention.' Of course, whatever the role of the Urals, the original frontier between Europe (that is the Hellenes) and the peoples defined as 'barbarians' by the Hellenes had run through the steppes north of the Black Sea. Southern Russia has been part of Europe far longer than many regions now automatically included in Europe, but about whose geographic classification geographers argued even in the late nineteenth century, for example Iceland and Spitsbergen.

That Europe is a construct does not, of course, mean that it did not or does not exist. There has always been a Europe, since the ancient Greeks gave it a name. Only, it is a shifting, divisible and flexible concept, though perhaps not quite so elastic as 'Mitteleuropa', the classic example of political programmes disguised as geography. No part of Europe except the area of the present Czech Republic and its adjoining regions appears on *all* maps of central Europe; but some of these reach across the entire continent except for the Iberian peninsula. However, the elasticity of the concept 'Europe' is not so much geographical – for practical purposes all atlases accept the Ural line – as political and ideological. During the Cold War the field 'European history' in the USA covered mainly western Europe. Since 1989 it has extended to central and eastern Europe as 'the political and economic geography of Europe is changing'.[3]

The original concept of Europe rested on a double confrontation: the military defence of the Greeks against the advance of an eastern empire in the Persian wars, and the encounter of Greek 'civilization' and the Scythian 'barbarians' on the steppes of South Russia. We see this, in the light of subsequent history, as a process of confrontation and differentiation, but it would be quite as easy to read into it symbiosis and syncretism. Indeed, as Neal Ascherson reminds us in his beautiful *Black Sea*,[4] following Rostovtzeff's *Iranians and Greeks in Southern Russia*, it generated 'mixed civilizations, very curious and very interesting', in this region of intersection between Asian, Greek and Western influences moving downstream along the Danube.

It would be equally logical to see the entire Mediterranean civilization of classical antiquity as syncretic. After all, it imported its script, as later its imperial ideology and state religion, from the Near and Middle East. Indeed the present division between Europe, Asia and Africa had no meaning – at least no meaning corresponding to the present – in a region in which the Greeks lived and flourished equally in all three continents. (Not until our tragic century have they finally been expelled from Egypt, Asia Minor and the Pontic region.) What meaning could it have had in the heyday of the undivided Roman Empire, happily tricontinental and ready to assimilate anything useful that came from anywhere?

Migrations and invasions from the regions of barbarian peoples were not new. All empires in the belt of civilization that ran from East Asia westwards into the Mediterranean faced them. However, the collapse of the Roman Empire left the Western Mediterranean, and rather later the Eastern Mediterranean, without any empires and rulers capable of dealing with them. From that point on it becomes possible for us to see the history of the region between the Caucasus and Gibraltar as a millennium of struggle against conquerors from east, north and south – from Attila to Suleiman the Magnificent, or even to the second siege of Vienna in 1683.

It is not surprising that the ideology which has formed the core of the 'European idea' from Napoleon via the Pan-European movement of the 1920s and Goebbels to the European Economic Community – that is to say a concept of Europe which deliberately *excludes* parts of the geographical continent – likes to appeal to Charlemagne. That Great Charles ruled over the only part of the European continent which, at least since the rise of Islam, had *not* been reached by the invaders, and could therefore claim to be 'vanguard and saviour of the West' against the Orient – to quote the words of the Austrian President Karl Renner in 1946, in praise of his own country's alleged 'historic mission'.[5] Since Charlemagne was himself a conqueror who advanced his borders against Saracens and eastern barbarians, he might even be seen, to use the jargon of the Cold War, to advance from 'containment' to 'roll-back'.

True, in those centuries nobody outside a tiny circle of classically educated clergymen thought in terms of 'Europe'. The first genuine counter-offensive of the West against Saracens and barbarians was conducted not in the name of the 'regnum Europaeum' of the Carolingian panegyrists, but in the name of (Roman) Christianity: as south-eastern and south-western crusades against Islam, north-eastern crusades against the heathens of the Baltic. Even when Europeans began their real conquest of the globe in the sixteenth century, the crusading ideology of the Spanish *reconquista* is easily recognizable in that of the *conquistadores* of the New World. Not before the seventeenth century did Europeans recognize themselves as a continent rather than a faith. By the time they were able to challenge the might of the major Eastern empires at the end of that century, the conversion of unbelievers to the true faith could no longer compete ideologically with double-entry book-keeping. Economic and military superiority now reinforced the belief that Europeans were superior to all others not as carriers of a civilization of modernity, but collectively as a human type.

'Europe' had been on the defensive for a millennium. Now, for half a millennium, it conquered the world. Both observations make it impossible to sever European history from world history. What has long been obvious to economic historians, archaeologists and other enquirers into the past fabric of everyday life (*Alltagsgeschichte*) should now be generally accepted. Even the very idea of a cartographically defined history of Europe became possible only with the rise of Islam, which permanently divorced the southern and eastern coasts of the Mediterranean from its northern shores. What historian of classical antiquity would insist on writing the history only of the North Mediterranean provinces of the Roman Empire, except out of caprice or ideology?

However, separating Europe from the rest of the world is less dangerous than the practice of excluding parts of the geographic continent from some ideological concept of 'Europe'. The last fifty years should have taught us that such redefinitions of the continent belong not to history but to politics and ideology. Until the end of the Cold War this was perfectly obvious. After the Second World War Europe, for Americans, meant 'the eastern frontier of what came to be called "western civilization"'.[6] 'Europe' stopped at the borders of the region controlled by the USSR, and was defined by the non-communism, or anti-communism, of its governments. Naturally the attempt was made to give a positive content to this rump, for example by describing it as the zone of democracy and freedom. However, this seemed implausible even to the European Economic Community before the middle 1970s, when the patently authoritarian regimes of southern Europe disappeared – Spain, Portugal, the Greek colonels – and Britain, unquestionably democratic but doubtfully 'European', finally entered it. Today it is even more obvious that programmatic definitions of Europe won't work. The USSR, whose existence cemented 'Europe' together, no longer exists, while the variety of regimes between Gibraltar and Vladivostok is not concealed by the fact that all, without exception, declare their allegiance to democracy and the free market.

Seeking for a single programmatic 'Europe' thus leads only to endless debates about the hitherto unsolved, and perhaps insoluble, problems of how to extend the European Union, that is how to turn a continent that has been, throughout its history, economically, politically and culturally heterogeneous into a single more or less homogeneous entity. There has never been a *single* Europe. Difference cannot be eliminated from our history. This has always been so, even when ideology preferred to dress 'Europe' in religious rather than geographical costume. True, Europe was the specific continent of Christianity, at least between the rise of Islam and the conquest of the New World. However, barely had the last pagans been converted when it became evident that at least two far from brotherly varieties of Christianity faced one another on the territory of Europe, and the sixteenth century Reformation added several others. For some (admittedly more often than not from Poland and Croatia) the border between Roman and Orthodox Christianity is 'even today, one of the most permanent cultural divides of the globe'.[7] Even today Northern Ireland demonstrates that the old tradition of bloody intra-European religious war is not dead. Christianity is an ineradicable part of European history, but it has no more been a unifying force for our continent than other even more typically European concepts, for instance the 'nation' and 'socialism'.

The tradition which regards Europe not as a continent but as a club, whose membership is open only to candidates certified as suitable by the club committee, is almost as old as the name 'Europe'. Where 'Europe' ends naturally depends on one's position. As everyone knows, for Metternich 'Asia' began at the eastern exit from Vienna, a view still echoed at the end of the nineteenth century in a series of articles directed against the 'barbarian–asiatic' Hungarians in the Vienna *Reichspost*. For the inhabitants of Budapest, the border of true Europe clearly ran between Hungarians and Croats, for President Tudjman it runs equally plainly between Croats and Serbs. No doubt proud Rumanians see themselves as essential Europeans and spiritual Parisians exiled among backward Slavs, even though Gregor von Rezzori, the Austrian writer born in the Bukowina, described them in his books as 'Maghrebians', that is 'Africans'.

The true distinction is thus not one of geography; but neither is it necessarily one of ideology. It demarcates felt superiority from imputed inferiority, as defined by those who see themselves as 'better', that is to say usually belonging to a higher intellectual, cultural or even biological class than their neighbours. The distinction is not necess-arily ethnic. In Europe as elsewhere the most universally acknowledged border between civilization and barbarism ran between the rich and the poor, that is to say between those with access to luxuries, education and the world outside, and the rest. Consequently the most obvious division of this sort ran across and not between societies, that is primarily between city and countryside. Peasants were unquestionably European – who was more indigenous than they? – but how often did the educated romantics, folklorists and social scientists of the nineteenth century, even as they often admired or even idealized their archaic system of values, treat them as a 'survival' of some earlier, and consequently more primitive, stage of culture, preserved into the present by virtue of their backwardness and isolation? Not city folk but country people belonged in the new ethnographic museums which the educated opened in several cities of eastern Europe between 1888 and 1905 (as in Warsaw, Sarajevo, Helsinki, Prague, Lemberg/Lwiw, Belgrade, St Petersburg and Cracow).

Nevertheless, only too often the line ran between peoples and states. In every country of Europe there were those who looked down across some frontier on barbarian neighbours, or at least on technically or intellectually lagging populations. The usual cultural–economic slope on our continent descends eastwards or towards the south-east from the Ile de France and Champagne, thus making it easier to classify undesirable neighbours as 'Asiatic', notably the Russians. However, let us not forget the slope from north to south, which told the Spaniards they 'really' belonged to Africa more than to Europe, a view shared by the inhabitants of northern Italy as they look down on their fellow-citizens south of Rome. Only the barbarians of the north, who ravaged Europe in the tenth and eleventh centuries, with nothing but Arctic ice behind them, could be assigned to no other continent. In any case, they have turned into the rich and peaceful Scandinavians, and their barbarism survives only in the bloodthirsty mythology of Wagner and German nationalism.

And yet the peaks of European civilization from which the slopes led down to other continents could not have been discovered until Europe as a whole had ceased to belong to the realm of barbarism. For even in the late fourteenth century scholars from the region of high culture like the great Ibn Khaldun had shown little interest in Christian Europe. 'God knows what goes on there,' he observed, two centuries after Sa'id ibn Akhmad, cadi of Toledo, who was convinced that nothing was to be learned from the northern barbarians. They were more like beasts than men.[8] In those centuries the cultural slope evidently ran in the opposite direction.

But here precisely lies the paradox of European history. These very historical U-turns or interruptions are its specific characteristic. Throughout its long history the belt of high cultures that stretched from East Asia to Egypt experienced no lasting relapses into barbarism, in spite of all invasions, conquests and upheavals. Ibn Khaldun saw history as an eternal duel between the pastoral nomads and settled civilization – but in this eternal conflict the nomads, though sometimes victorious, remained the challengers and not the victors. China under Mongols and Manchus, Persia, overrun by whatever conquering invaders from central Asia, remained beacons of high culture in their regions. So did Egypt and Mesopotamia, whether under Pharaohs and Babylonians, Greeks, Romans, Arabs or Turks. Invaded for a millennium by the peoples from steppe and desert, all the great empires of the old world survived with one exception. Only the Roman Empire was permanently destroyed.

Without such a collapse of cultural continuity, which made itself felt even at the modest level of gardening and flower-culture,[9] a 'Renaissance' – that is an attempted return, after a thousand years, to a forgotten, but supposedly superior, cultural and technical heritage – would have been neither necessary nor conceivable. Who, in China, needed to return to classics which every candidate had to memorize for the state examinations, held without a break annually since long before the Christian era? The erroneous conviction of Western philosophers, not excluding Marx, that a dynamic of historical development could be discovered only in Europe, but not in Asia or Africa, is due, at least in part, to this difference between the continuity of the other literate and urban cultures and the discontinuity in the history of the West.

But only in part. For from the end of the fifteenth century world history unquestionably became Eurocentric, and remained so until the twentieth century. *Everything* that distinguishes the world of today from the world of the Ming and Mughal emperors and the Mamelukes originated in Europe – whether in science and technology, in the economy, in ideology and politics, or in the institutions and practices of public and private life. Even the concept of the 'world' as a system of human communications embracing the entire globe could not exist before the European conquest of the western hemisphere and the emergence of a capitalist world economy. This is what fixes the situation of Europe in world history, what defines the problems of European history, and indeed what makes a specific history of Europe necessary.

But this is also what makes the history of Europe so peculiar. Its subject is not a geographical space or a human collective, but a process. If Europe had not transformed itself and thereby transformed the world, there would be no such thing as a single, coherent history of Europe, for 'Europe' would no more have existed than 'South-east Asia' as concept and history existed (at least before the era of European empires). And indeed a 'Europe' conscious of itself as such, and more or less coinciding with the geographical continent, emerges only in the epoch of modern history. It could emerge only when Europe could no longer be defensively defined as 'Christianity' against the Turks and, conversely, when the religious conflicts between Christian faiths retreated before the secularization of state policy and the culture of modern science and scholarship. Hence, from some time in the seventeenth century, the new and self-conscious 'Europe' appears in three forms.

First, it emerged as an international state system, in which state foreign policies were supposed to be determined by permanent 'interests', defined as such by a 'reason of state' which kept aloof from religious faith. In the course of the eighteenth century Europe actually acquired its modern cartographic definition, as the system took the form of a *de facto* oligarchy of what later came to be called the 'powers', of which Russia was an integral part. Europe was defined by the relations between the 'great powers' which, until the twentieth century, were exclusively European. But this state system has ceased to exist.

Second, 'Europe' consisted of a now possible community of scholars or intellectuals engaged, across geographical borders, languages, state loyalties, obligations or personal faiths in the construction of a collective edifice, namely that modern *Wissenschaft* which embraces the whole range of intellectual activity, science and scholarship. 'Science' in this sense emerged in the region of European culture and, until the beginning of our century, remained virtually confined to the geographical area between Kazan and Dublin – admittedly with gaps in south-eastern and south-western parts of the continent. What has become the 'global village' in which we live today, or at least pass some of our lives, was then the 'European village'. But today the global village has swallowed the European.

Third, 'Europe', especially in the course of the nineteenth century, emerged as a largely urban model of education, culture and ideology, though from the start the model was seen as exportable to overseas communities of European settlers. Any world map of the universities, opera houses and publicly accessible museums and libraries existing in the nineteenth century will rapidly establish the point. But so will a map showing the distribution of the nineteenth-century ideologies of European origin. Social democracy as a political and (since the First World War) a state-sustaining movement was and remains almost wholly European, as did the Second (Marxist–social democratic) International – but not the Marxist communism of the Third International after 1917. Nineteenth-century nationalism, especially in its linguistic forms, is hard to find outside Europe even today, although varieties with a primarily confessional or racial colouring unfortunately appear to be penetrating into other parts of the Old World in recent decades. These ideas may be traced back to the eighteenth-century Enlightenment. Here, if at all, we find the most lasting and specifically European intellectual heritage.

However, all these are not primary but secondary characteristics of European history. There is no historically homogeneous Europe, and those who look for it are on the wrong track. However we define 'Europe', its diversity, the rise and fall, the coexistence, the dialectical interaction of its components, is fundamental to its existence. Without it, it is impossible to understand and explain the developments which led to the creation and control of the modern world by processes which came to maturity in Europe and nowhere else. To ask how the Occident broke loose from the Orient, how and why capitalism and modern society came to develop fully only in Europe, is to ask the fundamental questions of European history. Without them, there would be no need for the history of this continent as distinct from the rest.

But just these questions take us back into the no-man's land between history and ideology or, more precisely, between history and cultural bias. For historians must give up the old habit of looking for specific factors, to be found only in Europe, which made our culture qualitatively different from, and therefore superior to, others – for instance, the unique rationality of European thinking, Christian tradition, this or that specific item inherited from classical antiquity, such as Roman property law. First, we are no longer superior, as we seemed to be when even all the world champions of the unquestionably Oriental game of chess were, without exception, Westerners. Second, we now know that there is nothing specifically 'European' or 'Western' about the *modus operandi* which, in Europe, led to capitalism, to the revolutions in science and technology, and the rest. Thirdly, we now know that we must avoid the temptations of *post hoc, propter hoc.* When Japan was the only non-Western industrial society, historians scoured Japanese history for similarities with Europe – for example in the structure of Japanese feudalism – which might explain the uniqueness of Japan's development. Now that there are plenty of other successful non-Western industrial economies, the inadequacy of such explanations leaps to the eye.

Yet the history of Europe remains unique. As Marx observed, the history of humanity is one of its growing control over the nature in which and by which we live. If we think of this history as a curve, it will be a curve with two sharp upward turns. The first is the late V. Gordon Childe's 'neolithic revolution' which brought agriculture, metallurgy, cities, classes and writing. The second is the revolution which brought modern science, technology and economy. Probably the first occurred independently, in varying degrees, in different parts of the world. The second occurred only in Europe and hence, for a few centuries, made Europe into the centre of the world and a few European states into the lords of the globe.

This era, 'The Age of Vasco de Gama', in the phrase of the Indian diplomat and historian Sardar Panikkar, is now at an end. We no longer know exactly what to do about European history in a world that is no longer Eurocentric. 'Europe' – to cite John Gillis again – 'has lost its spatial and temporal centrality'.[10] Some try, mistakenly and vainly, to deny the special role played by European history in world history. Others barricade themselves behind 'the "Fortress Europe" mentality that seems to be emerging', and is so much more readily recognizable on the other side of the Atlantic than here. What is to be the direction of European history? At the end of the first post-European century since Columbus, we, as historians, need to rethink its future both as regional history and as part of the history of the globe.

CHAPTER 18

The Present as History

This chapter, written as I was about to publish a history of the 'Short Twentieth Century' (1914–91), which almost coincides with my lifetime, was given as the Creighton Lecture at the University of London in 1993. The text was published as a pamphlet by the university under the title, The Present as History: Writing the History of One's Own Times.

It has been said that all history is contemporary history in fancy dress. As we all know, there is something in this. The great Theodor Mommsen was writing about the Roman Empire as a German Liberal of the '48 vintage reflecting also on the new German Empire. Behind Julius Caesar we discern the shadow of Bismarck. The same is even more plainly true of Ronald Syme. Behind *his* Caesar there is the shadow of the fascist dictators. Yet it is one thing to write the history of classical antiquity, or the Crusades, or Tudor England as a child of the twentieth century, as all historians of these periods must do, and quite another to write the history of one's own lifetime. The problems and possibilities of doing so are the subject of my lecture tonight. I shall consider mainly three of these problems: the problem of the historian's own date of birth, or, more generally, of generations; the problems of how one's own perspective on the past can change as history proceeds; and the problem of how to escape the assumptions of the time which most of us share.

I speak to you as one who, for most of his career as an essentially nineteenth-century historian, deliberately kept away, at least in his professional writings, though not in his extracurricular ones, from the world after 1914. Like Sir Edward Grey's lights of Europe, mine also went out after Sarajevo – or, as we must now learn to call it, the first Sarajevo crisis, the one of 1914, of which President Mitterrand tried to remind the world by visiting that city on 28 June 1992, the anniversary of the assassination of the Archduke Franz Ferdinand. Alas, so far as I can tell, not a single journalist picked up what, for all educated Europeans of my age, was an obvious reference.

Still, for various reasons I find myself finally writing about the history of the Short Twentieth Century – the period which begins at Sarajevo and (as we can now sadly recognize) also ends at Sarajevo, or rather with the collapse of the socialist regimes of the Soviet Union and, consequently, of the eastern half of Europe. This is what has led me to reflect on writing about the history of one's own lifetime, for as someone born in 1917 my own life virtually coincides with the period about which I am now trying to write.

Yet the very phrase 'one's own lifetime' begs a major question. It assumes that an individual life-experience is also a collective one. In some sense this is obviously true, though paradoxical. If most of us recognize the major landmarks of global or national history in our lifetime, it is not because all of us have experienced them, even though some of us may actually have done so or even been aware at the time that they were landmarks. It is because we accept the consensus that they are landmarks. But how is such a consensus formed? Is it really as general as we, from our British or European or Western perspective, assume? There are probably not more than a half-dozen dates which are simultaneous landmarks in the separate histories of *all* regions of the world. Nineteen-fourteen is not among them, though the end of the Second World War and the Great Depression of 1929–33 probably are. There are others which, though not particularly prominent in this or that national history, would have to enter it simply because of their worldwide repercussions. The October Revolution is one such event. Insofar as there is such a consensus, how far is it permanent, how far subject to change, to erosion, to transformation and how or why? I shall try to look at some of these questions later.

Yet if we leave aside this framework of contemporary history which is constructed for us and into which we fit our own experiences, they are our own. Every historian has his or her own lifetime, a private perch from which to survey the world. Perhaps it is shared with others in a comparable situation, but, among the 6,000 million human beings at the end of the century, such peer-groups are statistically insignificant. My own perch is constructed, among other materials, of a childhood in the Vienna of the 1920s, the years of Hitler's rise in Berlin, which determined my politics and my interest in history, and the England, and especially the Cambridge, of the 1930s, which confirmed both. I know that, presumably largely because of these things, my angle of vision is different even from that of other historians who share or shared my brand of historical interpretation and worked in the same field – let's say, nineteenth-century labour history – even when we came to the same conclusions about the same problems. In his or her own way every other historian with a taste for a little analytical introspection probably has the same feeling. And when one writes not about classical antiquity or the nineteenth century, but about one's own time, inevitably the personal experience of these times shape the way we see them, and even the way we assess the evidence to which all of us, irrespective of our views, must appeal and submit. If I were to write about the Second World War, through which I served as an entirely undistinguished serviceman who never fired a shot in anger, I must in some sense see things differently from my friends whose experience of war was different – for instance from the late E. P. Thompson, who served as a tank commander in the Italian campaign, or from the Africanist Basil Davidson, who fought with the partisans in the Voivodina and Liguria.

If this is so for historians of the same age and background, the difference between generations is enough to divide human beings profoundly. When I tell my American students that I can remember the day in Berlin on which Hitler became Chancellor of Germany, they look at me as though I had told them that I was present in Ford's Theatre when President Lincoln was assassinated in 1865. Both events are equally prehistoric for them. But for me 30 January 1933 is a part of the past which is still part of my present. The schoolboy who walked home from school with his sister that day and saw the headline is still in me somewhere. I can still see the scene, as in a dream.

These divisions of age apply to historians also. The debate about John Charmley's recent *Churchill, the End of Glory: A Political Biography* has illustrated this dramatically. The argument is not about the facts, even the facts of Churchill's very poor record of judgment as a politician and a strategist. These have not been in serious dispute for a long time. Nor is it only about whether Neville Chamberlain was more right than those who wanted to resist Hitler Germany. It is also about the *experience* of living through 1940 in Britain, which men of Dr Charmley's age cannot have had. Very few of those who were lucky enough to live through that extraordinary moment in our history doubted then, or doubt now, that Churchill put into words what most British people – no, what *the* British people – then felt. Certainly I did not doubt it at the time, a sapper in a very working-class unit trying to build some patently inadequate defences against invasion on the coasts of East Anglia. What struck me then was the automatic, unthinking, absolute assumption of my mates in the 560 Field Company RE that we would go on fighting. Not that we *had* to or *chose* to or followed our leaders, but that the option of *not* going on was simply not considered. No doubt this was the reflex of men too ignorant and unthinking to recognize the desperate predicament in which Britain found herself after the fall of France, and which was obvious even to a displaced young intellectual who had only the newsagents of Norfolk to inform him. And yet it was clear to me even then that there was an unassuming grandeur about this moment, whether or not we choose to call it 'Britain's Finest Hour'. *C'était magnifique – et c'était la guerre*: and Churchill put it into words. But then, I was there.

That does not mean that Charmley, Neville Chamberlain's biographer, is not right to revive the case for the appeasers – something that is quite easy for a historian in his thirties, but almost impossible for historians of the war-generation to envisage, let alone to do. The appeasers *had* a case, the force of which the young anti-fascists of the 1930s did not recognize, because our ends were not Chamberlain's and Halifax's. In their own terms, which were also Churchill's – the preservation of the British Empire – they had a better case than Churchill's, except in one respect. Like his greater contemporary Charles de Gaulle, he knew that the loss of a people's sense of dignity, pride and self-respect may be worse for it than the loss of wars and empires. We can see this as we look around Britain today.

And yet, as our generation knows without having to go to archives, the appeasers were wrong, and Churchill for once was right, in recognizing that a deal with Hitler was not possible. In terms of rational politics it made sense, on the assumption that Hitler's Germany was a 'great power' like any other, playing the game by the tested and cynical rules of power-politics, as even Mussolini did. But it was not. Almost everybody in the 1930s at one time or another believed that such deals could be made, including Stalin. The grand alliance which eventually fought and beat the Axis came into being not because the resisters won out over the appeasers, but because German aggression *forced* the future allies together between 1938 and the end of 1941. What faced Britain in 1940–1 was not the choice between a blind will to hold out without the slightest visible prospect of victory, and the search for a compromise peace 'on reasonable conditions', for even then the record suggested that such a peace was not possible with Hitler's Germany. What was on offer was, or seemed at best to be, a slightly more face-saving version of Pétain's France. And the fact that, whatever views to the contrary can be found in the archives, Churchill carried the government with him speaks for itself. Few thought that a peace would be more than a euphemism for Nazi domination.

I don't wish to suggest that only those who can remember 1940 are likely to come to this conclusion. However, for a young historian to reach it requires an effort of the imagination, a willingness to suspend beliefs based on his or her own life experience, and a lot of hard research work. For us it does not. Nor, of course, do I wish to suggest that Dr Charmley's assessment of the consequences of going on fighting in 1940 are as mistaken as his assessment of the situation in 1940. Arguments about counterfactual alternatives cannot be settled by evidence, since evidence is about what happened and hypothetical situations did not happen. They belong to politics or ideology and not to history. I don't think Charmley is right, but that argument does not belong in this lecture.

Please don't misunderstand me. I am not just making a case for old historians of the twentieth-century over young ones. I began my career as a young historian interviewing survivors of the pre-1914 Fabian Society about their times, and the first lesson I learned was that they were not even worth interviewing unless I had found out more about the subject of the interview than they could remember. The second lesson was that, on any independently verifiable fact, their memory was likely to be wrong. The third lesson was that it was pointless to get them to change their ideas which had been formed and set a very long time ago. Historians in their twenties and thirties no doubt have this experience still with their aged sources, which must, in principle, include historians who are also rather senior citizens. Nevertheless, we have some advantages. Not the least of them, for those who set out to write the history of the twentieth century, is the mere fact of knowing, without special effort, *how much things have changed.* The past thirty or forty years have been the most revolutionary era in recorded history. Never before has the world, that is to say the lives of the men and women who live on earth, been so profoundly, dramatically and extraordinarily transformed within such a brief period. This is difficult for generations to grasp intuitively, who have not seen what it was like before. A former member of the band of the Sicilian bandit Giuliano, returned after twenty years in jail to his native town near Palermo, once told me, lost and disoriented: 'Where once there were vineyards, now there are *palazzi*.' (He meant the apartment blocks of the real-estate developers.) Indeed, he was right. The country of his birth had become unrecognizable.

Those who are old enough to remember do not take these changes for granted. They *know*, as very young historians cannot, without a special effort, that 'The past is another country. They do things differently there.' This may have been a direct bearing on our judgment of both past and present. For instance, as someone who lived through the rise of Hitler in Germany, I know that the old streetcorner Nazis behaved quite differently from the neo-Nazis of today. For one thing, I doubt whether in the early 1930s there is a recorded case of a Jewish house being attacked and burned down with its inhabitants by young Nazis acting without specific orders, as happens quite often now to Turkish and other immigrant houses. The young men who do this may use the symbols of the Hitler era, but they represent a different political phenomenon. Insofar as the beginning of historical understanding is an appreciation of the *otherness* of the past, and worst sin of historians is anachronism, we have a built-in advantage to offset our numerous disadvantages.

However, whether or not we give old age the advantage over youth, in one respect the change in generations is patently central to both the writing and the practice of twentieth-century history. There is no country in which the passing of the political generation which had direct experience of the Second World War has not marked a major, if often silent, shift in that country's politics, as well as in its historical perspective on the war and – as is evident in both France and Italy – the Resistance. This applies, more generally, to the memory of any of the great upheavals and traumas in national life. I don't think it is an accident that a history of Israel which is not dominated by nationalist mythology and polemic did not appear in that country until the middle 1980s – say forty years after the establishment of the state, or that Irish history written by the Irish did not really emancipate itself from the heritage of both Fenian myth and unionist counter-myth until the 1960s.

Let me now turn to the second of my observations, which is the reverse of the first. It deals not with the effect of the historian's age or his perspective on the century, but with the effect of the passing years of the century on the historian's perspective, whatever his or her age.

I shall begin with a conversation between Harold Macmillan and

President Kennedy in 1961. Macmillan thought the Soviets 'have a buoyant economy and will soon outmatch capitalist society in the race for material wealth'. However preposterous the statement now seems, there were plenty of well-informed people at the end of the 1950s who took, or at any rate did not dismiss, this view, especially after the Soviets demonstrated that they had beaten the USA in space technology. It would not have been absurd for a contemporary historian writing in the 1960s to have accepted it. Our wisdom is not that we necessarily understand the mechanisms of the Soviet economy better than the economists of 1961, but that the passage of time has provided us with the historian's ultimate weapon, hindsight. In this instance hindsight is correct, but it can also be misleading. For instance, since 1989 it has become common among many observers, especially economists with a better understanding of market theory than of historical reality, to think of the Soviet and similar economies as a complete field of ruins, because that is what they became after the collapse of the Soviet bloc and the Soviet Union. In fact, though by the 1980s plainly quite creaky and inferior to capitalist economies both in technology and in the ability to provide their inhabitants with goods and services, and slowly running down, they were in their own way a working economic system. They were not on the verge of collapse. Indeed, my friend Ernest Gellner, a lifelong critic of communism, who spent a year in Moscow in the late 1980s, has recently suggested that, if the USSR could have isolated itself totally from the rest of the world as a sort of small planet of its own, its inhabitants would almost certainly have agreed that under Brezhnev they lived better and easier lives than any earlier generation of Russians.

What is at issue here is not simply the historian's or anyone else's capacity to predict. It might well be worth discussing why so very few of the dramatic events in world history of the past forty years have been predicted or even expected. I would even guess that the predictability of twentieth-century history has become distinctly lower since the Second World War. After 1918, another world war and even the world depression were quite often predicted. But, after the Second World War, did the economists predict the 'thirty glorious years' of the great world boom? No. They expected a post-war slump. Did they predict the end of the Golden Age at the start of the 1970s? The OECD predicted continued, even accelerated, growth of 5 per cent per annum. Did they predict the present economic troubles, which are sufficiently serious to have broken the half-century's taboo on the use of the word 'depression'? Not much. Predictions were and are being made on the basis of far more advanced models than were available between the wars, and on the basis of enormous and unprecedented inputs of data, processed at the speed of light by the most complex and sophisticated machinery. The record of the political predictors, amateurs by comparison, is no better. However, I have not the time to consider the nature and the methodological implications of these failures here. The point I want to concentrate on is that *even the recorded past* changes in the light of subsequent history.

Let me illustrate. Very few people would deny that an epoch in world history ended with the collapse of the Soviet bloc and the Soviet Union, whatever we read into the events of 1989–91. A page in history has been turned. The mere fact that this is so is enough to change the vision of every living historian of the twentieth century, for it turns a tract of time into a historic period with its own structure and coherence or incoherence – 'the short twentieth century' as my friend Ivan Berend calls it. Whoever we are, we cannot fail to see the century as a whole differently from the way we would have done before 1989–91 inserted its punctuation mark into its flow. It would be absurd to say that we can now stand back from it, as we can from the nineteenth century, but at least we can see it as a whole. In a word, the history of the twentieth century written in the 1990s must be qualitatively different from any such history written before.

Let me be even more concrete. When I was first asked to write a book on the twentieth century to round off or complement the three volumes I'd written about the nineteenth, that is to say about five years ago, I thought I could see the Short Century as a sort of diptych. Its first half – from 1914 to the aftermath of the Second World War – was plainly an age of catastrophe, in which every aspect of nineteenth-century liberal capitalist society collapsed. It was an era of world wars, followed by social revolutions and the collapse of the old empires, of the world economy close to breakdown, of the collapse or defeat of liberal democratic institutions almost everywhere. The second half, from the late 1940s on, was the exact opposite: an era when, in one way or another, liberal capitalist society reformed and restored itself to flourish as never before. And the extraordinary, unprecedented and unparalleled Great Leap Forward of this world economy in the third quarter of the (long) twentieth century seemed to me – and still seems to me – to be the feature of the twentieth-century landscape which observers will see as central in the third millennium. It was possible, even then, to see the socialist sector of the world not as a global economic alternative to capitalism – by the 1980s its inferiority was evident – but as a product of capitalism's age of catastrophe. In the 1980s it no longer looked like the global alternative to capitalism, as it had done to many in the 1930s. Though its future seemed problematic, it no longer looked central. Again, everyone was aware that the Golden Age of the world economy's Great Leap Forward had come to an end in the early 1970s. Economic historians are quite familiar with these long swings of twenty to thirty years of economic boom followed by a much more problematic period of about the same length. They can be traced back to at least the eighteenth century, they are best known as the Kondratiev long waves, and are so far quite inexplicable. Nevertheless, though these changes of, as it were, global pace have usually had fairly substantial political and ideological consequences, these did not yet seem sufficiently dramatic to disturb the general picture. You will recall that the later 1980s were a period of substantial boom in the developed capitalist world.

Within a year or two it plainly became necessary to rethink this binary shape of the twentieth century. On the one hand the Soviet world collapsed, with unpredicted but catastrophic economic consequences. On the other, it became increasingly evident that the Western world economy itself was in the most severe trouble it had known since the 1930s. By the early 1990s even Japan was shaky, and the economists once again began to worry about mass unemployment rather than inflation, as they had in the prehistoric days of the 1940s. Governments of all shapes and sizes, though now advised by greater armies of economists than ever before, once again found themselves not knowing what to do, or helpless. The ghost of Kondratiev had, after all, struck again. It also now appeared that, while the Eastern political systems ceased to exist, the stability of the non-communist ones, in both the developed and the third worlds, could also no longer be taken for granted. To put it briefly, the history of the Short Twentieth Century now looked much more like a triptych, or a sandwich: a comparatively brief Golden Age separating two periods of major crisis. We do not yet know the outcome of the second of these. That will have to be left to the historians of the next century.

When I first submitted an outline to my publishers, I did not see things this way. I could not have seen it this way, though perhaps a better historian might have. As I am fortunately a procrastinating author, by the time I began to write I did. What had changed was not the facts of world history since 1973 as I knew them, but the sudden conjunction of events in both East and West since 1989 which almost forced me to see the past twenty years in a new perspective. I cite my experience not because I want to persuade you to see the century in this perspective also, but simply to demonstrate what a difference living through two or three dramatic years can make to the way one historian can look at the past. Will a historian writing in fifty years' time see our century in this light? Who knows? It does not matter whether I care. But he or she will almost certainly be less at the mercy of relatively short-term movements of the historical weather, as experienced by those who live through them. This is the predicament of the historian of his or her own times.

Let me now turn to the third problem of writing twentieth-century history. It affects historians of all generations and is, unfortunately, less subject to rapid revision in the light of historical events, although it is fortunately not immune to the erosion of historical change. It brings me back to the question of historical consensus which I mentioned earlier on. I mean the general pattern of our ideas about our times, which imposes itself on our observation. We have lived through a century of wars of religion and this has affected all of us, including the historians. It is not only the rhetoric of politicians which treats the events of the century as a struggle between Good and Evil, Christ and Antichrist. The German *Historikerstreit* or 'Battle of the Historians' of the 1980s was not about whether the Nazi period should be seen as part of German history, rather than a strange nightmare parenthesis in it. There was no real disagreement about this. It was about whether any historical attitude to Nazi Germany other than total condemnation did not run the risk of rehabilitating an utterly infamous system, or at least of mitigating its crimes. At a lower level, many of us still find the behaviour of the sort of young men who become football hooligans more shocking and frightening when it is accompanied by swastikas and ss tattoos – and, conversely, the sub-cultures which deliberately adopt these fashions do so as a declaration of total rejection of the conventional standards of a society which sees these symbols as – literally – the marks of hell. The strength of these feelings is such that, while I am saying these sentences, I am uneasily aware that even today they may still be interpreted by some as a sign of being 'soft on Nazism', and so require some kind of disclaimer.

The danger of wars of religion is that we continue to see the world in terms of zero-sum games, of mutually incompatible binary divisions, even when the wars are over. Seventy-odd years of worldwide ideological conflict have made it almost second nature to divide the economies of the world into socialist and capitalist ones, state- and privately based economies, and to see an either/or choice between the two. If we see conflict between the two as normal, the 1930s and 1940s when liberal capitalism and Stalinist communism found themselves making common cause against the danger of Nazi Germany will look anomalous. They still seem so to me, though they were clearly in some sense the central hinge of twentieth-century history. For it was both the sacrifice of the USSR and the ideas of macro-economic planning and management pioneered there that saved liberal capitalism and helped to reconstitute it. It was the salutary fear of revolution that provided much of the incentive to do so.

But will these central decades of the century seem so anomalous to the historian of 2093, who, looking back, will observe that actually the mutual declarations of hostility between capitalism and socialism never led to real war between them, though socialist countries launched military operations against one another, and so did non-socialist countries?

If the famous imaginary Martian observer were to look at our world, would he, she or it actually choose to make such a binary division? Would the Martian classify the social and political economies of the USA, South Korea, Austria, Brazil, Singapore and Ireland under the same heading? Would the economy of the USSR which collapsed under the stress of reform be fitted into the same pigeonhole as that of China, which plainly did not? If we put ourselves in the position of such an observer, we would have no trouble finding a dozen other patterns into which the economic structures of the world's countries can be fitted more easily than into a binary bed of Procrustes. But we are once again at the mercy of time. If it is now possible at least to abandon the pattern of mutually exclusive binary opposites, it is as yet far from clear which of the thinkable alternatives can be most usefully substituted. Once again, we shall have to leave it to the twenty-first century to make its own decisions.

I have little to say about the most obvious limitation on the contemporary historian, namely the inaccessibility of certain sources, because this strikes me as among the least of his or her problems. Of course we can all think of cases where such sources are essential. Clearly much of the history of the Second World War had to be incomplete or even wrong until writing about the famous code-breaking establishment at Bletchley became permissible in the 1970s. Yet in this respect the historian of his own times is not worse off than the historian of the sixteenth century, but better off. At least we know what might, and in most cases sooner or later will, become available, whereas the gaps in the past record are almost certainly permanent. In any case the fundamental problem for the contemporary historian in our endlessly bureaucratized, documented and endlessly enquiring times is an unmanageable excess of primary sources rather than a shortage of them. Today even the last great archival continent, the public records of the Soviet bloc, has been opened to exploration. Inadequacy of sources is the last thing we can complain about.

You will, perhaps, be relieved that at the end of a lecture devoted to the difficulties of writing the history of one's own times, I seem to end on this note of modest encouragement. You may feel that it hardly compensates for the scepticism of my earlier remarks. But I wouldn't want to be misunderstood. I speak as someone who is actually trying to write about the history of his own times and not as someone who tries to show how impossible it is to do so. However, the fundamental experience of everyone who has lived through much of this century is error and surprise. What has happened has been, far more often than not, quite unexpected. All of us have been mistaken more than once in our judgments and expectations. Some have found themselves agreeably surprised by the course of events, but probably more have been disappointed, their disappointment often sharpened by earlier hope, or even, as in 1989, by euphoria. Whatever our reaction, the discovery that we were mistaken, that we cannot have understood it adequately, must be the starting-point of our reflections on the history of our times.

There are cases – perhaps mine is among them – where this discovery can be particularly helpful. Much of my life, probably most of my conscious life, was devoted to a hope which has been plainly disappointed, and to a cause which has plainly failed: the communism initiated by the October Revolution. But there is nothing which can sharpen the historian's mind like defeat. Let me conclude with a passage from an old friend of very different convictions, who has used this observation to explain the achievement of a whole range of historical innovators from Herodotus and Thucydides to Marx and Weber. This is what Professor Reinhard Koselleck writes:

The historian on the winning side is easily inclined to interpret short-term success in terms of a long-term ex-post teleology. Not so the defeated. Their primary experience is that everything happened otherwise than hoped or planned ... They have a greater need to explain why something else occurred and not what they thought would happen. This may stimulate the search for middle-range and long-term causes which explains the ... surprise ... generating more lasting insights of, consequently, greater explanatory power. In the short run history may be made by the victors. In the long run the gains in historical understanding have come from the defeated.

Koselleck has a point, even if he stretches it. (In fairness to him I should add that, knowing German historiography of both the postwar periods, he does not suggest that the experience of defeat *alone* is enough to guarantee good history.) Still, if he is even partly right, the end of this millennium should inspire a lot of good and innovatory history. For, as the century ends, the world is fuller of defeated thinkers wearing a very wide variety of ideological badges than of triumphant ones – especially among those old enough to have long memories.

Let us see whether he is right.

CHAPTER 19

Can We Write the History of
the Russian Revolution?

This text, here published for the first time, was given as the Isaac Deutscher Lecture in London on 3 December 1996. It is intended to discuss, among other matters, the problem of counterfactual ('what if') history.

I have chosen my subject as a tribute to Isaac Deutscher, whose most lasting work is a classic in the history of the Russian Revolution, namely his life of Trotsky. So the immediate answer to this question in my title is obviously yes.

But this still leaves open the wider question: can we *ever* write the definitive history of anything, not just history as seen today, or in 1945 – including, of course, of the Russian Revolution? Here, in an obvious sense the answer is no, in spite of the fact that there is in an objective historical reality, which historians investigate, to establish, among other things, the difference between fact and fiction. You are free to believe that Hitler escaped from the Russians and took refuge in Paraguay, but it isn't so. Still, every generation asks its particular new questions about the past. And they will go on doing so. And remember, in the history of the modern world we are dealing with an almost infinite accumulation of public and private records. There is no way of even guessing what future historians will look for and find in them that we haven't thought of. The French Revolutionary archives have kept historians busy for 200 years, and there's no sign of diminishing returns. We have only just started on the Himalayas of documentation in the Soviet archives. So a definitive history is not possible. And yet history as a serious activity is possible because historians can agree about what they are talking about, on what questions they are discussing, and even on enough of the answers to narrow down their differences sufficiently for meaningful debate.

In the field of twentieth-century Russian history this has long been almost impossible. Now the end of the Soviet Union has, inevitably, changed the way all historians see the Russian Revolution, because they are now able – they are, in fact, obliged – to see it in a different perspective, like a biographer of a dead, as distinct from a living, subject. It is, of course, patent that it will take a long time before the passions of those who write the history of the USSR will have cooled down to the tepid temperature of those who nowadays write the history of the Protestant Reformation, which used to be a matter for great bitterness between Catholic and Protestant scholars, or those who write about the Revolution of 1688 outside Martin McGuiness's Derry and the Rev. Ian Paisley's Bushmills, home of what was once described to me by an ideological Irish drinker as 'a Protestant whisky'. In the former USSR and the successors to the socialist states the history of the Russian Revolution is still written in this spirit, which is why nothing except new source-materials for history, but not good history, is likely to come out from there. Even outside, most of us are still too close in emotion and partiality to see the Cold War between capitalism and communism – because the two systems never actually fought each other on the field of battle – as we see the Thirty Years War.

There is another thing. We can make a judgment of the Revolution which started the USSR, but not yet of its end, and this will certainly affect historical judgment. The catastrophe into which the common people of the old USSR have been plunged by the end of the old system is not yet over. I suggest that the sudden, revolutionary leap from the old system to capitalism which has been imposed on them has disrupted the economy perhaps more than the Second World War, more than the October Revolution did, and the economy of the region has already taken longer to recover from it than it did in the 1920s and 1940s. Our assessment of the entire Soviet phenomenon remains provisional. Nevertheless, we can now begin to ask: on what can historians of the Russian Revolution legitimately agree today? Can we reach a consensus on some questions in the history of the Russian Revolution which need to be asked, and on some elements in it which can be firmly established by the rules of research and evidence, and therefore are beyond serious dispute?

One problem is that the most difficult such questions lie beyond the usual range of historical proof and disproof, because they are about might-have-beens. Much of what actually happened can now be known because information is available, although during practically all the life of the USSR much was inaccessible, hidden behind locked archive doors and barricades of official lies and half-truths.

This is why an enormous mass of the literature that appeared during that time will now have to be junked, whatever its ingenuity in using fragmentary sources and the plausibility of its guesswork. We just won't need it any more. Robert Conquest's *The Great Terror*, for instance, will drop out of sight as the major treatment of its subject, simply because the archival sources are now available, though these sources won't eliminate all argument. Conquest will be read as a remarkable pioneer effort to assess the Stalin Terror, but one which has inevitably become obsolete as a treatment of the terrible facts it tried to investigate. In short, he will eventually be read more for what his book tells us about the historiography of the Soviet era than for what it tells us about its history. When better or more complete data are available, they must take the place of poor and incomplete ones. This alone will transform the historiography of the Soviet era, although it won't answer all our questions, particularly those concerning the early Soviet period before the full bureaucratization of the regime, when the Soviet government and party actually didn't know much of what was going on in their territory.

On the other hand, the most burning debates about twentieth-century Russian history have not been about what happened, but about what might have happened. Here are some. Was a Russian revolution inevitable? Could Tsarism have saved itself? Was Russia on the way to a liberal capitalist regime in 1913? Once the Revolution had occurred, we have an even more explosive set of counter-factuals. What if Lenin had not got back to Russia? Could the October Revolution have been avoided? What would have happened in Russia if it had been avoided? More to the point of Marxists: what made the Bolsheviks decide to take power with an obviously unrealistic programme of socialist revolution? Should they have taken power? What if the European revolution – that is the German revolution, on which they put their money – had taken place? Could the Bolsheviks have lost the Civil War? But for the Civil War, how would the Bolshevik Party and Soviet policy have developed? Having won it, were there alternatives to the return to market economics under the NEP ('New Economic Policy')? What might have happened if Lenin had continued in full action? The list is endless, and I have merely mentioned some of the obvious counterfactual questions of the period up to Lenin's death. The object of my lecture isn't to give my answer to these questions, but to try and put such questions into the perspective of a working historian.

They cannot be answered on the basis of evidence about what

happened, because they are about what did not happen. Thus we can say, beyond serious doubt, that in the autumn of 1917 an enormous wave of popular radicalization, of which the Bolsheviks were the main beneficiaries, swept the provisional government aside, so that, by the time of the October Revolution, power didn't so much have to be seized as picked up from where it had been dropped. We have good evidence for this. The idea that October was nothing more than some sort of conspiratorial coup simply won't stand up. To recognize this you have only to read the report, written *before* the October Revolution by the then correspondent of the *Manchester Guardian*, Philips Price, after several weeks' tour of the Volga provinces. By the way, I know of no other foreign eyewitness, with a good knowledge of Russia and fluency in the Russian language, who made such a tour of the Russian heartland at that time. 'The Maximalist fanatics', he wrote, 'who still dream of a social revolution throughout all Europe have, according to my observations in the provinces, recently acquired an immense if amorphous following.' By the time this article, filed from Yaroslav, reached Manchester, the Bolsheviks had taken power, and so the paper published it in December 1917 under the headline 'How the Maximalists have come to gain control', but it had actually been sent off before October.

But of course questions about alternatives cannot be settled in this way – for instance, what might have happened if the Bolsheviks had not decided to take over, or had been willing to take over at the head of a broad coalition with the other socialist and social-revolutionary parties. How could we know? Philips Price, for instance, in the same dispatch, suggested the possibility that the enormous hatred of the war, which was, he thought, what held together 'the confused social mass' of revolution (his words) would produce 'a Napoleon – a peace dictator ... who will put an end to the war even at the cost of territorial losses to Russia and at the price of the political liberties won by the Revolution'. We know that something like this did happen. Looking back we can see that in the situation of 1917 he was certainly right in supposing that, one way or another, Russia would inevitably get out of the war soon. But he also thought once that happened the Revolution would break up into struggling bits and this would lead to its defeat. This didn't happen, but to a pretty good contemporary observer it also looked highly likely. As it didn't happen, even historians can't do more than go on speculating about it.

But how exactly do we speculate? And what is the point of at least some such speculations? The trouble is there are at least three different kinds of counterfactuals. One kind, though fascinating, is analytically useless. Take Lenin, or for that matter, Stalin. Without the personal input of these single men, the history of the Russian Revolution would certainly have been very different. In spite of a lot of general political and ideological waffle, individuals do not always make all that much difference in history. For instance, the USA has actually lost seven presidents before the end of their term by assassination or otherwise since 1865 but, seen in the century's perspective, it doesn't seem to have made much difference to the shape of US history. On the other hand, sometimes individuals do make a difference, as in the case of Lenin and Stalin – or, for that matter, in the last years of the USSR. A former director of the CIA told Professor Fred Halliday in a BBC interview: 'I believe that if Andropov had been fifteen years younger when he took power in 1982, we would still have a Soviet Union with us, continuing to decline economically, increasingly disadvantaged technically ... but still extant.'[1] I don't like to agree with CIA chiefs, but this seems to me to be entirely plausible. Yet, having said that, there's not much else you can say. You can analyse the kind of historic situations in which single persons can make such a dramatic difference, positively or negatively. Possibly, as Alan Bullock does in his parallel lives of Hitler and Stalin, we can investigate the ways in which they then arrange to reinforce their personal power, as Stalin certainly did, although Lenin plainly did not try to. We can establish the limits of what such individuals with absolute domestic power could achieve, or in what way their aims and policies were not specific to themselves as individuals, but characteristic of their time, place and situation.

For instance, you can argue quite plausibly that there was room for more or less harshness in the project of very rapid industrialization by Soviet state planning, but if the USSR was committed to such a project then, however great the genuine commitment of millions to it,[2] it was going to require a good deal of coercion, even if the USSR had been led by someone less utterly ruthless and cruel than Stalin. Or again you can argue, with Moshe Lewin, that even total power could not give Stalin control over the ever swelling bureaucratic machine into which the USSR necessarily turned. Only terror, the fear of death for temporarily all-powerful functionaries, could guarantee that they obeyed the autocrat and did not enmesh him in the bureaucratic spider-web. Or, again, you can show that, given a particular historical background, even what autocrats do follows old patterns. Both Stalin and Mao knew that they were the successors to absolute emperors, and modelled themselves, to some extent at least, on their imperial predecessors – certainly they were aware that they would be seen in this light by their subjects. But, when you have said all that and more, you have still not answered the question about historical alternatives. All you have said is: 'Things could have been different if Lenin had been unable to get out of Switzerland till 1918,' or, at most, 'Things could have been very different' or 'not very different'. And you can't get any further, except into fiction.

A second lot of counterfactuals are a bit more interesting, if only because they do help the history of the Revolution to take off the blinkers of ideological polemic. Let us take the fall of Tsarism. No serious observer even before 1900 expected Tsarism to survive far into the twentieth century. A Russian revolution was universally predicted. Marx himself, in 1879, looked 'for a great and not distant crash in Russia; thinks it will begin by reforms from above which the old bad edifice will not be able to bear and which will lead to its tumbling down altogether',[3] and the British politician who reported his views to the daughter of Queen Victoria thought this view was 'not unreasonable'. In retrospect it seems pretty undeniable that the chances of Tsarism after surviving its first revolution in 1905 were small, and virtually dead well before the Great War; and not very many people at the time thought otherwise for more than a moment. We need not seriously bother about the theory that Tsarist Russia was well on the way to becoming a prosperous liberal capitalist society when the First World War and the Bolsheviks, just out of the blue, came and ruined it. But for the requirements of anti-Marxist argument, it would never have been taken seriously.

By the way, not even liberals have argued with any confidence that a liberal, democratic-parliamentary Russia was much of a possibility *after* the fall of the Tsar. Many of them would like to believe that it was nothing but a Leninist putsch which cut the throat of a promising Russian liberal democracy, but they do so without conviction. I may just remind you, in passing, that in the only reasonably free elections, held just after the October Revolution, those for the Constituent Assembly, the bourgeois Liberals scored 5 per cent and the Mensheviks 3 per cent.

On the other hand, the communists also have their 'if only' myths. My generation, for instance, was brought up on the story of the betrayal of the German Revolution of 1918 by the moderate Social Democratic leaders. The Eberts and the Scheidemanns aborted the potentially socialist and proletarian German Revolution, Soviet Russia remained isolated – and the logical development hoped for by Marx and Engels did not happen, namely a Russian Revolution sparking off proletarian revolution in countries less obviously unprepared to build a socialist economy.

Now this myth differs from the one about a liberalized Tsarism in one important respect. No realistic observer before 1917 expected, for more than the odd moment, that Tsarism would survive, let alone overcome its problems, but in 1917–18 the Marx–Engels scenario seemed very much on the cards. I don't blame German and Russian revolutionaries in 1917–19 for having these hopes, though I have argued elsewhere that Lenin should have known better by 1920. For a few weeks or even months in 1918–19 a spread of the Russian Revolution to Germany could seem on the cards.

But it wasn't. I think today there is a historical consensus about this. The First World War profoundly shook all the peoples involved in it, and the revolutions of 1917–18 were, above all, revolts against that unprecedented holocaust, especially in the countries on the losing side. But in parts of Europe, and nowhere more so than in Russia, they were more than this: they were social revolutions, rejections of the state, the ruling classes and the *status quo* by the poor. I don't think Germany belonged to the revolutionary sector of Europe. I don't think a social revolution in Germany looked in the least likely in 1913. Unlike the Tsar, I do believe that, but for the war, the Kaiser's Germany could have solved its political problems. This doesn't mean that the war was an unexpected and unavoidable accident, but that is another question. Of course the moderate Social Democratic leaders wanted to stop the German Revolution falling into the hands of the revolutionary socialists, because they themselves were neither socialists nor revolutionaries. In fact they had not even wanted to get rid of the Emperor. But that is not the point. A German October revolution, or anything like it, was not seriously on and therefore didn't have to be betrayed.

I think Lenin was mistaken in putting his money on a German revolution, but I don't think Lenin could have seen this in 1917 or 1918. It just didn't look like that. This is where historical retrospection differs from the contemporary assessment of possibilities. If we are in politics to make decisions, as Lenin was, we play them as we see them – and it was natural for him to see them that way. But the past has happened, the match can't be replayed, and therefore we can see things more clearly. The German Revolution was not a game that was lost against the run of the team's previous play. The Russian Revolution was destined to build socialism in one backward and soon utterly ruined country, although I remain to be convinced by Orlando Figes, who argues that in 1918 Lenin had already given up thinking of a revolution spreading elsewhere in Europe. On the contrary, I suspect that the archives will show that for several more years the Soviet leadership, though not prepared to jeopardize its home base in Russia, remained as committed to international revolution as Fidel Castro and Che Guevara did, and, if I may say so, often with as many illusions and as much ignorance about the situation abroad as the Cubans.[4]

I am inclined to think that Lenin would have wanted to storm the Winter Palace even if he had been certain the Bolsheviks would be defeated, on what might be called by the Irish the 'Easter Rising' principle: to provide inspiration for the future, even as the defeated Paris Commune had done. Still, taking power and declaring a socialist programme made sense only if the Bolsheviks looked to a European revolution. Nobody believed Russia could do it on its own. So, should the October Revolution have been made at all? And if so, with what objects? This brings us to the third kind of counterfactuals which actually deal with alternatives considered possible at the time. Actually the question was not whether someone else should take over from the provisional government of Kerensky. This was already dead. It was not even who should take over, because the Bolsheviks were the only ones in a position to, alone or as the dominant partner in an alliance. It was *how*: whether with or without a planned insurrection, before, during or after the forthcoming Congress of Soviets, as part of a broad coalition or otherwise, and with what object, given that it was far from clear that a Bolshevik government, or any central Russian government, could survive. And on all these issues there were real arguments at the time, not only between Bolsheviks and others, but among the Bolsheviks themselves.

But remember: if we now, as historians, think that, say, Kamenev was right against Lenin, we are not actually assessing the chances of Kamenev convincing the Bolshevik Party in October 1917. We are saying: if we found ourselves in such a situation *today*, we should take his view. We are talking about the game now or in the future, not about the game in 1917, whose score can't be changed any more. And again, what exactly are we saying, if we decide in retrospect, say, that it would have been better if the Bolsheviks had not committed themselves to, in effect, single-party government? Are we suggesting that a coalition government would actually have been better at dealing with the desperate situation of Russia then, or in the long run – if there had been a long run? This, by the way, strikes me as excessively unlikely. Or are we simply saying with Gorbachev that we would have preferred the February Revolution to have evolved in a different way. That it would have been better if a democratic Russia had emerged from the revolution is something about which most people would agree. But it is a statement about our political ideas and not about history. In 1917 October followed February. History must start from what happened. The rest is speculation.

But at this stage we must leave speculation and return to the actual situation of a Russia in revolution. Great mass revolutions erupting from below – and Russia in 1917 was probably the most awesome example of such a revolution in history – are in some sense 'natural phenomena'. They are like earthquakes and giant floods, especially when, as in Russia, the superstructure of state and national institutions has virtually disintegrated. They are to a large extent uncontrollable. We must stop thinking of the Russian Revolution in terms of the Bolsheviks' or anyone else's aims and intentions, their long-term strategy, and other Marxists' critiques of their practice. Why, in fact, did they not collapse, or go down to defeat, which they could so easily have done? Initially the new regime had no power at all – certainly no significant armed power. The only real asset the new Soviet government had outside Petrograd and Moscow was their ability to articulate what the Russian people wanted to hear. What Lenin aimed at – and in the last analysis Lenin got his way in the Party – was irrelevant. He 'could have no strategy or perspective beyond choosing, day by day, between the decisions needed for immediate survival and the ones which risked immediate disaster. Who could afford to consider the possible long-term consequences for the revolution of decisions which had to be taken *now* or else there would be an end to the revolution and no further consequences to consider?'[5] Nothing was predetermined. At any time things could go wrong. Not until 1921 could the regime count on being permanent, could it take stock of the appalling state to which Russia had been reduced, or could it begin to think in years rather than months or even weeks. By this time its future course was more or less prescribed, and it was a long way from anything any Marxist, including Lenin, would have envisaged for Russia before the Revolution. Both orthodox Soviet doctrine and anti-communist conspiracy theory thought of the

Revolution as controlled and directed from above: Lenin knew better.

So how did the October Revolution come to survive? First – and here I agree very much with Orlando Figes' excellent *A People's Tragedy*[6] – the Bolsheviks won because they fought under the red flag and, however misleadingly, in the name of the Soviets. In the last analysis, the Russian peasants and workers preferred the Reds against the Whites who would, they thought, take away the land and bring back the Tsar, the gentry and the so-called 'boorzhooi' (bourgeois). They stood for the Revolution which most Russians had wanted. And the Russian Revolution, remember, was made by the masses and for its first ten years its fate was determined by the Russian masses – by what they wanted or wouldn't stand for. Stalinism put an end to that.

Second, the Bolsheviks survived because they were the only potential force of national government after the Tsar. The alternative in 1917 was not, and could not be, a democratic or a dictatorial Russia, but Russia or no Russia. Here the centralized Leninist structure of the Bolshevik Party, an institution constructed for disciplined action and therefore *de facto* for state-building, was essential, though at a greater cost to freedom than under Tsarism. But: if not the Bolsheviks, then nobody. In fact, one of the few achievements of the Russian Revolution which not even its enemies deny is that, unlike the other defeated multinational empires of the First World War, the Habsburgs and the Ottomans, Russia was not broken into pieces. It was saved as a multinational bi-continental state by the October Revolution. We consistently underestimate the appeal which Soviet Russia therefore had to non-political, even to right-wing patriotic, Russians, both during and after the Civil War: how else are we to explain the curious return of a small but influential number of Russian émigrés, civilian and military, in the Five Year Plan period? (Some may later have regretted it.)

Third, they survived because the appeal of their cause was not purely Russian. The foreign powers may have been half-hearted in supporting the various and mutually hostile White armies in the Civil War, for various reasons – but after the end of the Great War they knew that they could not have sent major forces of their own to carry on the war, least of all against the regime regarded by their soldiers as one of the workers' revolution. Again, the Bolsheviks recovered control of the Transcaucasus after the war essentially because Turkey saw them as a force against the imperialism of the British and French. Even defeated Germany, confident of its own immunity to Bolshevism, was prepared to come to terms with them. At all events, as the Red Army defeated the Polish aggression in 1920 and swept forward towards Warsaw, General Seeckt of the German army sent Enver Pasha to Russia to suggest something that sounds surprisingly like the 1939 partition of Poland in the secret clauses of the Molotov–Ribbentrop treaty. The defeat of the Red Army at the gates of Warsaw put an end to these suggestions.

But the international impact of October brings me to my last point, which is also my conclusion. The Russian Revolution really has two interwoven histories: its impact on Russia and its impact on the world. We must not confuse the two. Without the second, few except a handful of specialist historians would ever have been concerned with it. Outside the USA not many people know more about the American Civil War than that it is the setting of *Gone with the Wind*. And yet it was both the greatest war between 1815 and 1914 and by far the greatest in American history, and can also claim to have been something like a second American revolution. It meant and means much inside the USA but very little outside, for it had very little obvious effect on what happened in other countries, other than those beyond its southern borders.

On the other hand, both in Russian history and in twentieth-century world history the Russian Revolution is a towering phenomenon – but not the same kind of phenomenon. What has it meant for the Russian peoples? It brought Russia to the peak of its international power and prestige – far beyond anything achieved under the Tsars. Stalin is as certain of a major permanent place in Russian history as Peter the Great. It modernized much of a backward country, but although its achievements were titanic – not least the ability to defeat Germany in the Second World War – their human cost was enormous, its dead-end economy was destined to run down and its political system broke down. Admittedly, for most of its inhabitants who can remember, the old Soviet era certainly looks far better than what the former Soviet peoples are going through now, and will go on doing so for a good long while. But it is too early to draw up a historical balance-sheet.

We must let the various socialist and formerly socialist peoples come to their own judgment on the impact of the October Revolution on their history.

As for the rest of the world – we only knew it at second hand. As a force for liberation in the former colonial world and, in all Europe, before and during the Second World War; as the quintessential enemy for the USA and indeed all conservative and capitalist regimes for most of the century, except between 1933 and 1945; as a system profoundly (and understandably) disliked by liberals and parliamentary democrats, but at the same time recognized on the left in the industrial world from the 1930s on as something which frightened the rich into giving some political priority to the concerns of the poor. The terrible paradox of the Soviet era is that the Stalin experienced by the Soviet peoples and the Stalin seen as a liberating force outside were the same. And he was the liberator for the ones at least in part because he was the tyrant for the others.

Can historians ever come to an agreed consensus about such a figure and such a phenomenon? I don't see how they can, in the foreseeable future. Like the French Revolution, the Russian Revolution will continue to divide judgments.

CHAPTER 20

Barbarism: A User's Guide

This was given as an Amnesty Lecture in the Sheldonian Theatre, Oxford, in 1994. It was published in New Left Review *206 (1994), pp. 44–54.*

I have called my lecture 'Barbarism: A User's Guide', not because I wish to give you instructions in how to be barbarians. None of us, unfortunately, needs it. Barbarism is not something like ice-dancing, a technique that has to be learned – at least not unless you wish to become a torturer or some other specialist in inhuman activities. It is rather a by-product of life in a particular social and historical context, something that comes with the territory, as Arthur Miller says in *Death of a Salesman*. The term 'street-wise' expresses what I want to say all the better for indicating the actual adaptation of people to living in a society without the rules of civilization. By understanding this word we have all adapted to living in a society that is, by the standards of our grandparents or parents, even – if we are as old as I am – of our youth, uncivilized. We have got used to it. I don't mean we can't still be shocked by this or that example of it. On the contrary, being periodically shocked by something unusually awful is part of the experience. It helps to conceal how used we have become to the normality of what our – certainly my – parents would have considered life under inhuman conditions. My user's guide is, I hope, a guide to understanding how this has come about.

The argument of this lecture is that, after about 150 years of secular decline, barbarism has been on the increase for most of the twentieth century, and there is no sign that this increase is at an end. In this context I understand 'barbarism' to mean two things. First, the disruption and breakdown of the systems of rules and moral behaviour by which *all* societies regulate the relations among their members and, to a lesser extent, between their members and those of other societies. Second, I mean, more specifically, the reversal of what we may call the project of the eighteenth-century Enlightenment, namely the establishment of a *universal* system of such rules and standards of moral behaviour, embodied in the institutions of states dedicated to the rational progress of humanity: to Life, Liberty and the Pursuit of Happiness, to Equality, Liberty and Fraternity or whatever. Both are now taking place and reinforce each other's negative effects on our lives. The relation of my subject to the question of human rights should therefore be obvious.

Let me clarify the first form of barbarization, that is what happens when traditional controls disappear. Michael Ignatieff, in his recent *Blood and Belonging,* notes the difference between the gunmen of the Kurdish guerrillas in 1993 and those of the Bosnian checkpoints. With great perception he sees that in the stateless society of Kurdistan every male child reaching adolescence gets a gun. Carrying a weapon simply means that a boy has ceased to be a child and must behave like a man. 'The accent of meaning in the culture of the gun thus stresses responsibility, sobriety, tragic duty.' Guns are fired when they need to be. On the contrary, most Europeans since 1945, including in the Balkans, have lived in societies where the state enjoyed a monopoly of legitimate violence. As the states broke down, so did that monopoly. 'For some young European males, the chaos that resulted from [this collapse] … offered the chance of entering an erotic paradise of the all-is-permitted. Hence the semi-sexual, semi-pornographic gun culture of the checkpoints. For young men there was an irresistible erotic charge in holding lethal power in your hands' and using it to terrorize the helpless.[1]

I suspect that a good many of the atrocities now committed in the civil wars of three continents reflect this type of disruption, which is characteristic of the late-twentieth-century world. But I hope to say a word or two about this later.

As to the second form of barbarization, I wish to declare an interest. I believe that one of the few things that stands between us and an accelerated descent into darkness is the set of values inherited from the eighteenth-century Enlightenment. This is not a fashionable view at this moment, when the Enlightenment can be dismissed as anything from superficial and intellectually naive to a conspiracy of dead white men in periwigs to provide the intellectual foundation for Western imperialism. It may or may not be all that, but it is also the only foundation for all the aspirations to build societies fit for *all* human beings to live in anywhere on this Earth, and for the assertion and defence of their human rights as persons. In any case, the progress of civility which took place from the eighteenth century until the early twentieth was achieved overwhelmingly or entirely under the influence of the Enlightenment, by governments of what are still called, for the benefit of history students, 'enlightened absolutists', by revolutionaries and reformers, liberals, socialists and communists, all of whom belonged to the same intellectual family. It was not achieved by its critics. This era when progress was not merely supposed to be both material and moral but actually was, has come to an end. But the only criterion which allows us to judge rather than merely to record the consequent descent into barbarism is the old rationalism of the Enlightenment.

Let me illustrate the width of the gap between the period before 1914 and ours. I will not dwell on the fact that we, who have lived through greater inhumanity, are today likely to be less shocked by the modest injustices that outraged the nineteenth century. For instance, a single miscarriage of justice in France (the Dreyfus case) or twenty demonstrators locked up for one night by the German army in an Alsatian town (the Zabern incident of 1913). What I want to remind you of is standards of conduct. Clausewitz, writing after the Napoleonic Wars, took it for granted that the armed forces of civilized states did not put their prisoners of war to death or devastate countries. The most recent wars in which Britain was involved, that is to say the Falklands War and the Gulf War, suggest that this is no longer taken for granted. Again, to quote the eleventh edition of the *Encyclopaedia Britannica*, 'civilized warfare, the textbooks tell us, is confined, as far as possible, to the disablement of the armed forces of the enemy; otherwise war would continue till one of the parties was exterminated. "It is with good reason"' – and here the *Encyclopaedia* quotes Vattel, an international lawyer of the noble eighteenth-century Enlightenment – '"that this practice has grown in a custom within the nations of Europe".' It is no longer a custom of the nations of Europe or anywhere else. Before 1914 the view that war was against combatants and not non-combatants was shared by rebels and revolutionaries. The programme of the Russian Narodnaya Volya, the group which killed Tsar Alexander II, stated explicitly 'that individuals and groups standing outside its fight against the government would be treated as neutrals, their person and property were to be inviolate'.[2] At about the same time Frederick Engels condemned the Irish Fenians (with whom all his sympathies lay) for placing a bomb in Westminster Hall, thus risking the lives of innocent bystanders. War, he felt as an old revolutionary with experience of armed conflict, should be waged against combatants and not against civilians. Today this limitation is no more recognized by revolutionaries and terrorists than by governments waging war.

I will now suggest a brief chronology of this slide down the slope of barbarization. Its main stages are four: the First World War, the period of world crisis from the breakdown of 1917–20 to that of 1944–7, the four decades of the Cold War era, and lastly, the general breakdown of civilization as we know it over large parts of the world in and since the 1980s. There is an obvious continuity between the first three stages. In each the earlier lessons of man's inhumanity to man were learned and became the basis of new advances in barbarism. There is no such linear connection between the third and the fourth stage. The breakdown of the 1980s and 1990s is not due to the actions of human decision-makers which could be recognized as being barbarous, like the projects of Hitler and the terror of Stalin, lunatic, like the arguments justifying the race to nuclear war, or both, like Mao's Cultural Revolution. It is due to the fact that the decision-makers no longer know what to do about a world that escapes from their or our control, and that the explosive transformation of society and economy since 1950 produced an unprecedented breakdown and disruption of the rules governing behaviour in human societies. The third and fourth stages therefore overlap and interact. Today human societies are breaking down, but under conditions when the standards of public conduct remain at the level to which the earlier periods of barbarization have reduced them. They have not so far shown serious signs of rising again.

There are several reasons why the First World War began the descent into barbarism. First, it opened the most murderous era so far recorded in history. Zbigniew Brzezinski has recently estimated the 'megadeaths' between 1914 and 1990 at 187 million, which – however speculative – may serve as a reasonable order of magnitude. I calculate that this corresponds to something like 9 per cent of the world's population in 1914. We have got used to killing. Second, the limitless sacrifices which governments imposed on their own men as they drove them into the holocaust of Verdun and Ypres set a sinister precedent, if only for imposing even more unlimited massacres on the enemy. Third, the very concept of a war of total national mobilization shattered the central pillar of civilized warfare, the distinction between combatants and non-combatants. Fourth, the First World War was the first major war, at all events in Europe, waged under conditions of democratic politics by, or with the active participation of, the entire population. Unfortunately democracies can rarely be mobilized by wars when these are seen merely as incidents in the international power-game, as old-fashioned foreign offices saw them to be. Nor do they fight them like bodies of professional soldiers or boxers, for whom war is an activity that does not require hating the enemy, so long as he fights by the professional rules. Democracies, as experience shows, require demonized enemies. This, as the Cold War was to demonstrate, facilitates barbarization. Finally, the Great War ended in social and political breakdown, social revolution and counter-revolution on an unprecedented scale.

This era of breakdown and revolution dominated the thirty years after 1917. The twentieth century became, among other things, an era of religious wars between a capitalist liberalism, on the defensive and in retreat until 1947, and both Soviet communism and movements of the fascist type, which also wished to destroy each other. Actually the only real threat to liberal capitalism in its heartlands, apart from its own breakdown after 1914, came from the right. Between 1920 and Hitler's fall no regime *anywhere* was overthrown by communist or socialist revolution. But the communist threat, being to property and social privilege, was more frightening. This was not a situation conducive to the return of civilized values. All the more so, since the war had left behind a black deposit of ruthlessness and violence, and a substantial body of men experienced in both and attached to both. Many of them provided the manpower for an innovation, for which I can find no real precedent before 1914, namely quasi-official or tolerated strong-arm and killer squads which did the dirty work governments were not yet ready to do officially: *Freikorps*, Black-and-Tans, *squadristi*. In any case violence was on the rise. The enormous surge in political assassinations after the war has long been noticed, for instance by the Harvard historian Franklin Ford. Again, there is no precedent that I know before 1914 for the bloody street-fighting between organized political opponents which became so common in both Weimar Germany and Austria in the late 1920s. And where there had been a precedent, it was almost trivial. The Belfast riots and battles of 1921 killed more people than had been killed in the entire nineteenth century in that tumultuous city: 428 lives. And yet the streetcorner battlers were not necessarily old soldiers with a taste for war, though 57 per cent of the early membership of the Italian Fascist Party were. Three-quarters of the Nazi stormtroopers of 1933 were too young to have been in the war. War, quasi-uniforms (the notorious coloured shirts) and gun-carrying now provided a model for the dispossessed young.

I have suggested that history after 1917 was to be that of wars of religion. 'There is no true war but religious war' wrote one of the French officers who pioneered the barbarism of French Algerian counter-insurgency policy in the 1950s.[3] Yet what made the cruelty which is the natural result of religious wars more brutal and inhuman was that the cause of Good (that is of Western great powers) was confronted with the cause of Evil represented, most commonly, by people whose very claim to full humanity was rejected. Social revolution, and especially colonial rebellion, challenged the sense of a *natural*, as it were a divine or cosmically sanctioned, superiority of top people over bottom people in societies which were naturally unequal, whether by birth or by achievement. Class wars, as Mrs Thatcher reminded us, are usually conducted with more rancour from the top than from the bottom. The very idea that people whose perpetual inferiority is a datum of nature, especially when made manifest by skin colour, should claim equality with, let alone rebel against, their natural superiors was an outrage in itself. If this was true of the relation between upper and lower classes, it was even more true of that between races. Would General Dyer in 1919 have ordered his men to fire into a crowd, killing 379 people, if the crowd had been English or even Irish and not Indian, or the place Glasgow and not Amritsar? Almost certainly not. The barbarism of Nazi Germany was far greater against Russians, Poles, Jews and other peoples considered sub-human than against West Europeans.

And yet the ruthlessness implicit in relations between those who supposed themselves to be 'naturally' superior and their supposedly 'natural' inferiors merely speeded up the barbarization latent in any confrontation between God and Devil. For in such apocalyptic face-offs there can be only one outcome: total victory or total defeat. Nothing could conceivably be worse than the Devil's triumph. As the Cold War phrase went, 'Better dead than red', which, in any literal sense, is an absurd statement. In such a struggle the end necessarily justified *any* means. If the only way to beat the Devil was by devilish means, that is what we had to do. Why, otherwise, would the mildest and most civilized of Western scientists have urged their governments to build the atom bomb? If the other side is devilish, then we must assume that they will use devilish means, even if they are not doing so now. I am not arguing that Einstein was wrong to regard a victory by Hitler as an ultimate evil, but merely trying to clarify the logic of such confrontations, which necessarily led to the mutual escalation of barbarism. That is rather clearer in the case of the Cold War. The argument of Kennan's famous 'Long Telegram' of 1946, which provided the ideological justification of the Cold War, was no different from what British diplomats had constantly said about Russia throughout the nineteenth century: we must contain them, if need be by the threat of force, or they will advance on Constantinople and the Indian frontier. But during the nineteenth century the British government rarely lost its cool about this. Diplomacy, the 'great game' between secret agents, even the occasional war, were not confused with the apocalypse. After the October Revolution they were. Palmerston would have shaken his head; in the end, I think, Kennan himself did.

It is easier to see why civilization receded between the Treaty of Versailles and the fall of the bomb on Hiroshima. The fact that the Second World War, unlike the First, was fought on one side by belligerents who specifically rejected the values of nineteenth-century civilization and the Enlightenment speaks for itself. We may need to explain why nineteenth-century civilization did not recover from the First World War, as many expected it to do. But we know it didn't. It entered upon an age of catastrophe: of wars followed by social revolutions, of the end of empires, of the collapse of the liberal world economy, the steady retreat of constitutional and democratic governments, the rise of fascism and Nazism. That civilization receded is not very surprising, especially when we consider that the period ended in the greatest school of barbarism of all, the Second World War. So let me pass over the age of catastrophe and turn to what is both a depressing and a curious phenomenon, namely the advance of barbarism in the West after the Second World War. So far from an age of catastrophe, the third quarter of the twentieth century was an era of triumph for a reformed and restored liberal capitalism, at least in the core countries of the 'developed market economies'. It produced both solid political stability and unparalleled economic prosperity. And yet barbarization continued. Let me take, as a case in point, the distasteful subject of torture.

As I need not tell you, at various times from 1782 on, torture was formally eliminated from judicial procedure in civilized countries. In theory it was no longer tolerated in the state's coercive apparatus. The prejudice against it was so strong that torture did not return after the defeat of the French Revolution, which had, of course, abolished it. The famous or infamous Vidocq, the ex-convict turned police chief under the Restoration, and model for Balzac's character Vautrin, was totally without scruples, but he did not torture. One may suspect that in the corners of traditional barbarism that resisted moral progress – for instance in military prisons or similar institutions – it did not quite die out, or at any rate its memory didn't. I am struck by the fact that the basic form of torture applied by the Greek colonels in 1967–74 was, in effect, the old Turkish *bastinado* – variations on beating the soles of the feet – even though no part of Greece had been under Turkish administration for almost fifty years. We may also take it that civilized methods lagged where governments fought subversives, as in the Tsarist Okhrana.

The major progress of torture between the wars was under Communist and fascist regimes. Fascism, uncommitted to the Enlightenment, practised it fully. The Bolsheviks, like the Jacobins, formally abolished the methods used by the Okhrana, but almost immediately founded the Cheka, which recognized no restraints in its fight to defend the revolution. However, a circular telegram by Stalin in 1939 suggests that after the Great War 'application of methods of physical pressure in NKVD [the successor to the Cheka] practice' was not officially legitimized until 1937, that is to say it was legitimized as part of the Stalinist Great Terror. In fact it became compulsory in certain cases. These methods were to be exported to the European Soviet satellites after 1945, but we may take it that there were policemen in these new regimes who had experience of such activities in the regimes of Nazi occupation.

Nevertheless, I am inclined to think that Western torture did not learn much from, or imitate, Soviet torture, although techniques of mental manipulation may have owed more to the Chinese techniques of what journalists baptized 'brainwashing' when they came across it during the Korean War. Almost certainly the model was fascist torture, particularly as practised in the German repression of resistance movements during the Second World War. However, we should not underestimate the readiness to learn even from the concentration camps. As we now know, thanks to the disclosures of President Clinton's administration, the USA engaged, from shortly after the war until well into the 1970s, in systematic radiation experiments on human beings, chosen from among those felt to be of socially inferior value. These were, like the Nazi experiments, conducted or at least monitored by medical doctors, a profession whose members, I must say it with regret, too often allowed themselves to be involved in the practice of torture in all countries. At least one of the American medical men who found these experiments distasteful protested to his superiors that there seemed to be 'a smell of Buchenwald' to them. It is safe to assume that he was not the only one to be aware of the similarity.

Let me now bring in Amnesty, for whose benefit these lectures are held. This organization, as you know, was founded in 1961, mainly to protect political and other prisoners of conscience. To their surprise these excellent men and women discovered that they also had to deal with the systematic use of torture by governments – or barely disguised agencies of government – in countries in which they had not expected to find it. Perhaps only Anglo-Saxon provincialism accounts for their surprise. The use of torture by the French army during the Algerian war of independence, 1954–62, had long caused political uproar in France. So Amnesty had to concentrate much of its effort on torture and its 1975 Report on the subject remains fundamental.[4] Two things about this phenomenon were striking. In the first place its systematic use in the democratic West was novel, even allowing for the odd precedent of electric cattle-prods in Argentinian jails after 1930. The second striking fact was that the phenomenon was now *purely Western*, at all events in Europe, as the Amnesty Reported noted. 'Torture as a government-sanctioned Stalinist practice has ceased. With a few exceptions ... no reports of torture in Eastern Europe have been reaching the outside world in the past decade.' This is perhaps less surprising than it looks at first sight. Since the life-and-death struggle of the Russian Civil War, torture in the USSR – as distinct from the general brutality of Russian penal life – had not served to protect the security of the state. It served other purposes, such as the construction of show trials and similar forms of public theatre.

It declined and fell with Stalinism. Fragile as the communist systems turned out to be, only a limited, even a nominal, use of armed coercion was necessary to maintain them from 1957 until 1989. On the other hand it *is* more surprising that the period from the mid-1950s to the late 1970s should have been the classic era of Western torturing, reaching its peak in the first half of the seventies, when it flourished simultaneously in Mediterranean Europe, in several countries of Latin America with a hitherto unblemished record – Chile and Uruguay are cases in point – in South Africa and even, though without the application of electrodes to genitals, in Northern Ireland. I should add that the curve of Western official torturing has dipped substantially since then, partly, one hopes, because of the labours of

261

Amnesty. Nevertheless, the 1992 edition of the admirable *World Human Rights Guide* records it in 62 out of the 104 countries it surveyed and gave only fifteen a completely clean bill of health.

How are we to explain this depressing phenomenon? Certainly not by the official rationalization of the practice, as stated in the British Compton Committee, which reported rather ambiguously on Northern Ireland in 1972. It talked about 'information which it was operationally necessary to obtain as rapidly as possible'.[5] But this was no explanation. It was merely another way of saying that governments had given way to barbarism, that is that they no longer accepted the convention that prisoners of war are not obliged to tell their captors more than name, rank and number, and that more information would *not* be tortured out of them, however urgent the operational necessity.

I suggest that three factors are involved. The post-1945 Western barbarization took place against the background of the lunacies of the Cold War, a period which will one day be as hard to understand for historians as the witch craze of the fifteenth and sixteenth centuries. I shall not say more about it here, except to note that the extraordinary assumption that only the readiness to launch the nuclear holocaust at a moment's notice preserved the Western world from immediate overthrow by totalitarian tyranny was enough in itself to undermine all accepted standards of civility. Again, Western torturing clearly developed first, on a significant scale, as part of the doomed attempt by a colonial power, or at all events the French armed forces, to preserve its empire in Indochina and North Africa. Nothing was more likely to barbarize than the suppression of inferior races by the forces of a state which had recently experienced suppression by Nazi Germany and its collaborators. It is perhaps significant that, following the French example, systematic torture elsewhere seems later to have been primarily carried out by the military rather than the police.

In the 1960s, following the Cuban Revolution and the student radicalization, a third element entered the situation. This was the rise of new insurrectionary and terrorist movements which were essentially attempts by volunteer minority groups to create revolutionary situations by acts of will. The essential strategy of such groups was polarization. Either by demonstrating that the enemy regime was no longer in control, or – where the situation was less favourable – by provoking it into general repression, they hoped to drive the hitherto passive masses to support the rebels. Both variants were dangerous. The second was an open invitation for a sort of mutual escalation of terror and counter-terror. It took a very level-headed government to resist; even the British in Northern Ireland did not keep their cool in the early years. Several regimes, especially military ones, did not resist. I need hardly add that in a contest of comparative barbarism the forces of the state were likely to win – and they did.

But a sinister air of unreality surrounded these underground wars. Except in the remaining struggles for colonial liberation, and perhaps in Central America, the fights were for smaller stakes than either side pretended. The socialist revolution of the various left-wing terrorist brigades was not on the agenda. Their actual chances of defeating and overthrowing existing regimes by insurrection were insignificant, and known to be so. What reactionaries were really afraid of was not students with guns but mass movements which, like Allende in Chile and the Peronists in Argentina, could win elections, as the gunmen could not. The example of Italy demonstrates that routine politics could go on almost as before, even in the presence of the strongest force of such insurrectionaries in Europe, the Red Brigades. The main achievements of the neo-insurrectionaries was thus to allow the general level of force and violence to be ratcheted up by a few notches. The 1970s left behind torture, murder and terror in formerly democratic Chile, where its object was not to protect a military regime which ran no risk of overthrow, but to teach the poor humility and to install a system of free-market economics safe from political opposition and trade unions. In relatively pacific Brazil, not a naturally bloodthirsty culture like Colombia or Mexico, it left a heritage of death squads of policemen, scouring the streets to liquidate 'anti-socials' and the lost children of the pavements. It left behind, almost everywhere in the West, doctrines of 'counter-insurgency' which I can sum up in the words of one of the authors who surveyed these writings: 'Dissatisfaction there is always, but resistance only has a change of success against a liberal-democratic regime, or an old-fashioned, ineffectual authoritarian system.'[6] In short, the moral of the 1970s was that barbarism is more effective than civilization. It has permanently weakened the constraints of civilization.

Let me finally turn to the current period. The wars of religion in their characteristic twentieth-century form are more or less over, even though they have left behind a sub-stratum of public barbarity. We may find ourselves returning towards wars of religion in the old sense, but let me leave aside this further illustration of the retreat of civilization. The current turmoil of nationalist conflicts and civil wars is not to be regarded as an ideological phenomenon at all, and still less as the re-emergence of primordial forces too long suppressed by communism or Western universalism, or whatever else the current self-serving jargon of the militants of identity politics calls it. It is, in my view, a response to a double collapse: the collapse of political order as represented by functioning states – *any* effective state which stands watch against the descent into Hobbesian anarchy – and the crumbling of the old frameworks of social relations over a large part of the world – *any* framework which stands guard against Durkheimian *anomie*.

I believe the horrors of the current civil wars are a consequence of this double collapse. They are not a return to ancient savageries, however long ancestral memories may be in the mountains of Hercegovina and Krajina. The Bosnian communities were not prevented from cutting each other's throats by the *force majeure* of a communist dictatorship. They lived together peacefully and, at least among the 50 per cent or so of the urban Yugoslav population, intermarried to a degree inconceivable in really segregated societies like Ulster or the racial communities of the USA. If the British state had abdicated in Ulster as the Yugoslav state did, we would have had a lot more than some 3,000 dead in a quarter of a century. Moreover, as Michael Ignatieff has brought out very well, the atrocities of this war are largely committed by a typically contemporary form of the 'dangerous classes', namely deracinated young males between the ages of puberty and marriage, for whom no accepted or effective rules and limits of behaviour exist any longer: not even the accepted rules of violence in a traditional society of macho fighters.

And this, of course, is what links the explosive collapse of political and social order on the periphery of our world system, with the slower subsidence in the heartlands of developed society. In both regions unspeakable things are done by people who no longer have social guides to action. The old traditional England which Mrs Thatcher did so much to bury relied on the enormous strength of custom and convention. One did, not what 'ought to be' done, but what *was* done: as the phrase went, 'the done thing'. But we no longer know what 'the done thing' is, there is only 'one's own thing'.

Under these circumstances of social and political disintegration, we should expect a decline in civility in any case, and a growth in barbarism. And yet what has made things worse, what will undoubtedly make them worse in future, is that steady dismantling of the defences which the civilization of the Enlightenment had erected against barbarism, and which I have tried to sketch in this lecture. For the worst of it is that we have got used to the inhuman. We have learned to tolerate the intolerable.

Total war and cold war have brainwashed us into accepting barbarity. Even worse: they have made barbarity seem unimportant, compared to more important matters like making money. Let me conclude with the story of one of the last advances of nineteenth-century civilization, namely the banning of chemical and biological warfare – weapons essentially designed for terror, for their actual operational value is low. By virtually universal agreement they were banned after the First World War under the Geneva Protocol of 1925, due to come into force in 1928. The ban held good through the Second World War, except, naturally, in Ethiopia. In 1987 it was contemptuously and provocatively torn up by Saddam Hussein, who killed several thousands of his citizens with poison-gas bombs. Who protested? Only the old 'stage army of the good', and not even all of these – as those of us who tried to collect signatures at the time know. Why so little outrage? In part, because the absolute rejection of such inhuman weapons had long been quietly abandoned. It had been softened down to a pledge not to be the first to use such weapons, but, of course, if the other side used them ... Over forty states, headed by the USA, took this position in the 1969 UN resolution against chemical warfare. Opposition to biological warfare remained stronger. Its means were to be totally destroyed under an agreement of 1972: but not chemical ones. We might say that poison gas had been quietly domesticated. Poor countries now saw it simply as a possible counter to nuclear arms. Still, it was terrible. And yet – need I remind you – the British and other governments of the democratic and liberal world, so far from protesting, kept quiet and did their best to keep their citizens in the dark, as they encouraged their businessmen to sell Saddam more arms including the equipment to gas more of his citizens. They were not outraged, until he did something genuinely insupportable. I don't need to remind you what he did: he attacked the oil fields thought vital by the USA.

CHAPTER 21

Identity History Is Not Enough

This paper, which takes issue with the relativism of some current ('postmodern') intellectual fashions, was written for a special issue on history, edited by my friend Professor François Bédarida, long-time director of the Paris Institut pour l'Histoire du Temps Présent, for the journal Diogenes, *42/4 (1994), under the title: 'The Historian between the Quest for the Universal and the Quest for Identity'.*

I

It might be best to begin this discussion of the historian's predicament with a concrete experience. In the early summer of 1944, as the German army retreated northwards in Italy to establish a more defensible front against the advancing Allied forces along the so-called Gothic Line in the Apennines, its units carried out a number of massacres, usually justified as reprisals against local 'bandit' (that is partisan) activity. Fifty years later some of these village massacres in the province of Arezzo, hitherto left to the memories of the villages' own survivors and the local historians of the Resistance, provided the occasion for an international conference on the memory of German massacres in the Second World War.

The conference gathered together not only historians and social scientists from various countries in eastern and western Europe and the USA, but local survivors, old resisters and other interested parties. No subject could be less purely 'academic', even fifty years after 175 men were separated from their women and children in Civitella della Chiana, shot and dumped in the burning houses of their village. Hence, not surprisingly, the conference took place in an extraordinary atmosphere of tension and uneasiness. Everyone was aware that matters of major political, even existential, urgency were at stake. Every historian present could not fail to wonder about the relation of history and the present. After all, only a few weeks earlier Italy had elected the first government since 1943 to include fascists, and dedicated both to anti-communism and to the proposition that the Resistance of 1943–5 had not been a movement of national liberation and, in any case, that it belonged to a remote past which was irrelevant to the present and ought to be forgotten.

Everyone was uneasy. The survivors of the times of resistance and massacre were uneasy at the bringing into the open of things which, as every countryman and countrywoman knew, were best left unspoken. How, but by a tacit agreement to bury the conflicts of the past, could rural life have returned to any kind of 'normality' after 1945? (An American historian produced a perceptive paper about this mechanism of selective silence in his Croatian wife's Istrian village.) The old partisans, and indeed public opinion in the deeply left-wing region of Tuscany, were uneasy at living through a moment when the Italian Republic officially rejected the tradition of the Resistance against Hitler and Mussolini, which they (rightly) regarded as its foundation. The young, and presumably mainly left-wing, oral historians who had interviewed or re-interviewed the villagers in preparation for the conference, were shocked to find that, at least in one strongly Catholic village, the inhabitants blamed not so much the Germans for the massacre as the local youngsters who had joined the partisans and, they felt, had irresponsibly plunged their homes into disaster.

Other historians had their own reasons for unease. The German historians present were palpably haunted by what their fathers or grandfathers in 1944 had done, or failed to do. Virtually all non-Italian historians, and several Italian ones, had never heard of the massacres in whose memory the conference was organized: a troubling reminder of the sheer arbitrariness of historical survival and memory. Why had some experiences become part of a wider historical memory, but so many others not? The Russian participants made no secret of their belief that a concentration of scholarship on Nazi atrocities was a means of diverting attention from the horrors of Stalin. The specialists in the history of the Second World War, irrespective of their national backgrounds, could not avoid the question, fifty years after the event, of whether the massacres of the innocent that spring – amounting, it was said, to over 1 per cent of the total population of the province of Arezzo – were a justifiable price to pay for the relatively minor military harassment of a German force which was in any case planning to withdraw from the area within a matter of days or, at most, weeks.

The very subject-matter of the conference, atrocity, was impossible to contemplate dispassionately. Rightly, attention was not confined to local micro-history, but broadened out to consider the greater atrocities of genocide, some of whose leading historians were also present, and the wider problem of how such things are, or can be, remembered. Yet as we stood on the rebuilt piazza of a once destroyed village, listening to the elaborate commemorative narrative which the survivors and the children of the dead had constructed about that terrible day in 1944, how could we fail to see that our kind of history was not merely incompatible with theirs, but in some ways destructive of it? What was the nature of the communication between the historian, who presented the mayor of the village with the transcript of the enquiry into the massacre made by the British army a few days after it had occurred, and the mayor who received it? For one it was a primary archival source, for the other a reinforcement of the village's memorial discourse, which we historians easily recognized as partly mythological. Yet that memorial narrative was a way of coming to terms with a trauma which was as profound for Civitella della Chiana as the Holocaust is for the totality of the Jewish people. Was our history, designed for the universal communication of what could be tested by evidence and logic, relevant to their memorial, which, by its nature, belonged to no one but themselves? It was a memorial which, as we learned, the villagers had for decades kept to themselves for this reason, refusing, out of a tact which we did not share, to enquire into the details of a neighbouring village massacre because that was not their past but their neighbours'. Was our history comparable to theirs at all?

In short, no occasion could have better dramatized the confrontation between universality and identity in history, and the historians' confrontation with both past and present.

Nevertheless, this very confrontation demonstrated that for historians universality necessarily prevailed over identity. As it happened at least one historian present represented both in his own person. The organizer of the conference had himself stood on the piazza of Civitella as a small child with his mother as the Germans dragged away and slaughtered his father. He was still part of the village, where he spent the summer in the old family house. Nobody could possibly deny that for him, as for all his followers, the massacre held memories and meanings which it could not hold for the rest of us,

268

or that he would read even the archival records differently from any researcher who did not share the experience. And yet as a historian he confronted the memorial narrative which the village had constructed for itself in exactly the same way as the historians lacking this personal involvement, namely by applying the rules and criteria of our discipline. By his and our standards – by the universally accepted criteria of the discipline – the village narrative had to be tested against the sources, and by these standards it was not history, although the formation of this village memory, its institutionalization and its changes over the past fifty years were part of history. It was itself a subject for historical research by the same methods as the events of June 1944 with which it had tried to come to terms. Only in this respect was the 'culture of [Civitella's] identity' relevant to the historians' history of the massacre. In every other respect it was irrelevant.

In short, on the questions with which historical research and theoretical reaction can deal, there was and could be no difference in substance between scholars for whom the identity problems of Civitella were insignificant or uninteresting and a historian for whom they were existentially central. All historians present hoped to agree about the formulation of the questions about the Nazi atrocities, though one would not necessarily expect them to agree about them. All agreed about the procedures for answering these questions, the nature of the possible evidence which would allow them to be answered – insofar as the answers depended on evidence – and about the comparability of events which were experienced by the participants as unique and incommunicable. Conversely, those who were unwilling to submit their, or their community's, experience to these procedures, or who refused to accept the results of such tests, were outside the discipline of history, however much historians respected their motives and feelings. In fact, among the historians present there was an impressive consensus on matters of substance. It contrasted strikingly with the chaos of varied and conflicting emotions which agitated the participants.

II

The problem for professional historians is that their subject has important social and political functions. These depend on their work – who else discovers and records the past but historians? – but at the same time they are at odds with their professional standards. This duality is at the core of our subject. The founders of the *Revue Historique* were conscious of it when they stated, in the *avant-propos* to their first number that 'To study the past of France, which will be our main concern, is today a matter of national importance. It will enable us to restore to our country the unity and moral force of which it has need.'[1]

Of course, nothing was further from their confident, positivist minds than serving their nation otherwise than by the search for truth. And yet the non-academics who need and use the commodity which historians produce, and who constitute the largest and politically decisive market for it, are untroubled by the sharp distinction between the 'strictly scientific procedures' and the 'rhetorical constructions' which was so central to the founders of the *Revue*. Their criterion of what is 'good history' is 'history that is good for us' – 'our country', 'our cause', or simply 'our emotional satisfaction'. Whether they like it or not, professional historians produce the raw material for the non-professionals' use or misuse.

That history is inextricably bound to contemporary politics – as the historiography of the French Revolution continues to prove – is probably today not a major difficulty, for the debates of historians, at least in countries of intellectual freedom, are conducted within the rules of the discipline. Besides, many of the most ideologically charged debates among professional historians concern matters about which non-historians know little and care less. However, all human beings, collectivities and institutions need a past, but it is only occasionally the past uncovered by historical research. The standard example of an identity culture which anchors itself to the past by means of myths dressed up as history is nationalism. Of this Ernest Renan observed more than a century ago, 'Forgetting, even getting history wrong, is an essential factor in the formation of a nation, which is why the progress of historical studies is often a danger to nationality.' For nations are historically novel entities pretending to have existed for a very long time. Inevitably the nationalist version of their history consists of anachronism, omission, decontextualization and, in extreme cases, lies. To a lesser extent this is true of all forms of identity history, old or new.

In the pre-academic past there was little to prevent pure historical invention, such as the forgery of historical manuscripts (as in Bohemia), the writing of an ancient, and suitably glorious Scottish national epic (like James Macpherson's 'Ossian'), or the production of an entirely invented piece of public theatre purporting to represent the ancient Bardic rituals, as in Wales. (This still forms the climax of the annual National Eisteddfod or cultural festival of that small country.) Where such inventions have to be submitted to the tests of a large and established scholarly community, this is no longer possible. Much of early historical scholarship consisted of the disproof of such inventions and the deconstruction of the myths built on them. The great English medievalist J. Horace Round made his reputation by a series of merciless dissections of the pedigrees of British noble families whose claim to descent from Norman invaders he showed to be spurious. The tests are not necessarily only historic. The 'Turin shroud', to name a recent example of a holy relic of the kind that made the fortunes of medieval pilgrimage centres, could not resist the test of carbon-B dating to which it had to be submitted.

History as fiction has, however, received an academic reinforcement from an unexpected quarter: the 'growing scepticism concerning the Enlightenment project of rationality'.[2] The fashion for what (at least in Anglo-Saxon academic discourse) is known by the vague term 'postmodernism' has fortunately not gained as much ground among historians as among literary and cultural theorists and social anthropologists, even in the USA, but it is relevant to the question at issue, as it throws doubt on the distinction between fact and fiction, objective reality and conceptual discourse. It is profoundly relativist. If there is no clear distinction between what is true and what I feel to be true, then my own construction of reality is as good as yours or anyone else's, for 'discourse is the maker of this world, not the mirror'.[3] To cite the same author, the object of ethnography, as presumably of any other social and historical enquiry, is to produce a co-operatively evolved text, in which neither subject nor author nor reader, nor indeed anyone, has the exclusive right of 'synoptic transcendence'.[4] If, 'in historical as in literary discourse, even presumably descriptive language *constitutes* what it describes',[5] then no narrative among the many possible ones can be regarded as privileged. It is not fortuitous that these views have appealed particularly to those who see themselves as representing collectivities or milieux marginalized by the hegemonic culture of some group (say, middle-class white heterosexual males of Western education) whose claim to superiority they contest. But it is wrong.

Without entering the theoretical debate on these matters, it is essential for historians to defend the foundation of their discipline: the supremacy of evidence. If their texts are fictions, as in some sense they are, being literary compositions, the raw material of these fictions is verifiable fact. Whether the Nazi gas ovens existed or not can be established by evidence. Because it has been so established, those who deny their existence are not writing history, whatever their narrative techniques. If a novel were to be about the return of the living Napoleon from St Helena, it might be literature but could not be history. If history is an imaginative art, it is one which does not invent but arranges *objets trouvés*. The distinction may appear pedantic and trivial to the non-historian, especially the one who uses historical material for his or her own purposes. What does it matter to the theatrical audience that there is no historical record of a Lady Macbeth urging her husband to kill King Duncan, or of witches predicting that Macbeth would be king of Scotland, which indeed he became in 1040–57? What did it matter to the (pan-African) founding fathers of West African post-colonial states that they gave their countries the names of medieval African empires which had no obvious connection with the territories of the modern Ghana or Mali? Was it not more important to remind sub-Saharan Africans, after generations of colonialism, that they had a tradition of independent and powerful states somewhere on their continent, if not precisely in the hinterland of Accra?

Indeed, the historians' insistence, once again in the words of the first issue of the *Revue Historique*, on 'strictly scientific procedures, where every statement is accompanied by proofs, source-references and citations',[6] is sometimes pedantic and trivial, especially now that it no longer forms part of a faith in the possibility of a definitive, positivist scientific truth, which lent it a certain simple-minded grandeur. Yet the procedures of the law court, which insist on the supremacy of evidence as much as historical researchers, and often in much the same manner, demonstrate that the difference between historical fact and falsehood is not ideological. It is crucial for many practical purposes of everyday life, if only because life and death, or – what is quantitatively more important – money, depend on it. When an innocent person is tried for murder, and wishes to prove his or innocence, what is required is the techniques not of the 'postmodern' theorist, but of the old-fashioned historian.

Moreover, the historical verifiability of political or ideological claims can be vitally important, if historicity is the essential basis of such claims. This is true not only of territorial claims by states or communities, which are commonly historic. The anti-Muslim campaign [in 1992] by the integrist Hindu party BJP, which led to large-scale massacre in India, was justified on historical grounds. The city of Ayodhya was claimed to be the birthplace of the divine Rama. For this reason the construction of a mosque on a Hindu holy site, allegedly by the Mogul conqueror Babur, in such a holy place was a Muslim insult to the Hindu religion and a historic outrage. It had to be destroyed and replaced by a Hindu temple. (The mosque was actually torn down by a vast crowd of Hindu zealots, mobilized for this purpose by the BJP in 1992.) Not surprisingly, the leaders of that party declared that 'such issues cannot be resolved by court verdict', as the historic base of the claim was non-existent. Indian historians were able to show that nobody had regarded Ayodhya as the birthplace of Rama before the nineteenth century and that Mogul emperors had no specific association with the mosque, while legal regards showed that the Hindu claim to the site was in dispute. The specific tension between the religious communities was actually recent. It was a time-bomb whose fuse had been lit in 1949, when, in the aftermath of the partition of India and the establishment of Pakistan, a 'miracle of the images' appearing in the mosque had been fabricated.[7]

To insist on the supremacy of evidence, and the centrality of the distinction between verifiable historical fact and fiction, is only one of the ways of exercising the historian's responsibility, and, as actual historical fabrication is not what it once was, perhaps not the most important. Reading the desires of the present into the past, or, in technical terms, anachronism, is the most common and convenient technique of creating a history satisfying the needs of what Benedict Anderson has called 'imagined communities' or collectives, which are by no means only national ones.[8]

The deconstruction of political or social myths dressed up as history has long been part of the historian's professional duties, independent of his or her sympathies. British historians are, one hopes, as committed to British liberty as anyone, but that does not prevent them from criticizing its mythology. Every British child was once taught at school that the Magna Carta was the foundation of British liberties, but since McKechnie's monograph of 1914 every university student of British history has had to learn that the document extorted from King John by the barons in 1215 was not intended to be a declaration of parliamentary supremacy and equal rights for free-born Englishmen, even though it came to be regarded as such in British political rhetoric much later. The sceptical critique of historical anachronism is probably today the chief way in which historians can demonstrate their public responsibility. Their most important public role today, especially in the numerous states founded or reconstituted since the Second World War, is to practise his craft in such a way as to constitute 'pour la nationalité' (and for all other ideologies of collective identity) 'un danger'.

This is dramatically obvious in situations in which international conflicts hinge on historical argument, as over the present phase of the always explosive Macedonian question. Everything about this incendiary issue, which involves four countries and the European Union and may once again launch a Balkan war, is historical. The ostensible history brandished by the chief contending parties is ancient, for both Macedonia and Greece (which refuses any other independent state even the use of the name) claim the heritage of Alexander the Great. The real history is relatively contemporary, for the actual dispute between Green and its neighbours arises out of the division of Macedonia after the Balkan Wars of 1912 between Greece, Serbia and Bulgaria. All of it had previously been part of the Ottoman Empire. The Greeks ended up with the greater part of it. Which of the successor states has a claim to what part of the undefined but large territory of pre-1913 Macedonia (for the Ottoman Empire did not use the name) has always been argued in terms of academic scholarship, mostly ethnographic and linguistic. The Greek case, which is at present the most vocal, rests largely on anachronistic history because the ethnic and linguistic arguments are more likely to favour Slav and possible Albanian claimants. It is not much more convincing than the argument that France has a claim to Italy because Julius Caesar was the conqueror of Gaul. A historian who points this out is not necessarily moved by prejudice against Greeks or in favour of Slavs, though he or she will at present be more popular in Skopje than in Athens. If the same historian points out that the majority of the population of the greatest city of (undivided) Macedonia, Salonica, was identifiable neither as Greek nor as Slav but almost certainly as Muslim and Jewish, he or she will be equally unpopular among the nationalist zealots of three countries.

Yet cases such as this also suggest the limitations of the historians' function as destroyer of myth. In the first place, the strength of their critique is negative. Karl Popper taught us that the test of falsification can make a theory untenable, but does not in itself substitute a better one. In the second place, we can demolish a myth only insofar as it rests on propositions which can be shown to be mistaken. It is in the nature of historical myths, especially nationalist ones, that usually only a few of its propositions can be so discredited. The Israeli national ritual constructed round the siege of Masada does not depend on the historically verifiable truth of the patriotic legend learned by Israeli schoolchildren and visiting foreigners, and is therefore not seriously affected by the justifiable scepticism of historians specializing in the history of Roman Palestine. Moreover, even where the test can be applied, when evidence is absent, defective, conflicting or circumstantial it cannot convincingly refute even a highly implausible proposition. Evidence can show conclusively, against those who deny it, that the Nazi genocide of the Jews took place, but, though no serious historian doubts that Hitler wanted the 'Final Solution', it cannot demonstrate that he gave a specific order to this effect. Given Hitler's mode of operation, such a specific written order is unlikely, and none has been found. So, whereas it is not difficult to dismiss the theses of M. Faurisson, we cannot, without elaborate argument, reject the case made by David Irving, as most experts in the field do.

The third limitation on the historians' function as myth-slayer is even more obvious. In the short run they are impotent against those who choose to believe historical myth, especially if they hold political power, which, in many countries, and especially the numerous new states, entails control over what is still the most important channel of imparting historical information, the schools. And, let it never be forgotten, history – mainly national history – occupies an important place in all known systems of public education. The Indian historians' critique of the historic myths of Hindu fanaticism may convince their academic colleagues, but not the zealots of the BJP party. The Croatian and Serb historians who resist the imposition of a nationalist legend on the history of their states have had less influence than the long-distance nationalists of the Croat and Serb diasporas, moved by nationalist mythology immune to historical critique.

III

These limitations do not diminish the public responsibility of the historian. This rests, first and foremost, on the fact, already noted above, that historians as an occupation are the primary producers of the raw material that is turned into propaganda and mythology. We must be aware that this is so, particularly at a time when alternative ways of preserving the past – oral tradition, family memory, everything that depends on the effectiveness of intergenerational communications which are disintegrating in modern societies – are disappearing. In any case the history of large collectivities, national or other, has rested not on popular memory, but on what historians, chroniclers or antiquarians have written about the past, directly or through school textbooks, on what teachers have taught their pupils from those schoolbooks, on how writers of fiction, film producers or the makers of television and video programmes have transformed their material. Even Shakespeare's *Hamlet* was derived at various removes from the work of a historian, the Danish chronicler Saxo Grammaticus. It is quite essential that historians should constantly remember this. The crops we cultivate in our fields may end up as some version of the opium of the people.

It is true, of course, that the inseparability of historiography from current ideology and politics – all history, as Croce said, is contemporary history – opens the way to the misuse of history. Historians do not and cannot stand outside their subject as objective observers and analysts *sub specie aeternitatis*. All of us are plunged into the assumptions of our times and places, even when we practise something as far removed from today's public passions as the editing of old texts. Many of us, like the founder of the *Revue Historique*, are happy to produce work that can be of use to our people or cause. We will no doubt be tempted to interpret our findings in the way most favourable to the cause. We may be tempted to abstain from enquiring into topics likely to throw unfavourable light on it. It is not surprising that historians hostile to communism were considerably more likely to research into forced labour in the USSR than historians sympathetic to it. We may even be tempted to remain silent about unfavourable evidence, if we happen to discover it, though hardly with a good scholarly conscience. After all, no sharp line divides *suppressio veri* from *suggestio falsi*. What we cannot do without ceasing to be historians is to abandon the criteria of our profession. We cannot say what we can show to be untrue. In this we inevitably differ from those whose discourse is not so constrained.

Yet the major danger lies, not in the temptation to lie, which, after all, cannot easily survive the scrutiny of other historians in a free scholarly community, though political pressure and authority provide a buttress for untruth, even in some constitutional states. It lies in the temptation to isolate the history of one part of humanity – the historian's own, by birth or choice – from its wider context.

The internal and external pressures to do so may be great. Our passions and interests may urge us in this direction. Every Jew, for instance, whatever his or her occupation, instinctively accepts the force of the question with which, during many threatening centuries, members of our minority community confronted any and every event in the wider world: 'Is it good for the Jews? Is it bad for the Jews?' In times of discrimination or persecution it provided guidance – though not necessarily the best guidance – for private and public behaviour, a strategy at all levels for a scattered people. Yet it cannot and should not guide a Jewish historian, even one who writes the history of his own people. Historians, however microcosmic, must be for universalism, not out of loyalty to an ideal to which many of us remain attached but because it is the necessary condition for understanding the history of humanity, including that of any special section of humanity. For all human collectivities necessarily are and have been part of a larger and more complex world. A history which is designed *only* for Jews (or African-Americans, or Greeks, or women, or proletarians, or homosexuals) cannot be good history, though it may be comforting history to those who practise it.

Unfortunately, as the situation in large parts of the world at the end of our millennium demonstrates, bad history is not harmless history. It is dangerous. The sentences typed on apparently innocuous keyboards may be sentences of death.

NOTES

PREFACE

1. Joyce Appleby, Lynn Hunt and Margaret Jacob, *Telling the Truth about History* (New York, 1994).
2. Cited in Charles Issawi (ed. and trans.), *An Arab Philosophy of History: Selections from the Prolegomena of Ibn Khaldun of Tunis (1332–1406)* (London, 1950), pp. 26–7.

CHAPTER 2: THE SENSE OF THE PAST

1. I am indebted to John Womack's splendid biography of *Zapata* (New York, 1969) for the details of the Morelos movement.
2. Such pseudo-historical aspirations must not be confused with the attempts to restore historically remote regimes in traditional societies, which are almost certainly literally meant: for example the Peruvian peasant risings up to the 1920s which sometimes aimed to restore the Inca Empire, the Chinese movements, last recorded in the middle of this century, to restore the Ming dynasty. For Peruvian peasants the Incas were in fact *not* historically remote. They were 'yesterday', separated from the present merely by a readily telescoped succession of self-repeating peasant generations doing what their ancestors had done insofar as the gods and the Spaniards let them. To apply chronology to them is to introduce anachronism.
3. The mode of argument of revolutionary regimes after the triumph of their revolutions would be worth analysing in this manner. It might throw light on the apparent indestructibility of 'bourgeois survivals' or such theses as the intensification of the class struggle long after the revolution.
4. Of course if we assume that 'whatever is becoming is right', or at least inevitable, we may accept the results of extrapolation with or without approval, but this does not eliminate the problem.
5. See, for example, Alan B. Cobban, 'Medieval Student Power', *Past and Present* 53 (November 1971), pp. 22–66.
6. The stress of Russian historical popularization on the priority of Russian inventors during the later Stalin years, so excessive as to provoke foreign ridicule, actually concealed the altogether remarkable achievements of nineteenth-century Russian scientific and technological thought.
7. The number-magic which seems to be a natural by-product of at least written chronologies, even in very sophisticated societies, may be worth

investigation: even today historians find it hard to escape from the 'century' or other arbitrary units of dating.

CHAPTER 3: WHAT CAN HISTORY TELL US ABOUT CONTEMPORARY SOCIETY?

1. *Times Literary Supplement*, 16 March 1984.

CHAPTER 6: FROM SOCIAL HISTORY TO THE HISTORY OF SOCIETY

1. See the remarks of A. J. C. Rueter in *IX congrès international des sciences historiques* (Paris, 1950), vol. 1, p. 298.

2. George Unwin, *Studies in Economic History* (London, 1927), pp. xxiii, 33–39.

3. J. H. Clapham, *A Concise Economic History of Britain* (Cambridge, 1949), introduction.

4. Two quotations from the same document (Economic and Social Studies Conference Board, *Social Aspects of Economic Development*, Istanbul, 1964) may illustrate the divergent motivations behind this new preoccupation. By the Turkish president of the board: 'Economic development or growth in the economically retarded areas is one of the most important questions which confronts the world today ... Poor countries have made of this issue of development a high ideal. Economic development is to them associated with political independence and a sense of sovereignty.' By Daniel Lerner: 'A decade of global experience with social change and economic development lies behind us. The decade has been fraught with efforts, in every part of the world, to induce economic development without producing cultural chaos, to accelerate economic growth without disrupting societal equilibrium; to promote economic mobility without subverting political stability' (pp. xxiii, 1).

5. Sir John Hicks' complaint is characteristic: 'My "theory of history" ... will be a good deal nearer to the kind of thing that was attempted by Marx ... Most of [those who believe ideas can be used by historians to order their material, so that the general course of history can be fitted into place] ... would use the Marxian categories, or some modified version of them; since there is so little in the way of an alternative version that is available, it is not surprising that they should. It does, nevertheless, remain extraordinary that one hundred years after *Das Kapital*, after a century during which there have been enormous developments in social science, so little else should have emerged': *A Theory of Economic History* (London, Oxford and New York, 1969), pp. 2–3.

6. Thus Marc Ferro's sampling of the telegrams and resolutions sent to Petrograd in the first weeks of the February Revolution of 1917 is plainly the equivalent of a retrospective public opinion survey. One may doubt

whether it would have been thought of without the earlier development of opinion research for non-historical purposes. M. Ferro, *La Révolution de 1917* (Paris, 1967).

7. At the conference on New Trends in History, Princeton, New Jersey, May 1968.

8. I do not regard such devices for inserting direction into societies as 'increasing complexity' as historical. They may, of course, be true.

9. P. Baran, *The Political Economy of Growth* (New York, 1957), ch. 2.

10. For an English version of this important article, see *Social Science Information* 9 (February 1970), pp. 145–74.

11. Cf. 'At stake in a broader view of urban history is the possibility of making the societal process of urbanization central to the study of social change. Efforts should be made to conceptualize urbanization in ways that actually represent social change': Eric Lampard in Oscar Handlin and John Burchard (eds), *The Historians and the City* (Cambridge, Mass., 1963), p. 233.

12. For the possible divergences between reality and classification, see the discussions about the complex socio-racial hierarchies of colonial Latin America: Magnus Mörner, 'The History of Race Relations in Latin America', in L. Foner and E. D. Genovese (eds), *Slavery in the New World* (Englewood Cliffs, 1969), p. 221.

13. See A. Prost, 'Vocabulaire et typologie des familles politiques', *Cahiers de lexicologie*, 14 (1969).

14. T. Shanin, 'The Peasantry as a Political Factor', *Sociological Review* 14 (1966), p. 17.

15. A. Dupront, 'Problèmes et méthodes d'une histoire de la psychologie collective', *Annales: Economies, Sociétés, Civilisations* 16 (January–February 1961), pp. 3–11.

16. By 'fitting together' I mean establishing a systematic connection between different, and sometimes apparently unconnected, parts of the same syndrome – for example the beliefs of the classic nineteenth-century liberal bourgeoisie in both individual liberty and a patriarchal family structure.

17. We look forward to the time when the Russian Revolution will provide historians with comparable opportunities for the twentieth century.

18. R. Braun, *Industrialisierung und Volksleben* (Erlenbach and Zurich, 1960); *Sozialer und kultureller Wandel in einem ländlichen Industriegebiet ... im 19. und 20. Jahrhundert* (Erlenbach and Zurich, 1965); J. O. Foster, *Class Struggle and the Industrial Revolution* (London, 1974).

19. Eric Stokes, who is doing this, is conscious of applying the results of work in African history: E. Stokes, 'Traditional Resistance Movements and Afro-Asian Nationalism: The Context of the 1857 Mutiny–Rebellion in India', *Past and Present* 48 (August 1970), pp. 100–17.

20. *Centre Formation, Nation-Building and Cultural Diversity: Report on a Symposium Organized by UNESCO* (duplicated draft, n.d.). The symposium was held 28 August–1 September 1968.

21. Though capitalism has developed as a global system of economic interactions, in fact the real units of its development have been certain territorial-political units – British, French, German, US economies – which may be due to historic accident but also (the question remains open) to the necessary role of the state in economic development, even in the era of the purest economic liberalism.

CHAPTER 7: HISTORIANS AND ECONOMISTS I

1. Joseph A. Schumpeter, *History of Economic Analysis* (New York, 1954), pp. 836–7.

2. R. W. Fogel, 'Scientific History and Traditional History', in R. W. Fogel and G. R. Elton, *Which Road to the Past?* (New Haven and London, 1983), p. 68.

3. A. G. Hopkins, reviewing T. B. Birnberg and A. Resnick, *Colonial Development: An Econometric Study* (London, 1976), in *Economic Journal* 87 (June 1977), p. 351.

4. See Hans Medick, *Naturzustand und Naturgeschichte der bürgerlichen Gesellschaft* (Göttingen, 1973), p. 264.

5. J. R. Hicks, reviewing J. K. Whitaker (ed.), *The Early Economic Writings of Alfred Marshall (1867–1890)*, in *Economic Journal* 86 (June 1976), pp. 368–9.

6. E. von Böhm-Bawerk, 'The Historical vs the Deductive Method in Political Economy', *Annals of the American Academy of Political and Social Science* 1 (1980), p. 267.

7. Joseph A. Schumpeter, *Das Wesen und der Hauptinhalt der theoretischen Nationalökonomie* (Leipzig, 1908), p. 578. See also his *Economic Doctrine and Method: An Historical Sketch* (London, 1954), p. 189.

8. H. W. Macrosty, *The Trust Movement in British Industry* (London, 1907).

9. Schumpeter, *History of Economic Analysis*, p. 10.

10. Fogel and Elton, *Which Road to the Past?*, p. 38.

CHAPTER 8: HISTORIANS AND ECONOMISTS II

1. J. R. Hicks, *A Theory of Economic History* (London, Oxford and New York, 1969), p. 167.

2. Elaborated in R. Fogel and S. Engermann, *Time on the Cross* (London, 1974).

3. M. Lévy-Leboyer, 'La "New Economic History"', *Annales: Economies, Sociétés, Civilisations* 24 (1969), p. 1062.

4. Joel Mokyr, 'The Industrial Revolution and the New Economic History', in

Joel Mokyr (ed.), *The Economics of the Industrial Revolution* (London, 1985), p. 2.

5. Ibid., pp. 39–40. The matter is more fully discussed in 'Editor's Introduction: The New Economic History and the Industrial Revolution', in J. Mokyr (ed.), *The British Industrial Revolution: An Economic Perspective* (Boulder, San Francisco and Oxford, 1993), pp. 118–30, esp. 126–8.

6. Jon Elster, *Logic and Society: Contradictions and Possible Worlds* (Chichester and New York, 1978), pp. 175–221.

7. Ibid., p. 204.

8. Robert Fogel, *Railroads and American Economic Growth* (Baltimore, 1964).

9. Hicks, *Theory of Economic History*, p. 1.

10. Mokyr, *The Economics of the Industrial Revolution*, p. 7.

11. Mokyr, *The British Industrial Revolution*, p. 11.

12. Mokyr, *The Economics of the Industrial Revolution*, p. 6.

13. Paul Bairoch, *The Economic Development of the Third World since 1900* (London, 1975), p. 196.

14. Alan Milward, 'Strategies for Development in Agriculture: The Nineteenth-Century European Experience', in T. C. Smout (ed.), *The Search for Wealth and Stability: Essays in Economic and Social History Presented to M. W. Flinn* (London, 1979).

15. See E. J. Hobsbawm, 'Capitalisme et agriculture: les réformateurs Ecossais au XVIIIe siècle', *Annales: Economies, Sociétés, Civilisations* 33 (May–June 1978), pp. 580–601.

16. Maurice Dobb, *Studies in the Development of Capitalism* (London, 1946), p. 32.

17. Hicks, *Theory of Economic History*, p. 2.

18. Hla Myint, 'Vent for Surplus', in John Eatwell, Murray Milgate and Peter Newman (eds), *The New Palgrave: A Dictionary of Economics* (London, 1987), vol. 4, pp. 802–4.

19. Witold Kula, *Théorie économique du système féodal: pour un modèle de l'économie polonaise 16e–18e siècles* (Paris and the Hague, 1970).

20. Abraham Rotstein, 'Karl Polanyi's Concept of Non-Market Trade', *Journal of Economic History* 30 (1970), p. 123.

CHAPTER 9: PARTISANSHIP

1. For example in the article 'Parteilichkeit' in G. Klaus and M. Buhr, *Philosophisches Wörterbuch* (Leipzig, 1964).

2. Without entering into philosophical arguments, every historian is familiar with statements about the past which can be shown to be either 'true' or 'false', such as 'Napoleon was born in 1769' or 'the French won the Battle of Waterloo.'

3. *Leviathan*, cap. xi: 'For I doubt not, but if it had been a thing contrary to any man's right of domination, or to the interest of men that have dominion *that the three angles of a triangle should be equal to two angles of a square*; that doctrine should have been, if not disputed, yet by the burning of all books of geometry, suppressed, as far as he whom it concerned was able.'

4. J. A. Moore, 'Creationism in California', *Daedalus* (Summer 1974), pp. 173–90.

5. Cf. the late Zhdanov's rejection of the argument that technical and specialist questions be discussed in specialist journals rather than in *Bolshevik* (A. Zhdanov, *Sur la littérature, la philosophie et la musique* (Paris, 1950), pp. 57–8).

6. This is particularly thorny where orthodoxies of 'scientific politics' are split by schisms and heresies, as notably within the Trotskyist movement.

7. This has been well defined as 'an immediate reduction not only of science to ideology, but of ideology itself into an instrument of propaganda and petty justification of adventitious political positions, whereby the most abrupt changes of policy were in each instance legitimated with pseudo-theoretical arguments and presented as congruent with the most orthodox Marxism'. S. Timparano, 'Considerations on Materialism', *New Left Review* 85 (May–June 1974), p. 6.

8. Admittedly the most spectacular examples of such pseudo-scholarship, such as the forged Königinhof manuscripts among the Czechs, Ossian, or the invention of pseudo-Druidism among the Welsh, occurred before modern historical scholarship had made such patriotic fictions unconvincing. However, Czech nationalists did not, on the whole, thank T. G. Masaryk for demonstrating that they were fictions.

9. Cf. N. Pastore, *The Nature–Nurture Controversy* (New York, 1949). Karl Pearson, by the way, had earlier shown some interest in Marxism, thus confirming his interest in political ideologies.

10. Cf. N. J. Block and Gerald Dworkin (eds), *The IQ Controversy* (New York, 1976), and the review of this work by P. B. Medawar in the *New York Review of Books*.

11. The importance of such 'interdisciplinary' activity is not denied here, though it sometimes tends to be little more than a convenient way to carve out a new professional 'field' in which careers and reputations can be made and financial subsidies mobilized. The ways in which such interdisciplinary cross-fertilization operates is not yet quite clear. However, it is safe to say that in the social sciences it is not easily separable from non-academic ideological or political commitment: cf. the case of the rapidly developing field of 'socio-biology'.

12. For Crick, see R. Olby, 'Francis Crick, d.n.a., and the Central Dogma', *Daedalus* (Fall 1970), pp. 940, 943. The fact that Hoyle's theory of 'constant

creation', whose motives are largely anti-religious, is not at present accepted does not diminish the significance of his intervention into the modern debates on cosmogony. It is not the purpose of the present paper to argue that scientific partisanship always produces the correct answers. My case is that, whether it does or not, it may advance the scientific debate.

13. For earlier doubts about Burt's studies – expressed before Professor J. Tizard demonstrated that he almost certainly cheated – see L. J. Kamin, 'Heredity, Intelligence, Politics and Psychology', in Block and Dworkin (eds), *The IQ Controversy*, pp. 242–50. More recent attempts to rehabilitate him cannot be considered here.

14. Cf. G. T. Marx and J. L. Wood, 'Strands of Theory and Research in Collective Behaviour', *Annual Review of Sociology* 1 (1975), pp. 363–428.

15. L. Thurow, 'Economics 1977', *Daedalus* (Fall 1977), pp. 83–5.

16. T. C. Barker, 'The Beginnings of the Economic History Society', *Economic History Review* 30/1 (1977), p. 2; N. B. Harte, 'Trends in Publications on the Economic and Social History of Great Britain and Ireland 1925–1974', *Daedalus* (Fall 1977), p. 24.

17. K. O. May, 'Growth and Quality of the Mathematical Literature', *Isis* 59 (1969), p. 363; Anthony, East, Slater, 'The Growth of the Literature of Physics', *Reports on Progress in Physics* 32 (1969), pp. 764–5.

CHAPTER 10: WHAT DO HISTORIANS OWE TO KARL MARX?

1. Arnaldo Momigliano, 'One Hundred Years after Ranke', in *Studies in Historiography* (London, 1966).

2. *Encyclopaedia Britannica*, 11th edn (London, 1910), article 'History'.

3. *Enciclopedia Italiana* (Rome, 1936), article 'Storiografia'.

4. Indeed, for several years after 1950 they mounted a fairly successful counter-offensive, encouraged by the favourable climate of the Cold War, but also perhaps by the inability of the innovators to consolidate their unexpectedly rapid advance.

5. Cf. George Lichtheim, *Marxism in Modern France* (London, 1966).

6. *Times Literary Supplement*, 15 February 1968.

7. J. Bonar, *Philosophy and Political Economy* (London, 1893), p. 367.

8. These remarks were to give rise to one of the earliest penetrations of what is undoubtedly a Marxist influence into orthodox historiography, namely the famous theme on which Sombart, Weber, Troeltsch and others were to play variations. The debate is still far from exhausted.

9. One must agree with L. Althusser that his discussion of the 'superstructural' levels remained much sketchier and more inconclusive than that of the 'basis'.

10. It need hardly be said that the 'basis' consists not of technology or economics, but of 'the totality of these relations of production', that is social organization in its broadest sense as applied to a given level of the material forces of production.

11. Obviously the use of this term does not imply any similarity with the process of biological evolution.

12. There are historical reasons for this rebellion against the 'evolutionary' aspect of Marxism, for example the rejection – for political reasons – of the Kautskyan orthodoxies, but we are not here concerned with these.

13. Marx to Engels, 7 August 1866. Marx and Engels, *Collected Works*, vol. 42 (London, 1987), p. 304.

14. In the sense in which Lévi-Strauss speaks of kinship systems (or other social devices) as a 'coordinated ensemble, the function of which is to insure the permanency of the social group': Sol Tax (ed.), *Anthropology Today* (1962), p. 343.

15. 'It remains true ... even for a properly revitalized version of functional analysis, that its explanatory form is rather limited; in particular, it does not provide an explanation of why a particular item i rather than some functional equivalent of it, occurs in system s': Carl Hempel, in L. Gross (ed.), *Symposium on Social Theory* (1959).

16. As Lévi-Strauss puts it, writing of kinship models, 'If no external factor were affecting this mechanism, it would work indefinitely, and the social structure would remain static. This is not the case, however; hence the need to introduce into the theoretical model new elements to account for the diachronic changes of the structure': in Tax (ed.), *Social Anthropology*, p. 343.

17. 'Il est clair, toutefois, que c'est la nature de ce concept de "combinaison" qui fonde l'affirmation ... que le marxisme *n'est pas un historicisme*: puisque le concept marxiste de l'histoire repose sur le principe de la variation des formes de cette "combinaison".' Cf. L. Althusser, *Lire le Capital*, vol. 2 (Paris, 1965), p. 153.

18. R. Bastide (ed.), *Sens et usage du terme structure dans les sciences sociales et humaines* (Paris, 1962), p. 143.

19. 'On voit par là que certains rapports de production supposent comme condition de leur propre existence, l'existence d'une *superstructure* juridico-politique et idéologique, et pourquoi cette superstructure est nécessairement *spécifique* ... On voit aussi que certains autres rapports de production n'appellent pas de superstructure politique, mais seulement une superstructure idéologique (les sociétés sans classes). On voit enfin que la nature des rapports de production considérés, non seulement appelle ou n'appelle

pas telle ou telle forme de superstructure, mais fixe également de *degré d'efficace* délégué à tel ou tel niveau de la totalité sociale': Althusser, *Lire le Capital*, p. 153.

20. These may, of course, be described, if we find this useful, as different combinations of a given number of elements.

21. One may add that it is doubtful whether they can be simply classified as 'conflicts', though insofar as we concentrate our attention on social systems as systems of relation between people, they may normally be expected to take the form of conflict between individuals and groups or, more metaphorically, between value-systems, roles and so on.

22. Whether the state is the only institution which has this function has been a question that much preoccupied Marxists like Gramsci, but need not concern us here.

23. G. Lichtheim (*Marxism*, London, 1961, p. 152) rightly points out that class antagonism plays only a subordinate part in Marx's model of the break-up of ancient Roman society. The view that this must have been due to 'slave revolts' has no basis in Marx.

24. As Worsley, summarizing work along these lines put it, 'change within a system must either cumulate towards structural change of the system, or be coped with by some sort of cathartic mechanism': 'The Analysis of Rebellion and Revolution in Modern British Social Anthropology', *Science and Society* 25/1 (1961), p. 37. Ritualization in social relations makes sense as such a symbolic acting-out of tensions which might be otherwise intolerable.

25. Cf. the great quantity of research and discussion on Oriental societies, deriving from a very small number of pages in Marx, of which some of the most important – those in the *Grundrisse* – were not available until fifteen years ago.

26. For example in the field of prehistory, the work of the late V. Gordon Childe, perhaps the most original historical mind in the English-speaking countries to apply Marxism to the past.

27. Compare, for instance, the approaches of Dr Eric Williams' *Capitalism and Slavery* (London, 1964), a valuable and illuminating pioneer work, and Professor Eugene Genovese to the problem of American slave societies and the abolition of slavery.

28. This is particularly obvious in fields such as the theory of economic growth as applied to specific societies, and the theories of 'modernization' in political science and sociology.

29. The discussion of the political impact of capitalist development on preindustrial societies, and more generally of the 'prehistory' of modern social movements and revolutions, is a good example.

CHAPTER 11: MARX AND HISTORY

1. J. R. Hicks, *A Theory of Economic History* (London, Oxford and New York, 1969), p. 3.
2. Quoted from Karl Marx, *Capital* (Harmondsworth, 1976), vol. 1, p. 513.
3. Karl Marx and Friedrich Engels, *The German Ideology*, in *Collected Works* (London, 1976), p. 24 (translation modified).
4. Ibid., p. 37.
5. Ibid., p. 53.
6. Eric R. Wolf, *Europe and the People without History* (Berkeley, 1983), p. 74.
7. Ibid., p. 75.
8. Marx and Engels, *German Ideology*, p. 37.
9. Wolf, *Europe*, pp. 91–2.
10. Ibid., p. 389.
11. Maurice Bloch, *Marxism and Anthropology* (Oxford, 1983), p. 172.

CHAPTER 14: THE REVIVAL OF NARRATIVE

1. Lawrence Stone, 'The Revival of Narrative: Reflections on a New Old History', *Past and Present* 85 (November 1979), pp. 3–24.
2. Arnaldo Momigliano, 'A Hundred Years after Ranke', in his *Studies in Historiography* (London, 1966), pp. 108–9.
3. Fernand Braudel, *La Méditerranée et le monde méditerranéen à l'époque de Philippe II* (Paris, 1960); Emmanuel Le Roy Ladurie, *Le Carnaval de Romans* (Paris, 1979); Emmanuel Le Roy Ladurie, *Les Paysans du Languedoc*, 2 vols (Paris, 1966), vol. 1, pp. 394–9, 505–6.
4. Christopher Hill, 'The Norman Yoke', in John Saville (ed.), *Democracy and the Labour Movement: Essays in Honour of Dona Torr* (London, 1954), repr. in Christopher Hill, *Puritanism and Revolution: Studies in Interpretation of the English Revolution of the Seventeenth Century* (London, 1958), pp. 50–122.
5. Stone, 'Revival', pp. 3, 4.
6. Fernand Braudel, 'Une Parfaite Réussite', reviewing Claude Manceron, *La Révolution qui lève, 1785–1787* (Paris, 1979), in *L'Histoire* 21 (1980), pp. 108–9.
7. Stone, 'Revival', p. 19.
8. Ibid., p. 13.
9. Ibid., p. 20.
10. Theodore Zeldin, *France, 1848–1945*, 2 vols (Oxford, 1973–7), trans. as *Histoire des passions françaises* (Paris, 1978); Richard Cobb, *Death in Paris* (Oxford, 1978).
11. Braudel, 'Une Parfaite Réussite', p. 109.
12. Stone, 'Revival', pp. 7–8.
13. J. Le Goff, 'Is Politics Still the Backbone of History?', in Felix Gilbert and

Stephen R. Graubard (eds), *Historical Studies Today* (New York, 1972), p. 340.

14. Clifford Geertz, 'Deep Play: Notes on the Balinese Cock-Fight', in his *The Interpretation of Cultures* (New York, 1973).

15. Carlo Ginzburg, *Il formaggio ed i vermi* (Turin, 1976); Carlo Ginzburg, *I benandanti: ricerche sulla stregoneria e sui culti agrari tra Cinquecento e Seicento* (Turin, 1966).

16. Maurice Agulhon, *La République au village* (Paris, 1970).

17. Le Roy Ladurie, *Les Paysans du Languedoc*; Emmanuel Le Roy Ladurie, *Montaillou, village occitan de 1294 à 1324* (Paris, 1976), trans. B. Bray as *Montaillou: Cathars and Catholics in a French Village, 1294–1324* (London, 1978); Georges Duby, *Le dimanche de Bouvines, 27 juillet 1214* (Paris, 1973); E. P. Thompson, *The Making of the English Working Class* (London, 1963); E. P. Thompson, *Whigs and Hunters* (London, 1975).

18. Stone, 'Revival', p. 23.

19. Ibid., p. 4.

CHAPTER 15: POSTMODERNISM IN THE FOREST

1. Miguel Barnet (ed.), *The Autobiography of a Runaway Slave* (New York, 1968). The title of the original was *Cimarrón* (Havana, 1967).

2. Richard Price (ed.), *Maroon Societies: Rebel Slave Communities in the Americas* (Baltimore, 1979); Eugene D. Genovese, *From Rebellion to Revolution: Afro-American Slave Revolts in the Making of the Modern World* (Baton Rouge, 1979).

3. Richard Price, *First Time: The Historical Vision of an Afro-American People* (Baltimore, 1983).

4. Price, *Maroon Societies*, p. 12n.

5. The quotations are from a breast-beating session of postmoderns, 'Critique and Reflexivity in Anthropology', *Critique of Anthropology* 9/3 (Winter 1989), pp. 82, 86.

6. Ibid., p. 83.

7. George E. Marcus, 'Imagining the Whole: Ethnography's Contemporary Efforts to Situate Itself', *Critique of Anthropology* 9/3 (Winter 1989), p. 7.

8. However, the author is to be congratulated for deliberately avoiding references to Barthes, Bakhtin, Derrida, Foucault *et al.*

CHAPTER 17: THE CURIOUS HISTORY OF EUROPE

1. Edward Said, *Orientalism* (London, 1978).

2. Bronislaw Geremek, in *Europa-aber wo liegen seine Grenzen?*, 104th Bergedorfer Gesprächskreis, 10 and 11 July 1995 (Hamburg, 1996), p. 9.

3. John R. Gillis, 'The Future of European History', *Perspectives: American Historical Association Newsletter* 34/4 (April 1996), p. 4.

4. Neil Ascherson, *Black Sea* (London, 1995).

5. Cited in Gernot Heiss and Konrad Paul Liessmann (eds), *Das Millennium: Essays zu Tausend Jahren Österreich* (Vienna, 1996), p. 14.

6. Gillis, 'Future of European History', p. 5.

7. Geremek, *Europa*, p. 9.

8. M. E. Yapp, 'Europe in the Turkish Mirror', *Past and Present* 137 (November 1992), p. 139.

9. Jack Goody, *The Culture of Flowers* (Cambridge, 1993), pp. 73–4.

10. Gillis, 'Future of European History', p. 5.

CHAPTER 19: CAN WE WRITE THE HISTORY OF THE RUSSIAN REVOLUTION?

1. Fred Halliday, *From Potsdam to Perestroika: Conversations with Cold Warriors* (London, 1995).

2. As shown, for example, in Jochen Hellbeck (ed.), *Tagebuch aus Moskau 1931–39* (Munich, 1996), a valuable example of the unofficial records of ordinary Russians – private diaries and so on – which have become available since Gorbachev.

3. Karl Marx and Friedrich Engels, *Collected Works* (London, 1976), vol. 24, p. 581.

4. See Richard Gott's account of 'Guevara in the Congo', *New Left Review* 220 (December 1996), pp. 3–35.

5. Eric Hobsbawm, *The Age of Extremes* (London, 1994), p. 64.

6. Orlando Figes, *A People's Tragedy: The Russian Revolution 1891–1924* (London, 1996).

CHAPTER 20: BARBARISM: A USER'S GUIDE

1. Michael Ignatieff, *Blood and Belonging: Journeys into the New Nationalism* (London, 1993), pp. 140–1.

2. Wolfgang J. Mommsen and Gerhard Hirschfeld, *Sozialprotest, Gewalt, Terror* (Stuttgart, 1982), p. 56.

3. Walter Laqueur, *Guerrilla: A Historical and Critical Study* (London, 1977), p. 374.

4. Amnesty International, *Report on Torture* (London, 1975).

5. Ibid., p. 108.

6. Laqueur, *Guerrilla*, p. 377.

CHAPTER 21: IDENTITY HISTORY IS NOT ENOUGH

1. G. Monod and G. Fagniez, 'Avant-propos', in *Revue Historique* 1/1 (1876), p. 4.

2. Michael Smith, 'Postmodernism, Urban Ethnography, and the New Social Space of Ethnic Identity', in *Theory and Society* 21 (August, 1992), p. 493.

3. Stephen A. Tyler, *The Unspeakable* (Madison, 1987), p. 171.

4. Stephen A. Tyler, 'Post-Modern Ethnography: From Document of the Occult to Occult Document', in James Clifford and George Marcus (eds), *Writing Culture: The Poetics and Politics of Ethnography* (New York, 1986), pp. 126, 129.

5. Smith, 'Postmodernism', p. 499.

6. Monod and Fagniez, 'Avant-propos', p. 2.

7. Romila Thapar, 'The Politics of Religious Communities', in *Seminar 365* (January 1990), pp. 27–32.

8. Benedict Anderson, *Imagined Communities: Reflections on the Origin and Spread of Nationalism* (rev. edn, London, 1991).

INDEX

academic
  history 142–2, 155, 201
  institutions, Boston 139
academics 138
Accra 272
Acton, Lord 60, 64
  Cambridge Modern History 142
advocacy, historians and 132
aerial photography 209
Afghanistan 53
Africa, South 261
Africa 16, 53, 219–20, 222–4
  history 176, 206
  North 262
  pan-Africa 272
  peasantry 68
  rites 197
  slaves from 193
  studies 91
  sub-Saharan 272
  West 272
agriculture 78–9, 112, 119
Agulhon, Maurice 182, 190
Akhmad, Sa'id ibn 223
Alaska 151
Albania 2, 6, 274
Alexander the Great 7, 274
Algeria, war of independence (1954–62) 261
Allardt, Eric 91
Allende, Salvador 263
Alps 2
Althusser, Louis 151–2
America
  pre-Columbian 175, 176
  Indians 11, 25, 122, 172, 173, 176, 198
  see also United States *and under names of specific countries*
American
  economics 98, 99, 101, 104, 105, 139

National Bureau of Economic Research 104
American Historical Review 60
Amin, Samir 166
Amish 12
Amnesty Report on torture (1975) 261–2
Amritsar 258
anachronism 7, 29, 210, 270, 274
anarchism 47, 209, 264
Anderson, Benedict 273
Andropov, Yuri 245
Anglo-Saxons 72, 96, 132, 135, 261, 271
  England 81
  Free 15–16
Angoulême 205
Ankara 5
Annales
  d'Histoire Economique et Sociale 62, 72
  Economies, Sociétés, Civilisations 73, 178–85, 189
  school 145, 182
anthropology 50, 52, 74, 78–9, 84, 88, 151, 153, 171, 183, 192–3, 195–6, 206, 213
  see also social anthropology
anti-imperialism 192
anti-intellectual leftist history 188
Aodhya mosque 6, 273
Apennines, Gothic Line 266
appeasement policy 231–2
Arezzo province, massacres 266–7
Argentina 130, 261, 263
Armenians 6
artisans 210
Ascherson, Neal, *Black Sea* 219
Asia, Asians 217–20, 224
  East 176, 218, 224
  economic model 218
  Marxism 145
  Minor 220
  peasantry 68

291

Frank, A. Gunder 175
free-market capitalism 4, 107
French Revolution 89, 141, 145, 168,
    187, 203–5, 208, 241, 252, 259,
    270
Freud, Sigmund 184
Friedman, Milton 109, 135
futurology 55

Galbraith, J.K., *The New Industrial State*
    105
Galiani, Ferdinando 135–6
Galton, Francis 134
Geertz, Clifford 190
Geldwirtschaft 153
Gellner, Ernest 31, 234
Gemeinschaft-Gesellschaft 79
genealogy 20–1, 59
generations 10, 25, 27, 29, 175, 206,
    230–3
Geneva Protocol (1925) 265
Genovese, Professor Eugene 137
    From Rebellion to Revolution 193
geologists 190
Geremek, Bronislaw 218
Germany 16, 232–3
    administrators and executives 102
    army 255, 266
    Bielefeld school 169
    Democratic Republic (GDR) 4, 130
    division (1945) 44
    East and West division 65, 130
    economics 2–3, 98–9, 100–3
    Empire 134, 228, 247
    Federal Republic 130
    Great War defeat 250
    history/historians 62, 69, 73, 104, 120,
        148, 169, 237, 240, 267
    Historikerstreit (Battle of the Historians)
        237
    Kaiser 247
    Ordensburgen of National Socialist 16
    philosophy and ideology 160
    professors 136
    refugees 53
    Revolution (1918) 243, 246–8
    Social Democratic Party 134, 246–7
    theorists 100
    Weimar 62, 257

West 62
    see also First World War, Second World
        War
Gesell, Silvio 95
Ghana 16
Gibbon, Edward 57–8
Gilbert, Felix 71
Gillis, John R. 227
Ginzburg, Carlo 190
Girard, L. 87
Giuliano (Sicilian bandit) 232
Gladstone, William 64–5
Glass, David 37, 51–2
global
    economy 28, 34, 107
    free-market system 107
Gluckman, Max 154, 183
Goebbels, Joseph 220
Gorbachev, Mikhail 249
Goubert, Pierrre 189
Governments and economists 99–104,
    133
Grammaticus, Saxo 276
Gramsci, Antonio 183
Grant and Temperley, *Europe in the
    Nineteenth and Twentieth Centuries*
    63
grassroots history 88–9, 201–6, 209–10,
    215–16, Chapter 16 *passim*
Graubard, Stephen R. 71
Great Depression (1929–33) 3, 104, 177,
    229
Great War *see* First World War
Great Soviet Encyclopedia 129
Greeks 2, 7, 81, 219–20, 260, 274
    ancient 24
    civilization 219
    colonels 221, 260
Guevara, Che 248
Gulf War 255
gun culture 254
Guyana 193, 198

Habsburg Empire 2–3, 207, 250
Hagen, Everett 76
Haldane, J.B.S. 134
Halifax, Lord 231
Halliday, Professor Fred 245
Han, societies 81